DATE DUE

GAYLORD   PRINTED IN U.S.A.

SOCIAL BEING

Social Being

Rom Harré

Second Edition

BLACKWELL
Oxford UK & Cambridge USA

Copyright © Rom Harré 1979, 1993

The right of Rom Harré to be identified as author of this work has been asserted
in accordance with the Copyright, Designs and Patents Act 1988.

First published 1979
Second edition 1993

Blackwell Publishers
108 Cowley Road
Oxford OX4 1JF
UK

238 Main Street, Suite 501
Cambridge, Massachusetts 02142
USA

British Library Cataloguing in Publication Data

A CIP catalogue record for this book is available from the British Library.

Library of Congress Cataloging-in-Publication Data
Harré, Rom.
Social being / Rom Harré.
p.   cm.
Includes bibliographical references and index.
ISBN 0-631-18782-0
1. Social psychology.   I. Title.
HM251.H243   1993
302 – dc20   92-29854   CIP

Typeset in 10 on 12 pt Times by Best-set Typesetters Ltd, Hong Kong
Printed in Great Britain by Biddles Ltd, Guildford

Contents

Preface

This is the second edition of my 1979 *Social Being*. The decision to produce a second edition has given me the opportunity not only to bring the argument up to date, but also to rewrite the text extensively. The original edition was written as a sequel to Secord's and my (1973) *Explanation of Social Behaviour*, to remedy certain important omissions. In our book the social dimension was very schematic and, like many social psychologists of that era, we had neglected time and change. The argument of the second edition is in most respects the same as that of the first. The role of 'rules' in social psychology has been more carefully explained and the methodological sections completely rewritten in the light of the rapid development of non-experimental methods of empirical research since 1979.

Once again I am grateful to the editors of *Advances in Experimental Social Psychology* and to the editors and publisher of *Structure, Consciousness and History* for their permission to make use of certain passages first published with them.

I owe debts of gratitude to many, but particularly to Michael Argyle and Jean-Pierre de Waele. To the former I owe innumerable opportunities to witness social psychologists at work and at play. To the latter I am grateful not only for allowing me to dip into his unrivalled knowledge of the literature of psychology, but for his unfailing critical support.

Oxford and Georgetown
1993

Introduction: Ways of Being

The original (1979) edition of this book was intended as the first of three studies, exploring three main human ways of being, *Social Being, Personal Being* (1983) and *Physical* Being (1991). In the course of this exploration it became increasingly clear that the 'discursive turn' in psychology was here to stay. Furthermore, during that period many new insights have been achieved by others who have come to adopt this point of view. It now seems right to incorporate some of these insights into a new edition of *Social Being*, fitting it in hindsight for its role in the wider study. The preparation of a second edition has also given me the opportunity to eliminate some of the errors, false emphases and infelicities of the first edition.

This introduction is meant to serve as a sketch or outline of the argument of the whole project, the attempt to found a general psychology on the thesis that human psychology is best understood as coming into existence in the enormously variable discursive or symbolic interactions of persons, grounded in a common biological inheritance.

We exist as persons for other people and for ourselves. As individuals we each have a social and a personal being. It is evident however that our individuality in each of these modes of being is bound up with the fact of embodiment. We are also physical beings, each in his or her own fleshly envelope.

In developing theories of human ways of being many attempts have been made to find a unity in this threefold diversity. All sorts of reduction programmes have been tried. Marx looked for the roots of human ways of being in the social relations of material production. Sociobiology was originally directed to the aim of reducing all forms of human interaction to the manifestation of action patterns genetically programmed into the human nervous system. Neither programme has been convincing. The three ways of being are mutually supportive and closely interrelated, but they are coincident nodes in different networks. There are many people who would insist on adding a fourth category of existence or mode of being to my list of three. For Christians, Muslims and Jews the fourth way of being is to be in relation to a personal God. Other religious stances to the universe require us to conceive of spiritual being in other ways. For many deeply religious people the three ways of being to the understanding of which the human sciences are directed are superficial consequences of their spiritual being. This point of view plays a not inconsiderable role in contemporary medical ethics and in moral theology.

To be fully human, from the point of view of the philosophical anthropology to the development of which my studies are directed, it is enough that we each have an intuition of ourselves as existing in the three mundane modes: social, personal and corporeal. In researching into these three modes of being two ranges of problems can be distinguished. The first concerns how we exist in each of the three realms. The second range concerns how we acquire the knowledge and skill so to exist. We must each have a certain repertoire of discursive and practical skills for living in each mode of being. For me, psychology can be nothing but the study of the acquisition, maintenance and coordinated application of those skills. This, at least, is hardly to be disputed as a universal feature of all forms of human life. These skills must be learned from others and they can be employed more or less expertly. If to be a person consists in having and using such skills, people are artifacts. We are the products of all sorts of processes and procedures of people making. These processes and procedures are also the exercise of skills and so can be done well or ill. We can apply them to ourselves.

'Identity' is a complex concept. It can refer to the oneness of each of us as unique and individual human beings. Philosophers usually call this 'personal identity'. It can also refer to the similarities we bear to others, the types we exemplify. Psychologists usually call this 'social identity'. An identity crisis is prompted by the question 'What sort of person am I?' not by the question 'Which person am I?' I can be mistaken about the former, and may even need to take trouble to find out. I cannot be mistaken about the latter and the idea of finding out makes no sense. These identities are linked. To be recognized as a person amongst and by others I must exemplify characteristics typical of and appropriate to persons of the kinds recognized in my tribe, as well as being uniquely identifiable by my distinctive bodily appearance.

SOCIAL CONSTRUCTIONISM: WHAT IT IS NOT

The general spirit of these studies is social constructionist. I share with many the idea that people and what they do are artifacts, products of social processes. In particular I believe that the most important of the processes through which the psychological phenomena that they jointly create are brought about are discursive. Without language there would be neither people as we know them nor the forms of life that we take unhesitatingly to be human. However there are two implications that some have drawn from the thesis of social constructionism from which I particularly want to dissociate myself.

The fact that people are created by other people and that their actions are in essence joint actions does not mean that the actions people perform are socially caused. People, as we construct them, are built to be capable of autonomous action, to engage, usually with others, in reflective discourse on possible courses of action, and to be competent in the discursive presentation of and taking up of personal responsibility. There are some criminal acts for which it is entirely proper to assign responsibility to some socially constructed individual. The very idea of 'could have done otherwise' is itself a social construct.

More importantly, social constructionism has sometimes been presented as a radically anti-foundationalist theory of human nature. If each culture is socially constructed it could presumably have been put together in some other fashion. And no one culture can claim to be representative of human nature in itself. Indeed it is sometimes claimed that on the social constructionist view there is no common human nature. Dispelling these errors of interpretation will involve a wide variety of considerations. It is of course not an integral part of the metaphysics of social constructionism to suppose that cultures could have been constructed in some other way than they are. And this for the very important reason that each form of life is firmly founded in the local form of personhood. We could no more genuinely adopt another way of life than we could take up another biology. To do so would require us not to be the people we are. People and their form of life are correlative with one another. The question of the existence of a common human nature is more subtle. There is at least one way in which there must be such a thing. All human beings have various generic capacities to acquire skills, which, though they differ in their specific forms from tribe to tribe, are nevertheless of the same general kind. Most important of all these is the capacity to acquire and use language.

The question of what is universal in all human associations cannot be answered as a straight empirical query. All depends on the level of generality and abstraction at which the question is posed. At the most abstract level there are the transcendental social conditions for the possibility of linguistic communication. I take these to be moral conditions, in a broad sense. They reflect norms of interpersonal relationships. There could hardly be linguistic interchanges in the absence of interpersonal trust. As Holiday (1987) has argued, there is a case to be made for other moral universals as transcendental conditions for the possibility of language. At the most concrete level there are the material conditions for the maintenance of life itself. There must therefore be a rudimentary conceptual system immanent in the most basic practices of living, such as eating, drinking, reproducing and so on, however elaborate and culturally specific are the forms of life built upon them. But it is easy to make far too much of these commonalities. I have gradually become convinced that the idea that there are basic *human* emotions is a mistake, and not much more than an illegitimate a priori projection of a local biologism onto other forms of life. However I shall be defending at least one claim for the universality of a generic social practice at the same level of abstraction as the transcendental conditions for possibility of language, namely the universal tendency of human beings to rank themselves hierarchically.

The self is a location, not a substance or an attribute. The sense of self is the sense of being located at a point in space, of having a perspective in time and of having a variety of positions in local moral orders. It is not having an awareness of some kind of being, particularly not an awareness of an entity at the core of one's being. The central thesis of this study is that human beings become persons by acquiring a sense of self. But that can only occur in social milieu in which they are already treated as persons by the others of their family and tribe. The public-social concept of person then serves as a model for the private-individual concept of self. One may, of course, represent one's sense of location in all sorts of ways, not least by such models as individual souls. After all one does much the same in one's management of geographical locations. One represents to oneself the abstract location of oneself and one's home and so on, which would be more transparently rendered in terms of latitude and longitude, in terms of other physical entities occupying neighbouring places in the abstract grid. Only the unsophisticated are deeply disappointed when they fail to find the ring of the equator clearly marked upon the ocean. It is that kind of lack of sophistication that leads some to take entity – like self-talk, seriously as metaphysics. It is, though, a sophisticated lack of sophistication, since it is just the error of assuming that every substantive must refer to a substance that Wittgenstein spent the second half of his life trying to eradicate.

Studies in cultural psychology, for instance Rosaldo (1980), have shown that human beings can function psychologically, that is are capable of engaging in those symbolic practices we call the mental, in two sharply differentiated modes. In one mode the selves that are created in the practices of person-making could exist in the absence of all other persons, since they exist as nodes or centres of perception, action and memory in relation only to themselves. In the other mode the selves therein created would be greatly diminished, and perhaps cease to exist in the absence of others, since they exist only as nodes in a network of relations with others. In both cases, as I have emphasized, the self, in the sense of the bearer of personal responsibility, is not an entity but a location.

Part of what it is to be just this person is to be embodied in just this flesh, to be just this body. But the body's role in our identities is complex. The uniqueness of the physical body is criterial for personal identity for all others than myself. But it plays only an indirect or supporting role in my sense of my own identity. It is the material basis for that singularity of point of view and in a less determinate way, for my point of action in the world, upon which the indexical features of the use of the first person depend. While it is nature that gives me the capacity to initiate action, a sense of power in the world, it is only language and a social order which can give me a sense of responsibility for what I do. Nature provides the 'can', but culture and language provide the 'may' and 'must'.

THE CONCEPTS OF 'CULTURE' AND 'FORM OF LIFE'

It has become a commonplace that much of what we take to be psychological is local, that is exists only within a culture and not across cultures. The exact distribution of the culturally specific, such as emotions, and the anthropologically universal, such as the use of language, among psychological phenomena has yet to be determined. I tried to lay out some guidelines for the discussion above. The surd element in all of this has been the concept of 'culture' itself. The term 'culture' has been used in so many and diverse ways that I shall try to avoid it in what follows. Wittgenstein's notion of 'form of life' is more or less what we are looking for. Wittgenstein used the notion in two ways. There is the human form of life, as distinct say from the form of life of lions or Martians. But there is also the form of life of each of the human tribes. In the former sense biological universals are prominent. In the latter, and it is to that we will turn for our purposes, a form of life is a cluster of material and symbolic *practices*. In Wittgenstein's eccentric but powerful image, a form of life, in the tribal sense, is constituted by a cluster of 'language games', activities in which the tongue and the hand play essential parts. The metaphysical background to the studies that follow in all of my three studies of our ways of being is just this: To explain a practice by suggesting some hypothetical information processing mechanism at work 'behind' the performing of the necessary actions, or to account for the regularities to be observed in human practices by treating some set of rules as analogous to the programmes the running of which accounts for regularities in the output of the machine, is to slide back to a Cartesianism which, in the end, can lead nowhere.

In developing a new paradigm for a well-established field of enquiry one is at risk of many misunderstandings. Among the most persistent is the assumption that the shift to a psychology of discursive practices is somehow a denial of the existence of any native 'mental' endowments in the nascent human being. But as Wittgenstein (1953) emphasized again and again, it would be impossible to acquire the skills necessary to engage in symbolic (and I would add material) practices unless there already existed all sorts of natural regularities in our behaviour. In *Personal being* (1983) I developed an account of the nature of persons in which they are seen as the products of the imposition of the structures of language on the native endowments of the 'general animate being'. Among the most salient of these endowments are conscious awareness, agentive powers and recollection. I simply assume that these features of the infant are capacities it has by virtue of a developing nervous system. But to become a person the infant's native endowments must be synthesized into a coherent and unified structure. It is the great achievement of Vygtosky to have realized that this synthesis (prefigured in the writings of Kant) comes about by the acquisition of *both symbolic and practical skills* in symbiosis with more competent members of the infant's immediate circle. In particular, conscious awareness becomes self-consciousness, agency becomes moral responsibility and recollection becomes the ordered memories of an autobiography through the acquisition, above all, of ways of making indexical reference to self and others, in short the pronoun system and its equivalents.

Life is a game, at once frivolous and serious, played on several different levels, a game in which there are no given rules, the game consists precisely in trying to discover the rules according to which it should be played . . . In the Absurd world, all rules are provisional and few are rarely fully understood, even when we are obeying them or trying to subvert them.

J. Weightman (1990)

The principles more or less universally operative in human physiology, and on which the basic processes of perception, learning, motivation and emotion are organized, cannot explain the immense variety of cultural practices and productions. The *physiological* psychology of causes is distinct from the anthropological psychology of motives and reasons. Both, however, are amenable to disciplined modes of inquiry. Both, therefore, will benefit from the progress of such disciplined inquiry, though the inquiries themselves cannot be of the same *genre*. It is not merely a matter of choice to study some things in a laboratory and others *in situ*. There are certain phenomena that derive their ontological standing solely from the context.

D. Robinson (1992)

I entirely agree . . . that there is a meaningful distinction to be made between facts and fictions . . . On the other hand, it seems to me equally obvious that as soon as 'facts' are articulated in a discourse, interpretation begins, and an interpretation is a kind of fiction (not to be confused with a falsehood).

D. Lodge (1992)

PART I

The Basic Concepts of a Social Psychology

1

THE PROBLEM OF SOCIAL BEING

ANTICIPATORY SUMMARY

The version of social psychology to be presented in this book can be defined by reference to certain basic contrasts. The most fundamental concerns the working ontology within which social psychological enquiry is to be framed. Are human beings to be taken to be active agents using their social knowledge jointly to accomplish certain ends? Or are they information-processing automata, the behaviours of which are the effects of causal processes? The studies to be reported in what follows and the methods of investigation to be recommended are based absolutely on the former picture.

A more subtle contrast appears in the uses of neo-Darwinian theory in sociobiology. I shall argue that we must accept the existence of 'fixed action patterns', but that these patterns are elaborated and transformed as they are absorbed into the symbolic universe of actual human associations. Though we cannot do without human ethology, it cannot serve as the only arm of social psychology.

In repudiating the once popular 'automaton' view of human action I am also denying the existence of common abstract information-processing mechanisms at the heart of human activity. Instead I shall be emphasizing the ubiquitous role of skilled employment of diverse discursive practices in the creation and maintenance of human social relations.

Finally the implicit sociology of these investigations can be spelled out in terms of distinctions drawn from Veblen and Goffman. In different ways they each distinguished between expressive activities, subserving honour, and practical activities, subserving biological survival and perhaps well being. For human beings in most times and places, but not in all, the weight in motivation for action has been on the former.

IDENTIFYING THE PROBLEMS OF SOCIAL PSYCHOLOGY

Human beings are fully persons only as members of social groups. Each person is a social being, equipped with a dual identity, and recognized as such by others who are also persons. I hope to show that we exist as social beings only by virtue of networks of relations in which we stand to other beings of our kind. My aim is to steer a middle course between individualism and collectivism. The studies reported in this volume, though conceived in the spirit of philosophical anthropology, are directed to the development of a well-rounded social psychology. My aim is in part methodological. I hope to provide a massive demonstration of the inadequacy of the attempt to frame psychological science in some version of the causal metaphysics of the natural sciences. I am not the first to believe that psychology belongs with the sciences of the artificial. In psychology we are or should be studying forms of symbolic interaction. Psychology, from my point of view, belongs with cultural sciences such as anthropology, jurisprudence and linguistics. This is not only because they share a common metaphysics, but because, as I hope to show, the broad range of phenomena we take to be psychological are at bottom discursive, they are produced in interactional processes which are best conceived on the model of a conversation.

The original edition of this book was written in the mid seventies, to develop and expand the argument of Secord's and my attempt at a critical reform of the foundations of social psychology, published as *The explanation of social behaviour*. At that time there were three major paradigms competing for hegemony over the human sciences; Marxism, sociobiology and naive experimentalism. Of these three only the last remains as a serious obstacle to the spread of the new approach. Marxist ways of explaining human life have so completely vanished that in this new edition, they will be mentioned no more. Sociobiology has become a great deal more sophisticated since that time. There is certainly a place for genetically programmed fixed action patterns in the explanatory framework of an adequate general psychology, but they fall far short of providing the materials needed for a comprehensive social psychology.

In this chapter I shall try to define the field of problems that must be tackled in attempts to understand the nature and genesis of our social being. As social beings we identify ourselves and others as sharing certain characteristics. One aspect of our social being is group membership, with all that entails. It is to investigating that aspect of social being that most academic social psychology has been addressed.

How do people come to seem to others to be, and to believe themselves to be, beings of this or that kind? The members of a group share common attributes and in the respect of their group membership they are all alike. I shall call aggregates of this sort 'taxonomic groups'. Such groups exist only as labels or concepts. Most of the human collectivities to which we belong are quite unlike taxonomic groups. They are internally structured, and each person plays a distinctive part, related to the others in different ways. If membership of a social class or an ethnic group is typical of the former aspect or dimension of social being, membership of a family or an institution is typical of the latter aspect or dimension of social being. Both of these aspects belong, as one, might say, to the statics of psychological science.

But social life is an interlocking weave of processes. Above all the paradigm of the naive laboratory tradition neglects process. There is almost no attempt to create a dynamics of psychological science. Such work as there is has been conceived in the static framework. For example studies of aggression (for instance Berkowitz 1962) typically involve the creation in laboratories of unusual types of episode in which one or more people are brought to act aggressively. The aim is to find the causal conditions that engender the disposition to be aggressive. They do not focus on the structure and dynamics of the unfolding of episodes in which aggressive acts have a specific and proper place. Secord's and my plea for a dynamics of social life has remained virtually unheard. In this new edition I shall be emphasizing the processual aspect of social life even more than in the original.

THE TWO MAIN APPROACHES TO THE PROBLEM OF UNDERSTANDING SOCIAL LIFE

Every science is shaped by its ontology, that is by the set of assumptions about the nature of its subject matter that are shared by the community of practitioners. From time to time the ontological assumptions that have been buried in the working practices and taken-for-granted concepts of the vocabulary of a science are subject to explicit scrutiny, and sometimes displaced by new ontological foundations. In the history of the physical sciences the demonstration of the inadequacy or incoherence of an ontology has led to its abandonment, usually within a fairly short time. Psychology is unique, even among the human sciences, for the fact that this does not happen. As an editor of an encyclopedia of psychology I have been very much aware of the multiplicity of ontologies that are alive amongst practitioners, long after their weaknesses have been exposed. Reflecting on the reasons for this, one is struck by the extent to which a certain methodology, incorporating an ontology and making sense only in that metaphysical context, seems to have a life of its own. But why in psychology do demonstrably inadequate methodologies persist? The answer to that question must be looked for not only from sociological studies of the relevant institutions, but also from the ontology, rarely explicitly formulated, that animates the enterprise of academic psychology. The investigation of the sociological dimension I shall leave to others. My interest is in the more basic question of choice of ontology.

Starting with the dynamic point of view in social psychology the subject matter of such a field could be loosely defined as 'coordinated behaviour'. The two approaches, still aptly named the old and the new paradigm, take opposing metaphysical stances to the nature of this subject matter. For adherents of the old paradigm coordinated behaviour is the effect of causal processes, triggered by the stimuli to which the subjects are exposed. The job of the experimenter is to look for correlations between elementary stimuli and elementary behaviours, usually by the use of statistical analyses to identify central tendencies. Individual people are the vehicles for causal processes. For adherents of the new paradigm coordinated behaviour is the product of the joint action of human agents acting intentionally according to local norms to accomplish certain projects. The job of the observer is to look for patterns of meaningful action, by attending to the plans and intentions of the actors and the rules and conventions accepted as valid in their community, and which are known to the members. Apart from some brief critical remarks in the chapter on methodology I shall from henceforth have little to say about old paradigm metaphysics and methodology.

An important point about the knowledgeability of actors must be made at this point, to prevent a common misunderstanding of new paradigm methods. In all human contexts one must recognize that there are two kinds of knowledge, practical ('knowing how') and discursive ('knowing that'). Much of the knowledge that people display in managing joint action is practical, and usually tacit. That is it is not easy for someone to express their practical knowledge discursively, for instance in a manual. One could define the task of social psychology, in new paradigm style, as the work of making the tacit, practical knowledge of a community explicit by representing it discursively. For new paradigm practitioners, rules (in the literal sense) are elements in a discursive presentation of social knowledge. It is only as potent metaphor that psychologists ought to refer to what actors know as 'the "rules"'.

A body of social knowledge can be in the possession, tacitly or explicitly, of everyone competent in a certain mode of social action. But it has been frequently demonstrated that it is more common for the total body of 'knowledge how' to be distributed amongst the relevant community. The coordinated behaviour of family members is a case in point. Studies have shown that the family knowledge base is fragmented and distributed amongst the family members, access to it being controlled by internal relations of asymmetrical power and differential rights of display in that micro-community. In the first case social psychology will come up with ways in which people resemble one another, while in the second it will come up with ways in which people differ from one another. This is a fact of the very greatest methodological importance and will be developed much more fully in the sections on methodology.

The limits of sociobiology

The idea behind sociobiology is an attractive one. Human beings have evolved in Darwinian fashion from primate ancestors. Like other animals they will have inherited certain genetic complexes which so order the human nervous system that a certain number of behavioural routines, condusive to optimum distribution of the genes controlling reproductive strategies, will be displayed in human social life. Neo-Darwinian evolutionary theory is based on the principle that those patterns of behaviour will survive which lead to the maximum spread of their genetic basis in the next and subsequent generations. Individual organisms will then display optimum reproductive strategies. Males will tend to mate with as many females as possible, while females will tend to so behave as to raise as many of their own offspring as possible. The actual situation is more complicated, since there is an interaction between these diverse patterns which leads to a certain number of each sex displaying something like the pattern of behaviour of the other, the whole system finally reaching equilibrium in an array of patterns of individual action, the 'evolutionarily stable strategy'. How much of the patterning of human social life can be explained within this theory?

I shall argue that there are very likely to be a certain number of 'fixed action patterns' whose origin must be looked for in human biology. A social psychology without a dimension of human ethology would be seriously impoverished. But humankind is symbol-using. In this simple and almost banal observation lies the possibility for the extraordinary degree of elaboration and diversification we find in human social life. Intentional structures overlay the biological patterns that Chance (1988) has called 'attentional structures', the patterns of dominance and submission which subserve optimum reproductive strategies. I shall look at three examples of behaviour patterns which seem to be based upon inherited routines and yet which take forms in human life that seem to display discursive patterns of interaction supervenient on the biological basis. The examples are chosen to illustrate three ways in which a purely sociobiological account is too narrow. I shall call these ways 'universalization', 'elaboration' and 'inversion' respectively.

Universalization: the case of altruism

Why should people help one another? Of all the people we encounter which categories deserve our help? The first question seems at first sight to have a simple moral answer, namely one has a duty to do so. Moral philosophies differ over the origin of this duty, though most seem to draw eventually on some version of the Golden Rule: Do unto others as you would be done by. To the second question a simple answer seems obvious, too, namely that one helps the destitute and the needy. This is sometimes qualified by adding some such condition to the actual giving of help as that the recipient is 'deserving'. Someone whose destitution is due to indulgence in some vice or folly is sometimes held not to be deserving of succour. In this framework the decision to help someone or some category of persons is arrived at discursively, through the examination of the case in point in accordance with some system of moral categories. We also find that sometimes there is a kind of impulsive generosity. People differ enormously in the extent to which they are willing to help others. We can define altruism as that degree of help-giving which requires some sacrifice on the part of the giver.

In contrast are the conclusions one would draw from gene-selection theory. If the inherited patterns of behaviour, including altruistic behaviour, of an organism have evolved to promote the spread of that organism's own genes, then the only beings which will be helped will be those which bear the same genes. Blood relatives will be helped, in inverse degree to the distance of their relationship to the helper. Other organisms of the same species and the same sex as the organism in question will be ignored or even hindered. Helping will be related directly or indirectly to reproductive success.

Our question must be: Can the forms of distinctively human moral orders be derived from this biological basis? In particular how can we explain the fact that anyone who satisfies the local 'need' condition is thought to be deserving of help, and that help is not confined to ameliorating the conditions which contribute to reproductive success.

Why help the deserving poor and the aged? The usual sociobiological answer in a way concedes the limits of sociobiological explanation. The general pattern of altruism is inherited in neo-Darwinian style, but in the case of human beings this pattern is universalized.

Elaborations: the case of marriage patterns
It can hardly be denied that the basic structure of relations between the sexes is almost certainly based on a repertoire of genetically-determined fixed action patterns. But the way the locally optimum number of mates is arrived at is very various. There are monogamous systems, polygynous and polyandrous systems, but so far as one knows there are no promiscuous systems. All societies impose a structure of duties and obligations, social and economic roles, and so on, on the basic pattern of reproductive pairing. Furthermore there are wide variations in the way parenting is accomplished. These range from societies in which fathers have almost no role in the upbringing of infants to those in which they play a major part. In some societies it is the mother's brother who provides the support for the mother-infant pair. In others the tasks of upbringing are divided temporally, so that at a certain age a boy child goes to live in the men's house while the girl child remains among the women. Societies differ greatly in the age at which reproductive mating is permitted. In Ireland it may be postponed until the thirties. In the European Middle Ages it began in the teens.

The interaction between social and biological patterns of sexual interaction is complicated by the fact that sexual intercourse plays two distinct roles in the parenting process. In the one it results, sometimes, in pregnancy. In the other it seems to function as one of the means by which the parents are bonded as a couple. Realistically one must acknowledge a third role, namely as a recreation or pastime. The regulation of these three roles is complex and easily demonstrated to take widely different forms at different times and in different cultural environments. There is a fourth role, sometimes to be found in human societies. It can be used as one of the many possible bases for a display of male personhood, the phenomenon of *machismo*. The corresponding feminine value is more complex, and much less dependent on real or fictitious claims about sexual conquests.

Similar elaborations can be discerned in studies of the role of meals in human society. There is a biological imperative to eat and drink. But there are elaborate ceremonial dinners, and there is anorexia as well. Mary Douglas (1972) has charted the semantics of those meal progressions through which friendship is tentatively initiated, confirmed and maintained. We might well ask too why so many people in

Western countries, living on diets which are adequate in every nutritional respect, yet publicly and systematically take vitamins and other dietary supplements, biologically appropriate only in the Third World.

Inversion: the case of the potlatch

It would seem obvious at first glance that the acquisition of material goods, of wealth, would subserve the biology of reproduction as it is understood in gene-selection theory. Yet in many societies the value of wealth suffers an inversion. The point of the custom of 'potlach', a term in use among native Americans, is to give away or destroy the stock of material goods that one has accumulated. One is honoured for divesting oneself of wealth. I have seen references in newspapers to the persistence of this custom among the Duhkabors, a clannish sect that still exists in parts of Canada. A member of the sect, having acquired a fine house stocked with valuable goods, will set fire to it, reducing himself and his family to penury. Which is the programmed action pattern – the urge to accumulate wealth or the urge to destroy it? Among the Maori, before their civilization was transformed by the assimilation of many nineteenth century European social practices, another form of potlach existed. Maori social psychology was built around the practices by which a distinctive form of honour, *mana*, was gained and lost. It could be gained by displays of bravery and prowess in battle, by stoic acceptance of the pain of tattooing, but also by munificence. A Maori and his family having saved up much in the way of the food items and tools, clothes and weapons that constituted wealth in that society, would host a great feast and give it all away. It is worth emphasizing for future reference that these acts of divestment of wealth, were accomplished by men. I know of no case of a custom of women's potlach.

Genetic programming can take us no great distance in the understanding of human social being. Let us call the other dimension, emphasized in the three cases I have cited, the cultural dimension of human life. The job of the social psychologist is to describe, analyze and account for the activities that constitute this dimension.

The variety of action patterns

One way of summing up the relationship between sociobiological and sociocultural aspects of interpersonal interaction draws on the distinction between *action* and *act*. An action is an individual person's intended public performance. An act is what is accomplished through the recognition of that action as locally significant in some way. Thus a certain shaping and moving of the hand is an action, while the greeting that that movement is taken to accomplish is an act. This distinction will play a ubiquitous role in the rest of this book. For the moment I want only to illustrate the way biology and culture are interrelated by crossing the act/action distinction with another way that human performances can be classified. If a pattern of action is the result of a neurological process the neural structures underlying which have been genetically determined I shall say that that pattern has a biogenic origin. If the pattern of action seems to be result of an active agent following a rule or convention I shall say that that pattern has a sociogenic origin. The situation, as we find it, can be summed up in a table (table 1).

Table 1

Action		**Act**	
Biogenic	frowning	Biogenic	warning
Biogenic	handshake	Sociogenic	betting
Sociogenic	giving flowers	Biogenic	courting
Sociogenic	signing	Sociogenic	contracting

The variety of combinations of origins and meanings displayed in this table demonstrates in a very simple way the impossibility of achieving a reduction of the biological to the cultural or of the cultural to the biological.

What are the media through which social relations are created and maintained and by means of which social episodes unfold? On the one hand there are bodily interconnections and mutual influences, ranging from actual body contact through postures and facial expressions to local repertoires of gestures. On the other hand is discourse. I shall call these corporeal and symbolic media respectively. At the polar extremes lie very different phenomena. On the one hand there are physically mediated interrelations such as the action of pheromones and on the other such customs as funeral orations. However there is an important intermediate class of interactional devices which, though corporeal, have many of the properties of the linguistic interchanges which make up the main substance of discourse. I have in mind such relatively static background features of social interaction as clothing, domestic furnishings and meals, as well as the more dynamic and foreground features such as gestures, gift exchanges and the like. Most of the devices typical of this intermediate class can best be understood in relation to their roles in social life in terms of the analytical categories appropriate to the investigation of discourse. They belong, I believe, in the cultural dimension.

In the course of this study I shall be deploying the consequences of the idea that some social activities can best be analysed as if they were efforts at solving problems, in a way that supports the expressive aims of the preservation of dignity and mutual respect of all those concerned. There are many sources of problems in human life. Amongst the most pervasive and perennial are the problems posed by the need to provide secure conditions for the slow maturation and long dependence of human infants, to regulate the relations between the sexes, to apportion food, and to dispose of dead bodies in a way commensurate with the dignity of these persons as they were in life; and many, many more. The biological basis of life should be seen, I suggest, as a source of problems for which social solutions must be invented.

THE PSYCHOLOGICAL BASIS OF SOCIAL PSYCHOLOGY

The elements of a psychology of social action

How can individual human beings function as social actors, and so come to exist as social beings? The way this question is answered will determine how the task of formulating a psychology of social action will be tackled. Two concepts are needed. The one is the idea of competence or skill. The second basic concept appears in the main foundational principle of the social psychology to be expounded in this study which runs as follows:

> A person is competent or skilled in some practice in so far as they have the requisite knowledge.

This principle was implicit in the introductory discussion of the kinds of knowledge to the revealing of which social psychology ought to address itself.

The results of social psychological investigations undertaken within this framework will not be expressible in terms of statistical correlations. The result of a study of social psychological phenomenon, let us say 'helping', will be an ordered corpus of rules, conventions, ideals and interpretative principles upon which adequate action in some concrete situation of need will be based. Once again let me enter a caution about the use of the word 'rule' and other expressions from the same lexicon. Rules, principles, moral dictates and so on figure in discursive *accounts* of action, both lay and professional. The giving of accounts is just as much a social practice as the act/action performances which are the subject matter of those accounts. There are rules and conventions for the giving of accounts, which will figure in the social psychological presentation of the knowledge base needed for competent accounting. How the knowledge base exists in individual human beings is not well described by the word 'rule' unless it is clearly and overtly being used as a metaphor linking the content of individual forms of knowledge to the discursive presentation of that knowledge in an account, be it first or second order. The same caution must be entered for the useful but potentially misleading explanatory concept of 'rule-following'. All this has been gnomically but thoroughly explored by Wittgenstein in the *Philosophical investigations* Part I. Social psychologists cannot be excused from acquainting themselves with it.

One final word of warning. The fact that much social pychological research has been conducted by and among North Americans has had an influence on how it has been assumed a knowledge base is located. The American moral universe is built on the idea of atomic individuals, severally responsible for and therefore presumptively knowledgeable about how to produce intelligible and warrantable social action. The experimental methodology which subjects participants to 'stimuli' individually, incorporates that assumption about the corpus of knowledge. Observational and participant studies of the way knowledge bases are located in real life disclose a very different pattern of distribution. The total corpus necessary for the performance of some complex social activity may be distributed through a group of people, some individuals having some of it, others having other bits. What is more, access to that corpus is controlled by social relations between the members of the group. Not only are there monopolies of knowledge, there are also monopolies of the rights to display knowledge. There are many situations in which certain members have the necessary knowledge to contribute competently to a skilled group performance but by reason of their social location in the group, may not manifest it. And that too is an element in that body of knowledge. The main concepts then of social psychology in the new paradigm mode are knowledge and skill.

But what of social phemomena themselves? This question provides the opportunity for introducing a third basic concept, that of joint action. I shall take it as a fundamental principle that a social phenomenon exists only when the intentions displayed by individual actors are reflected in or transformed by the understandings and interpretations displayed in the actions of those jointly engaged in the activity in question.

The universalizability issue

The basic question of course is whether there is a common core to the various apparently different forms of human social life. It is hard to imagine how such a question could be tackled head on, so to say. One way to approach it would be to ask the more tractable question: can the same descriptive and analytical concepts be used to record and analyze patterns of social action in all cultures? Can the same explanatory concepts be used to account for those patterns? And then one would perhaps hope to answer by reference to some reasonable standard of adequacy. This topic has been elegantly examined by R. Shweder and I can do no better than to quote his exposition of it, as he draws a contrast between 'general psychology' and 'cultural psychology'. By the latter he means pretty much what Secord and I meant by our term 'ethogenics'. Neither term now strikes me as particularly apt.

> Ontologically speaking, knowledge in general psychology is the attempt to imagine and characterize the form of shape of an inherent central processing mechanism for psychological functions (discrimination, categorization, memory, learning, motivation, inference, and so on). Epistemologically speaking, knowledge seeking in general psychology is the attempt to get a look at the central processing mechanism untainted by content and context, and so on.
> The main force in general psychology is the idea of that central processing device. The processor, it is imagined, stands over and above, or transcends, all the stuff upon which it operates. It engages all the stuff of culture, context, task and stimulus material as its content.
> Given that image the central processor itself must be context and content independent. That means, in effect, that the processor must be describable in terms of properties that are either free of context/content (abstract, formal, structural properties) or general to all contexts/contents (invariant, universal properties). (Shweder 1991:80)

In the context of the problems I am intending to tackle in this volume the central processor is to all intents and purposes a myth. There is no context-free knowledge and no universal practices. It can be ignored. But it may be that this strategy is apposite in the context of the psychology of social action just because of the level of abstraction of the structures that are processed in the general cognitive machine. The possibility would remain open that attention would have to be paid to that level of functioning in some other context. I must confess that I think that the central processor does not exist and that the attempts to study it are the pursuit of a will-o'-the-wisp. Interestingly one could translate the passage I have quoted from Shweder into a description of the logicist myth in general philosophy of science. Throughout the thirties and forties philosophers based their attempts to understand the nature of science on the idea that there was a content-free formal structure reproduced in every instance of scientific theorizing. This idea still has a few adherents. Just the same myth can be found in the idea of transformational linguistics which is based on the idea of a formal syntax.

The accuracy of Shweder's diagnosis of the ontological illusion that fosters so much seemingly risible academic social psychology can be confirmed by a glance at any 'block-buster' textbook. On p. 564 Wrightsman and Deaux (1981) at least take note of Gergen's famous criticism of mainstream social psychology, that all the data is context bound and historically particular. But they reject the criticism on the grounds that there are at least some universal facts about the social behaviour of human beings, which would be grist to the central processing mill. They cite a probable relationship between temperature and aggression as a candidate for a universal psychological law. Why should we accept this as a *psychological* law? Barry Schlenker, they assure us, has looked into the matter, and pronounced in favour of something they call 'scientific method'. This appears at the end of a book which could be described as an ethnography of the American middle class, excellent in its way. It is, at least, unfortunate that generations of trusting undergraduates are put through courses based on such very local ethnographics, presented as expositions of the psychology of all humankind.

The issue can be aproached in yet another way and in the light of yet another controversy. There has been much discussion of the status of so-called 'folk psychology'. By a folk psychology is meant the system of descriptive, analytic and explanatory concepts embedded in 'ordinary language'. Folk use this system to manage their lives. Is it primitive? Is it false? Could it be eliminated and replaced by something more sophisticated? In other words is there a root 'general psychology' which refers to the real source of human patterns of thought, feeling and action? The controversy over the character and status of folk psychology is, I believe, the same controversy as that which Shweder addresses in his discussion of the Platonistic myth of the existence of a ubiquitous but hidden general cognitive processor. The key issue is surely level of abstraction. The phenomena studied by social psychologists are extremely concrete and demonstrably culture bound. If we want to know what knowledge and skill is required to create and maintain a friendship in India it is almost wholly useless to transfer the conventions of friendship current in the American middle west to that distant subcontinent. The 'almost' defines an important programme of research, which, one might hope would displace the some of the older programmes of cross-cultural psychology, which assumed the scientific hegemony of the folk concepts of middle class Western academics. The matches and mismatches that we can identify in such matters as the genesis and maintenance of close and distant social relations can be defined only generically.

The psychological dimension of social activity, I have argued, following the observations of Shweder, is best confined to the attempt to understand the specific activities involved in the maintenance and creation of social order. However at the centre of any theory of people in society there must be some general conception of the nature of the human person. What are people generally disposed to do?

Throughout this study I shall be taking up the Renaissance image of architectonic humanity, *homo sapiens* the structure maker. The forms of life, for whatever purpose they are brought into being, are created according to various conceptions of harmony and order. As Coleridge argued, the imagination is central to human functioning since it is there that we generate the iconic, sensual representations of structures, that we hope to bring into existence. The creation, maintenance and recreation of local social orders is, I shall be demonstrating, just such a work of structure making. We owe to Durkheim (1915) the remarkable insight that certain social episodes, particularly folk rituals, can serve as representations of the common abstract structures of social orders in general.

We are also *homo loquens*. What are we saying? Much of human talk is performative, through which the forms of social order are realized in concrete episodes. But much talk effort is devoted to accounts, justificatory interpretations of what went on in this or that episode. *Homo loquens* is a rhetorician. The structures of ceremonies, institutions, life careers and so on 'fluoresce' only in the light of a rhetoric. As rhetorics shift and change so do the structures that they make visible. All are real. For example, when the structure of the social life within a mental hospital is made luminous by interpreting the activities therein according to the official rhetoric for such places, it appears as a place where sick and helpless people are cared for and sometimes cured by other healthy and competent people. But in the light of Goffman's (1968) dramaturgical rhetoric another social order is revealed, of a different structure. The institution can now be seen as a staging for dramas of character. Neither picture is false. Neither is wholly true. Each picture is a resource that members can draw on in making sense of their daily activities within the institution. One way of seeing the project of this book is as an argument that the ultimate source of each structured cluster of episodes we encounter in observing social life is the transformation of some social icon into concrete form of act-action sequences.

THE SOCIOLOGICAL BASIS FOR SOCIAL PSYCHOLOGY

The discursive skills, upon which social psychology should focus, are deployed in the joint production of the episodes of everyday life. There already exists a powerful and mature sociology for the analysis of such episodes. It can be found in the writings of Erving Goffman (1968, 1972) and in the work of the ethnomethodologists, inspired by Harold Garfinkel (1967). This is a microsociology, the central theme of which is that creation and maintenance of small-scale social order is an artful achievement of active human agents. It is to that sociology I believe social psychologists should turn for their conception of 'the social'.

The routines of social life are directed to the realization of all sorts of projects and ends. I shall be making use of a broad distinction between those aspects of social activity that are directed to material and biological ends, which I shall call 'practical aspects of joint-action', realized as a practical order, and those directed to such ends as the presentation of the self as valuable and worthy of respect, which I shall call 'expressive aspects of joint-action', realized as an expressive order. The concept of the expressive order, as I shall use it, owes a great deal to the writings of Thornstein Veblen (1899).

The expressive aspects of an activity usually appear in the way the practical side of the activity is carried out; and would often be described in adverbs of action: 'She typed the letter resentfully' and the like. But the distinction between practical and expressive activity or modes and aspects of activity is not absolute. It may re-emerge at a higher order of analysis if the expressive aspect of an activity becomes the dominating instrumentality, for there may be all kinds of practical tasks that need to be performed so as to achieve the expressive presentations aimed at. One needs to have cooked an *haute cuisine* meal successfully in order to be able to serve it with the studied nonchalance that gives the impression that it is one's everyday fare.

A rough guide as to whether an activity or mode of activity is predominantly practical or expressive is to see whether the relation of means to end is causal, as for example, digging is related to cropping; or conventional, as for example wearing one's hair short in the eighteenth century advertised a radical or even a revolutionary stance to society (Schama, 1989). Even this distinction is not quite adequate since we shall see that conventions play a certain role in the causal account of action. Though it is perhaps a little early in the argument to introduce the point, it might be better to make this distinction in terms of that between physical and psychological (and social) causality; though the full explication of that distinction must await a theory of actors and of the production of their performances.

But even this more refined distinction is subject to exceptions. For example a change in material organization of the world, involving at least some principles of physical causality, such as the orientation of door to door-frame may involve a sequence in which one or more steps are mediated by convention, as for instance that the sound sequence 'Close the door' means close the door; and the conventions that orders are to be obeyed and not to be challenged, debated or used as an occasion of self-presentation by staging a public refusal. (Though all of these may be uses to which orders are put, they were not on this occasion.) More positively, if an outcome of an action sequence is taken to be supportive of or demeaning to a reputation then the activity is to be treated as primarily expressive. This implies that the distinction practical-expressive is not given in any of the occurrent properties of the action sequence.

In the expressive aspects of social activity we make a public showing of skills, attitudes, emotions, feelings and so on, providing, sometimes consciously, the evidence upon which our friends, colleagues, neighbours, rivals and enemies are to draw conclusions as to the kind of person we are. The expressive aspect will include both natural and conventional signs. For instance, an agitated way of going about our work is a natural sign of our anxiety about its outcome, and how we will be judged by reference to it, even though we may deliberately assume an appearance of agitation for expressive purposes – while shrugging the shoulders with both palms raised is a conventional sign of our regret at the incompetence of another motorist; to be sharply distinguished from reproof. However, the distinction between natural and conventional signs is not an exhaustive and exclusive dichotomy, but a polar opposition. There are many signs that have a colour of both, and assumed agitation might be an example. While it is natural for some people it has become a convention for others.

Our general schema for the development of explanatory theories in social science can be set out as follows:

Practical aspects of activity }
Expressive aspects of activity } jointly explain social formations

But the relative weight of each in an explanation will depend upon historical conditions. In the nineteenth century, *for most people*, the practical aspect of an activity so absorbed the time and energy available for living that it had a dominant role in the genesis of social formations. But in the European Middle Ages or in near contemporary Melanesia the practical aspect occupies so little of the time available for social activity and its cognitive and imaginative preparation that the expressive aspect becomes the dominant influence on social formations. I take modern Western society to be more like Melanesian social formations in this regard that it is like the social world of the English midlands in the nineteenth century. Anthropologists give us a figure of between 8 to 10 per cent of living time devoted to sustenance of life in most pre-industrial societies (Sahlins, 1974). That leaves a lot of social space and time for dressing up, gossiping and chasing other people's spouses.

LINKING MICROSOCIOLOGY TO A PSYCHOLOGY OF ACTIVE AGENTS

Ritual markings of respect and contempt

Both practical and expressive aspects of social activity should be looked at teleologically. By this I mean that the full understanding of an activity, or of that aspect of it to which we are attending, could not be achieved without our viewing it as having an upshot or outcome, as culminating or issuing in a result. This allows for the possibility but does not enjoin the necessity of people intending those outcomes when they act.

But more importantly for present purposes it allows for the possibility of success or failure in bringing about the outcome. For those who share our evaluation of our goals our success would normally lead to their respect, if perhaps only grudging, while our failure would merit their contempt, derision, pity or sympathy. But for those who put different evaluations upon the upshot of our activities, our very success may merit their contempt, and our failure at least their indifference. A keen young bank clerk may be pitied or even despised by former school friends, bent on different goals, on his appointment as assistant branch manager – while the successful seduction of a child may be admired by fellow paedophiles.

I shall be supposing that common experiences of human life suggests that private knowledge of and satisfaction in success is worthless to most human beings. We prefer to risk the contempt or pity consequent upon public failure for the chance of the respect and even admiration accorded to public success. The concepts of respect and contempt have a useful duality. They are the names of feelings and of the attitudes which those feelings mark. But they are also the subject of public and ceremonial display. 'They showed him,' we say, 'the marks of respect (or contempt).' And of course they may have showed him those marks not because they had the feelings or attitudes to go with them, but because of the social demands of the occasion, the public role of the man, and so on. It is part of the point of this study to emphasize the degree to which progress in social life is forwarded by ritual and ceremonial activities, regardless of the flux of feelings and attitudes the very people who engage in them may be experiencing. It is only in very exceptional circumstances indeed that feeling will break through so to speak against the almost overwhelming power of ritual. I take it as almost (but not quite) unexceptionable that any public ritual of respect is dominant over personal feeling in human social activity. So too a public ritual of respect is not to be taken to imply of necessity feelings of admiration in those who perform it – nor one of contempt or disdain that the ritual practitioners feel dislike or disgust.

I do not propose to hazard any hypothesis as to the origins of the specific respect/contempt hierarchies that are found so variously and so widely in human social affairs. I shall be building the analysis in this work on the idea that ritual marking of respect and contempt do play a large part in human life, creating social relations of unique importance. But 'respecting' and 'despising' others take very different forms in different social systems, and differ greatly in the content and complexity of local criteria by means of which the judgements upon which the giving and withholding of respect and contempt are based. There is enormous variety, too, in the symbolic apparatus by which the results of these judgements are marked.

The continuum defined by this concept pair will be used as a basic analytical tool in this work. I am claiming that in the absence of any other social universal – and we shall see that there are good reasons for being sceptical of most proposals for universal principles – a continuum between generic relations of respect and contempt will serve to bring to light similarities in a wide variety of societies and social practices.

I shall try to prove the viability of this hypothesis in the course of the work in that the illuminations, which I believe it will be seen to cast upon the enigmatic and problematic issues of the understanding of human social activity, will be enough to confirm its value if not its truth.

Like many of the concepts we need for the understanding of the psychology of social life respect and contempt refer both to publicly expressed attitudes and to private feelings one may have for another.

In general we must not assume that where there is the one there will be the other. Much giving of public respect and contempt is ritualized and independent of feeling, while the demands of social propriety require the concealment or even the suppression of respectful or contemptuous feelings. We shall suppose then that real people on real occasions are seeking out occasions for acquiring respect while risking pity or disdain, and they may find these occasions in almost any social activities. But people hand out marks of respect and contempt not only for success and failure in the activities of social life, but on the basis of relatively permanent attributes and properties of other human beings. For example reasons for respecting or disdaining people may be found in their colour, stature, sex, accent, job, age, ethnicity and so on. I shall be arguing that it is impossible to predict in principle what any given society will select from the enormously complex system of properties and activities available to find occasions for dealing out marks of respect and contempt.

Respect, as I have argued above, is more than an attitude and not necessarily linked to an emotion. It is a socially marked relation, shown by deference and reciprocated by condescension. The associated presentational style of one who has respect, is dignity. In societies as we know of them, the showing of deference, the reciprocation by condescension, and the illustration of the propriety of the giving of respect in a show of dignity, have become largely ritualized. Contempt, on the other hand, is shown by disdain, and is reciprocated by grovelling. It is important to realize that both respect and contempt are reciprocal relations between people and marked in reciprocal and complementary forms of presentational style. It is not, of course, that the one who shows respect is thereby brought into contempt from the other: rather, for any attribution and ritual marking of respect or contempt, two people are required who must reciprocally publicly represent their place in the relation. Respect is reciprocated by affable condescension, while contempt, which is marked by the showing of disdain, must be reciprocated by the grovelling and servility of the one who accepts the contempt shown by the other. But of course one may deal with shown contempt by resentment and even retaliation.

Respect and contempt, then, are illustrated or shown, and ritually symbolically marked in the course of particular activities of daily life. Sometimes they may be the result of specific institutions whose function in the society is the generation of respect and contempt. These I shall call 'hazards'. A simple hazard, for example, is an examination in an educational system. Associated with these momentary phenomena is a social entity which I shall follow Goffman in calling 'character': that is, public social reputation. A single human individual may have more than one character, since character is what is attributed to him or her by a certain set of others. Human social life is sufficiently complex, at least in modern society, for someone to interact with several non-overlapping sets of others, and perhaps to acquire several characters. Public social reputation can be sought, risked, gained or lost in public, in the course of those conventional trials I have called hazards. It can be the subject of a progress, and acquired step by step in which I shall follow Goffman in calling 'a moral career'. But the existence of hazards and of the institutions for the giving and marking of respect and contempt allow for the possibility of a downward moral career through failure at hazard. Failure is defined reciprocally to the success from which one gains respect and dignity, and it is marked by humiliation. The experience of humiliation is the reciprocal of the maintenance of dignity. Some recent studies of adolescence have shown many young people to have an almost obsessive interest and preoccupation with the maintenance of dignity and the careful scanning of the social environment for occasions and acts of possible humiliation. When such acts have been identified some adolescents may undertake violent retaliation, which in their view has the aim of restoring the dignity that they have lost in the eyes of their peers before whom, and only before whom, they have been humiliated.

Finally, it is worth noticing that the conceptual system of which I have given the barest outline in this introduction allows for a disparity between a person's conception of themselves and the character, or characters, which are the public representations of what sort of human being they are taken to be. This introduces a dynamical tension into social life, a tension which we shall find to be powerfully explicatory of much social activity. The resolution of this tension requires the possibility of deliberately contrived action aimed at the management of public persona, which by influencing the way others perceive us, influences their attribution of character to us. We shall be returning, from time to time, to this distinctive type of presentational activity. It is at a different order from the expressive qualification of actions in the way they are performed – since the expressive aspects become instrumental goals.

I shall not be concerned in this study with the analysis and understanding of all those practical activities which human beings undertake for the purposes of the maintenance of life and the production of goods. I shall take them to be a groundswell of activity on the surface of which, in pursuit of expressive aims, people reveal the central preoccupations of human life. I take it the extraordinary degree to which the daily activity of the industrial workers of the nineteenth century was absorbed in the mere business of staying alive was a tragic aberration of the usual conditions of human life. It is in the froth or efflorescence, as it were, of life, in presentational and expressive activities of human beings, that I propose to locate the central dynamics of society. We shall see, however, that it is possible to acknowledge the fundamental truth that Marx perceived, namely the powerful role that the system of production, in both its material and social aspects, plays in social life. But its entry into and effect upon social activity, according to this theory, will be utterly different from the way Marx is popularly supposed to have conceived it. So his intuition will be preserved at the small cost of abandoning his implausible and ill-defined causal theory as to how it might be that the system of material production and distribution generates in all its essentials the super-structure in which social lives are actually led.

THE TONE OF THIS UNDERTAKING

Moscovici's accusation that 'mainstream' social psychologists have concentrated on, and so promoted, only a rosy picture of human life, is well founded. Human beings do the most appalling things to each other, often in pursuit of lamentable ends. Cruelty and prejudice are far more widespread than benevolence and kindness. Most people are generally miserable, bored and resentful most of the time. Occasionally a social psychologist can be found who has realized that there is a darker side to human social interactions. Milgram, despite serious defects in his methodology, must be given the greatest credit for turning away from the study of the 'good guys'. Even in the heartland of the 'smile' culture the social relationships in most academic institu-tions are poisoned by such divisive practices as 'merit raise' evaluations.

I am not disposed to take an optimistic view of human life. The hopes of most young people come to nothing. The disappointments of the middle years of life are followed, for those who survive them, by the ugliness, pain and despair of old age. Most human effort, it seems to me, is ill directed or dissipated in acts of folly. The pervasive tone of life for most people is boredom, but a boredom made more acute by resentment. Our imaginations offer us visions of all kinds of possibilities of action we are usually too idle to realize. As J.S. Mill put it, '. . . Those who, while desiring what others possess, put no energy into striving for it, are either incessantly grumbling that fortune does not do for them what they do not attempt to do for themselves or overflowing with envy and ill-will towards those who possess what they would like to have'.

But at the same time people have a deep sense of their own dignity, and craving for recognition as beings of worth in the opinion of others of their kind. I shall be arguing that the pursuit of reputation in the eyes of others is the overriding preoccupation of human life, for which people will often set aside life itself. Of course the means by which reputations are established can be extraordinarily various. Here we touch on the Shweder point yet again. Categorization and comparison must be available as discursive skills to those who live by social emulation, and that is all of us. Though people compete individually for honour and reputation in our society, reputation is a corporate matter and its acquisition a cooperative achievement. It is the product of the recognition of one's worth by others. Whether value accrues from one's personal or social identity is one of the great variables that distinguish human cultures so deeply that their moral orders, their conceptions of justice and so on are almost wholly incommensurable.

SUMMARY: SOME GENERAL PRINCIPLES THAT WILL GUIDE THIS ENQUIRY

1 Social life is a cultural achievement, an enormous elaboration on the biological processes necessary for organic survival.
2 Social acts are achieved by conventional means, often in the form of ritual.
3 Human beings can distance themselves from any of the rule-systems that underpin their culture, but only if they are prepared to pay the social and practical costs.
4 Lives are lived according to the local patterns of exemplary biographies, creating moral careers, ups and downs in reputation in the eyes of others.
5 A person's character transcends their roles, but is not, at bottom, a personal achievement. It is a cluster of theories and expectations held about that person by others in their circle, often revealed in personal gossip.
6 Episodes interact and interweave with one another. The whole may have a larger pattern unknown to those who actively and intentionally create its parts.
7 Disappointment and resentment encourage some to search for other icons of alternative social orders.

But envisaging a possible future, more satisfactory than the world of the present, is an empty exercise unless there are ways to bring those futures about. This introduces an inevitable political dimension into social psychology. However, we have learned, albeit reluctantly, that attempts to manage new worlds into existence have *always* failed. The final phase of the analysis presented in this book will be occupied with an attempt to understand why this is so and to redefine the nature of political reform in the light of that understanding.

2

PEOPLE IN GROUPS

ANTICIPATORY SUMMARY

In this chapter the interplay between individuals and the groups to which they belong will be analyzed from the point of view of one of the basic ontological concepts of social psychology, namely structure. I begin with the important distinction between a taxonomic group or class, constructed logically by attending to the balance of locally relevant similarities and differences between its members, and a structured group or collective, constituted effectively by social interactions and relations among its members. To develop a social psychology for various human forms of group life one of the great metaphysical issues in social science must be faced, namely the nature of the relations between individuals and collectives.

Acting together people produce structures, orderly assemblages of elements. In this chapter a general definition of the concept of structure is given. It is intended to be applicable both to relatively static social entities such as institutions, for instance business firms, and to dynamic interactional episodes, such as a meeting of the board of directors of that firm. In each of these structures people are present not only as individuals, but also as social beings, as representatives of types.

From this discussion the important conclusion emerges that structured groups, that is collectives, are ontologically prior to individuals. Human beings are constituted as people by their interpersonal relations. This does not mean that there is really no such thing as personal responsibility. In many societies people are brought up to be agents, that is to be capable of responding to the demands of individual moral responsibility for action. The distinction between ephemeral social groupings, institutions and large scale collectives, like nations, is brought out along the way.

THE STATUS OF HUMAN GROUPS

The longest-running, and perhaps the deepest philosophical issue in the theory of the social sciences has to do with the metaphysics of the groups in which human beings associate. The many discussions and controversies can, I think, be simplified and condensed into two issues:

1   Do groups of human beings in interaction with one another have properties which are different in any causally significant way from the aggregate of the properties of the individuals? We notice, of course, that one individual can influence all the others in a group, for instance, by putting poison in their water supply, or by sending each of them a copy of a pamphlet setting out his or her views on some matter (which need not be of common concern). But these are mere aggregates of individual influences. The question could be answered shortly and sharply if it could be shown that the groups had no properties of any kind other than aggregates of individual properties. Some groups of things, particularly structured groups such as cells congregated as organs and interconnected as organisms clearly do have emergent properties – a person's capacity to think is not the aggregate of the thinking capacities of each of their cells, nor indeed is their capacity to run an aggregate of the moving capacity of each of their limbs. It is looking to this kind of analogue for the relation between people and their groups that has been one historically potent source for the idea that societies as human collectives have emergent properties.

2   Do groups of people formed as collectives have the status of supra-individuals? Do they have some of the metaphysical properties of individuals, such as continuity and identity through time? Are there criteria by which they can be individuated one from another? It seems obvious that some forms of human groupings are supra-individuals. Armies and other military formations when they are in the field, teams on tour, families on holiday, business firms and many other collectives seem to display individualistic properties. But would it be right to attribute the same kind of supra-individuality to nations, to a work force, to a bureaucracy or to other such associations, even though grammar points directly to it?

In this chapter I shall be trying to steer a course between the extremes in the classical arguments – and to forge a plausible account of people in structured groups from a judicious blending of half-truths culled from the works of each party to the dispute.

It is necessary to develop suitable notions of individual and of collective which can be fitted together into a unified conceptual system adequate to control the analysis of human groups and associations. Any discussion of this perennial problem area must take account of the existence of two extreme metaphysical positions. According to one view there are no individuals, except in a bare spatio-temporal sense. There are only intersection-points of relational properties of collectives. According to the other view there are no collectives, only aggregates, that is only unstructured accidental assemblages of people. A subtle new form of this doctrine has recently been proposed. It is argued that to study collectives we need study only individuals and their properties. Both extreme theories will be examined and both will be found wanting (Ryan, 1970:177ff.).

COLLECTIVISM EXAMINED

The extreme collectivist position holds that each human being is wholly constituted as a social person by collective properties of the groups to which he or she belongs and in which he or she participates as a member of the society. These collective properties are not themselves constituted of individual properties but rather are the very structural properties which are the basis of the properties of the collective. So, by a double transition from the claim that an individual is constituted by their relations to other members of their collective, and that those relations are the structural properties of the collective itself, the individual as a social being is reduced to an entity wholly defined in terms of the properties of the collective. We are each nothing but the totality of our roles and the totality of roles constitutes the collective.

The extreme positions on this matter are defined not just by differences of opinion about matters of fact. Are the attributes of individual people *really* properties of the relevant collectives and vice versa? They also express moral stances. For instance the extreme positions incorporate different ideas of how moral responsibility for actions should be distributed. Arguments for and against the extreme individualist and extreme collectivist positions must take account of both empirical and moral considerations.

If people really are wholly constituted by their social roles how is it possible for any person to have distinctive, original or creative thoughts or to conduct themselves in other than stereotypical ways? The fact that people do have such thoughts, that these thoughts can be expressed and understood by others, and that they do engage in eccentric conduct that is not construed as mere madness, surely shows that the extreme ontological version of collectivism must be false. But that conclusion depends on both parties to the dispute agreeing that the creative individual is still a person – both an avant garde poet and a member of society.

A stern collectivist, of the kind so dominant in the late unlamented régimes of Eastern Europe, would be unmoved by this argument. 'Autonomy' and 'creativity' would more properly be called 'deviance'. In consequence an individual who has characteristics which are not reducible to the properties which he or she possesses by virtue of membership of the collective is, for that reason, a distorted or defective human being, scarcely a person at all. It follows, if one accepts this point of view, that remedial action, political, psychological, or otherwise, can be taken to restore the defect in the individual, making them once more a perfect member of the collective. The reasoning is fairly simple. If the collectivist theory is true, an individual who shows deviant properties is an imperfect representation of the ideal member of the collective. By the definition of a person as one fulfilling the demands of the collectivist theory, such deviant individuals are not truly persons. Hence it is proper to reconstitute or even, in the extreme, to eliminate them. It is clear that arguments against extreme collectivism cannot be based simply upon the empirical fact that deviant individuals exist. An argument would have to be constructed on the basis of a valuation of autonomous and creative individuals with respect to the higher development of the collective itself in such a way as to undermine the argument that all non-standard individuals are deviant. Such an argument can, indeed, be formulated. As I shall show, the only truly radical theory of social change requires that change should proceed through the differential selection of new social practices and institutions created by non-standard individuals within their collectives. Only in this way can the collective evolve to a higher form. In short, the extreme collectivist thesis is essentially conservative.

It sometimes happens that the society may be convinced of its perfection and consequently may wish to maintain itself in the state in which it presently finds itself. Such a belief in the actual perfection of an existing society is likely to be associated with an extreme collectivist theory and consequently with recognizable institutionalized practices for defining non-standard individuals as deviant, sick, mad and so on. The argument moves from a sociological to a moral plane.

INDIVIDUALISM EXAMINED

The extreme individualist thesis, that is the theory that each individual is wholly autonomous and could exist as a person independently of the

collectives to which he or she belongs, is a reflection of the theory that
the relations which a person has to the relevant collectives are wholly
external, and consequently quite contingent. This theory too cannot be
effectively sustained. Again, the reasons for repudiating an extreme
individualism are partly empirical and partly moral in character.

It is fairly easy to show, simply by drawing attention to uncontroversial facts available to anyone, that many properties characteristic of fully developed human beings are dependent upon that
person being a member of a collective. For example, I think it would
be readily conceded that for any anthropoid to be properly considered
a person, it must be capable not only of the use of language but
actually to use it in day-to-day social activity and in cognitive and
reflective life. I think it is also indisputable that there could not be a
language-user who was not a member of a language community.

Political and moral arguments against individualism are a little more
difficult to formulate than those against collectivism since they have to
do with the basis for responsibility to others. I would take it to be part
of the necessary conditions for an anthropoid to be a person that he or
she recognized him or herself as responsible to and for others in daily
life. The second component of that condition – namely responsibility
for others – is clearly an empirically grounded necessary condition
since it is an essential feature of anthropoid parenthood that the
caretaking individual should be responsible for the helpless infant.
However, one could imagine an anthropoid race in which that relation
did not obtain. Once again, as in the critique of collectivism, one could
maintain that an extreme moral individualism was in itself a self-
contradictory principle since it would be impossible for an individual to
attain true moral stature if it were not attained through the exercise of
responsibility to and for others. According to this line of thought the
very idea of a person is bound up with the possibility of that person
taking moral action. This in itself is bound up with the idea of action in
the interests not only of oneself but of others. And this is a collectivist
conception.

The distinction between internal and external relations

The distinction drawn in the last section between extreme collectivism
and extreme individualism can be looked at from the point of view
of the distinction between internal and external relations amongst
individuals.

Two or more individuals are internally related in case they are
wholly or partly constituted as beings of a certain type by virtue of

standing in that relation. For example, a person is constituted as a 'husband' by virtue of standing in the sociolegal relation of marriage with another person as 'wife'. It is not possible for a husband or a wife to be unmarried. Should a person by some misfortune lose the other member of the relation which is constituent of husbandhood, he or she becomes a member of a socially different type – for example 'widowed'. The relation of 'being married' is internal to and a constitutive of part of the meaning of 'husband' together with its correlative 'wife'.

There are subtleties with respect to the level of organization within which we are considering the members of a type. For example, when we are considering human beings for social or psychological purposes the spatio-temporal relations which individuate them as material objects are not usually amongst the relations. Nevertheless these play a role as necessary conditions for the coming into existence of those relations which do make human individuals persons of this sort or that. For most social categories a person is already taken to be in existence as a spatio-temporal enduring entity. We are considering him or her as coming into other kinds of relations, while maintaining basic individuating relations to space-time and the material system of which space-time is a property. Spatio-temporal continuity is not entirely irrelevant to the constitution of a human being as a social person, in that birth and death, which commonly result from spatial convergence and dispersal of material over time, are important markers in a social career.

A relation is external in case the individuals so related do not change their category or type when they cease to stand in that relation. For most purposes we can regard persons as beings for which spatio-temporal relations are external. Spatial and temporal propinquity and contemporaneity are involved in people finding themselves within the same nationstate or living in the same epoch but clearly the spatio-temporal relations are germane only in so far as they involve distinctive social conditions. I shall be assuming that there are almost no external social relations.

If we refer back now to the considerations advanced in the previous section concerning the individualist and collectivist points of view, it is apparent that these points of view could be expressed in terms of the distinction between internal and external relations.

If, as seems plausible, most social relations are internal, the nature of structured groups would seem to fit the metaphysics of collectivism better than that of individualism. However, as I have pointed out, the distinction between an individualist and a collectivist ontology is not only an empirical matter but expresses a fundamental cleavage in conceptions of moral responsibility. An emphasis on the moral integrity of persons can shift the weight of argument back towards individualism. In the framework of this analysis moral individualism, which is sustained by the existence of personal agency, is not only compatible with a theory of collectives based on internal relations which assigns a social origin to persons, but flows from it. Societal processes of person creation, examined in detail in *Personal being*, produce agents, with the degree of moral autonomy proper to the prevailing form of life. The thesis of the social construction of persons does not entail moral collectivism, the thesis that human actions are predominantly the effects of social causes.

Taking collectivism ontologically requires one to give an account of the way a structured group or collective of people see each other in terms of the cycle of internal relations constitutive of the group. Such a group could have properties different from an accidental aggregate or concourse of human beings. I shall begin an investigation of this question by briefly sketching the theory of social collectives, expounded directly and indirectly by Leon Tolstoy.

According to Tolstoy's theory, the only collective properties of a mass of human beings are very large scale, temporally and spatially, and partly as a consequence of that, very simple. His favourite example of a genuine collective property is migration, particularly the ebb and flow of people from west to east and east to west across the European continent.

In contrast, groups of people in social interaction on a smaller scale have no properties which are not imposed upon them by the human imagination, that is smaller groups are not collectives at all. They have no properties. Small groups of human beings engage in activities which are strictly inchoate. For example, the battles that were fought between the Russians and the French in the time of Napoleon are not structured events having collective properties, but chaotic and disorderly whirlpools in the tide of migration. However, according to Tolstoy, human beings are quite unable to accept that the events in which they feel themselves to have taken part are strictly disorderly and inchoate. In consequence they undertake an active, interpretative process in the course of which these events and the masses of people involved in them are represented as orderly and controlled. There may even come into existence a special profession, the profession of historian, whose task it is to create these orderly interpretations in which collectives are generated out of nothing but chaotic aggregates.

It is as an exemplification of this theory that the Battle of Borodino forms the centre-piece of Tolstoy's great novel, since it is both an illustration of the theory and a microcosm of human affairs. Neither Napoleon or Kutuzov were really in command of the men who took part in the battle. The fighting was joined by accident and the result was a victory for neither side if the events are viewed dispassionately. Yet, as Tolstoy shows, historians from both sides had reconstructed the 'reality' of what happened at Borodino so as to contrast the tactical genius of Napoleon with the strategic mastery of Kutuzov and to represent the happenings on the day of the battle as having properties that endowed them with an existence as a collective, an orderly assemblage of men and events.

However attractive this theory may be, it makes too extreme a case. One obvious difficulty is posed by the possibility of intermediate cases which are neither as grand as national migration nor as short-lived and small-scale as battles. For example, those organizations and collocated social practices we ordinarily call institutions seem to be both orderly in fact, and created and sustained in being by human interpretative activities and normative prescriptions.

Deeply embedded in Tolstoy's theory of collectives and their properties is a theory about the causes of social events. For him large-scale human phenomena have causes, small-scale human phenomena happen by accident. Only later, as a deliberate act of interpretation are they redefined so that they can be thought of as caused. But this development of the theory opens up the possibility of the question, 'How are the large-scale collective properties of masses of human beings caused?' One solution might be to claim that, strictly speaking, the collective properties are not caused at all, but are the aggregate of activities of individuals as, for example, a tribe migrates to the west because each member goes to the west. And this 'because' is not the 'because' of causation. The statement becomes, the tribe migrates to the west means "each member goes to the west"'. This solution is inadequate since it does not at all follow that if each member goes to the west the tribe goes to the west. For the tribe to go to the west its organization, its internal structure, social practices, its representations of its own history, its language, must go with it, whatever may be the account of those collective properties given by members of the tribe. It would be absurd to claim that because the slaves from the Dahomey were moved to the West Indies and the United States, so were their tribes.

Individual and collective properties in a relational theory

It may be possible to make a successful distinction between individuals and collectives by attacking the problem of their differentiation indirectly. Distinctions might be able to be drawn between the kinds of properties characteristic of collectives and those characteristic of individuals. Individuals and collectives could then be distinguished through the conditions they must satisfy for each to be able to take on its appropriate range of attributes. However, it should be noticed at the outset that the distinction between collectives and individuals is a relative distinction. An individual considered with respect to one kind of collective may be able to be treated as a collective with respect to another kind of individual. Similarly entities which are to be considered collectives with respect to a certain category of individuals may themselves be individuals with respect to some category of superordinate collectives. It may be the distinction between collective and individual properties must also be relativized to the kind of entity to which they are attributed. For example, though 'tall' is a non-collective property of a person, it might arguably be treated as a collective property of an assemblage of limbs or bones. It would be analysable as a relational attribute of the collection as collective.

So it seems that a circle of differentiations links the collective/individual distinction as conceived ontologically with the empirical distinctions we might draw between properties appropriate to collectives as against those attributable to individuals, with respect to some given level of analysis. Such a circle is not vicious since it could be broken anywhere and the pragmatic advantages of the distinction−drawing at that point displayed or demonstrated: 'Take "it" to "bits" before you fix "it"' for example.

One way of distinguishing collective from individual properties might be to propose that collective properties are structural properties − that is, they are based upon, but not reduceable to, relations between more than one individual. Not all relational properties are collective properties. For a relational property to be a collective property it must be that two or more individuals, standing in that relation or relations, constitute a superordinate individual, the collective. One way in which this more stringent condition might be achieved is to require that at least one of the relations in which the elements of the collective stand should be invariant under a wide range of transformations. For example, if the relation between two elements is a distance, then if that distance is invariant under translation and rotation of the pair of elements, we might with reason take that pair to be a simple collective; that is the pair behave in certain respects as an individual. Examples of more interesting structural properties, on the basis of which a set of elements might be thought to be a collective, would be, for example, an order of battle defined in terms of spatial relations between the units of an army in which order rather than absolute distance was held invariant; or a power hierarchy, based on asymmetrical relations of obedience, decision making, the giving of respect and deference, the showing of condescension, etc., among a fixed group of people. It is clear that in both these cases certain invariants have to be maintained for the collective constituted by these relational properties to be maintained. For example, certain geometrical relations must continue to obtain between the units of the army. Should they break down the army ceases to exist and a new collective, which perhaps ought more properly to be called an aggregate – in some circumstances it might be called a rabble – could come into existence, and the battle – an event collective – be transformed into a rout. Similarly, a power hierarchy constitutes an institution just so long as asymmetrical relations remain invariant over time and over the conditions of the life of the people who make up its elements.

For many collectives the internal structure – the kind of property to which I have been drawing attention so far – is not in general perceptible as such, when the collective is viewed as an individual. Many structural properties appear as simple qualities, often in a different sensory mode, when a collective is perceived as an individual. In general, secondary qualities are related to structural properties of an individual considered as a collective of elements in this way. For example, a melody is an epiphenomenal or secondary quality of the time and pitch structure of a collective of individual notes; a colour is an epiphenomenal quality of a particular orderly arrangement of the components of molecules, and so on.

There are endowments from the endo-collective, that is the internal structure of the relatively elementary parts of the individual, to that individual. For example, many of the properties we are accustomed to call 'powers' are such endowments. For example, the valency of a chemical atom is a power which it has by virtue of the structural properties of the endo-collective, that is the structured set of individual microparticles which make it up. Many human powers too we regard as endowments from structural properties of the nervous system or some other part of the anatomy.

It is worth remarking that for a structural property to be manifested as an epiphenomenal property – that is as a property of the collective considered as an individual – there must be something on which that collective has an effect. An obvious example is the effect the collective has on an observer by virtue of the possession of that structure, but we might equally well be inclined to use the concepts I have just sketched to understand the effect of a collective considered as an individual on some other collective, which is not itself sentient, as for example, the magnetic field of a bar magnet has an effect on the iron filings strewn on a piece of glass.

Many important properties of individuals are endowments to an individual from the exo-collective – that is the external structure within which an individual is an element. For example, according to Mach's theory, the mass of an individual material body in the material universe is an endowment from the exo-collective to that individual by virtue of the relations in which that individual stands to the collective. To take up an example I have already discussed briefly, social role as attributed to an individual member of an institution could be regarded as an endowment to that individual from the institution – that is the exo-collective – by virtue of their relations to that collective.

It is not without significance that most of the examples I have chosen to illustrate the points I want to make about the way collective properties exist have been made with examples chosen from the material world and from the physical sciences. This raises the question of whether there are any socially epiphenomenal properties, that is structural properties of collectives which are experienced as, or could be treated as, simple properties in another mode from those in which they exist as relations in the collective. I think it is not unreasonable to suggest that role is just such a property, since for many people role is experienced, not as a relational property in which the individual stands to the collectives of which he or she forms a member, but rather as a systematic set of psychological and microsocial imperatives and constraints. The relational property is experienced as an individual property, perhaps because the individual receives this endowment from the exo-collective by a long process of learning and conditioning. However, the properties of the exo-collective – for example institutions or even societies – which are not represented in individual consciousness in such a way as role might be thought to be represented, are not in general experienced at all. If we know about them it is only by round-about and frequently dubious macrosociological methods whose epistemology, as it is at present constituted, has been much called in question: in particular the usual methods for generating 'data' by giving standard questionnaires to each member of an exo-collective, and from some totalization of their replies hypothesizing properties of the collective. Even official statistics are highly suspect, for they are often constructed for some practical purpose, quite distinct from 'the aim of finding scientific truth'.

Structure

Under what conditions should we say a collection of individuals has a structure? I propose the following:

1 There is a set, or there are sets of individuals of one or several categories, for which determinate criteria of identity and individuation can be given.

2 There is a set, or there are sets of relations of one or more categories in which the individuals specified above can stand. The set of relations defining a structure is in principle richer than the relations actually realized at any time.

These conditions are meant to cover both those cases where the individuals can be specified as to kind, whether or not they stand in the relations which determine structure, or whether they are in part or whole constituted as members of kinds by virtue of standing in those relations.

3 There is at least one kind of relation in which the individuals forming a structure stand, which is invariant under transformation of some or all of the remaining kinds of relations in which they stand. Satisfaction of this principle I shall call the maintenance of the integrity of the structure.

The distinction between actual structures and latent structures will prove useful in addition. For the purposes of social analysis the institutions of society considered structurally are certainly not in actual being continuously over time. For example, when the pupils leave and the doors are shut and the teachers go home, schooling as a social activity ceases. However, to conclude that the school as a social entity has only intermittent existence would be unwarranted. So long as certain beliefs, commitments and rule systems are represented in the cognitive resources, whether conscious or not, and if all the people who are involved in that institution on the occasions when it is actual continue to exist, the school as a latent structure remains, as an institution of the society. Indeed it will emerge from our investigations that most of the social entities with which we are concerned are more latent than actual, that is exist more in the powers, capacities, knowledge, beliefs and expectations of the folk, than they do in continuously realized social practices.

Templates and jigsaws
There are a number of different cases which fall under the general template principle. The product may have a structure extended over time. For example, a musical score is the structure which generates a time-extended tune, a melodic structure through the activity of the pianist as an agent following the score. On the other hand a house-plan is responsible for the time-independent structure that is eventually realized as a house by the activities of the builder in following the plan. In both these cases the relationship between template and product is at

least potentially one: many, since many different performances of the same score and many different houses based upon the same plan can be constructed.

An important application of the distinction between types and tokens can be found in the relationship between template and product. In the examples just given, where the template is a physically realized structure, it can function as the bearer of a type, each individual product generated from it being a token of that type. Of course, the plan and the score are not themselves types, but by virtue of their re-usability, are the bearers of types. There are a number of different ways in which the temporal properties of templates and products may be related.

The template may be structured synchronically, that is realized at a moment in time, as for example, a printed Order of Service exists as a structure enduring in time, but the product created in accordance with it may be diachronic. For example, the ceremony which is produced by participants as agents following the Order of Service, is a structure of actions sequentially ordered in time.

A template may be all in being synchronically and endure through time, as in our example of the house-plan, and the product may also be synchronically organized and enduring as well. Such, for example, is the well-built house.

It is worth noticing that in practice synchronic organization of physical structures is often spatial and diachronic organization temporal, though as we shall see in the case of structural properties of society formations of synchronic organizations are not necessarily spatial.

There are cases where the template is realized diachronically, as for example the development by an Indian musician, in advance of his performance, of the conception of the melodic structure he is improvising. In this case the product, the musical performance, is also diachronic.

There are cases where the template exists as a temporal sequence laid out diachronically, but in following it through the agent produces a synchronically structured entity, for example, it may be that by following his developing conception an artist produces a product which is a synchronically structured and enduring work of art.

We must also differentiate those cases where the template survives the production of the product and can be used again – cases which I shall call 'replication' – from those where the productive process is, in one way or another, an absorption of the template into the product. The latter process I shall call 'transformation'.

A clay model for a statue is usually built onto an 'armature', a metal framework which becomes part of the model and so cannot be reused as a template for other copies. Something like this happens when the conversational intentions of a group are uniquely realized in a negotiation, for example, which, in the nature of the case could never be repeated. For instance the intentions of Czar Alexander and Napoleon were uniquely jointly realized in the their negotiations on a barge moored in the middle of a river.

The jigsaw style of structure production is just as common as template production in the ordering of social episodes and of social institutions. In the case of a repetitive process of production, units are assembled according to their own individual properties, but when they are put together the overall assemblage exhibits a pattern which is not simply the replication or transformation of the structural properties of any given constituent. A very simple example is the structure of ordinary conversations between two people, A and B. They have a straightforward turn-taking pattern, A B A B . . . generated by the end-properties and start-properties of each speech contribution, together with accompanying paralinguistic signs. Taken together these lead to the overall pattern of the conversation exhibiting the simple repetitive pattern. The problem of the understanding of the origins and nature of macrosocial structures will have to be solved in part by drawing upon the idea of a genesis of pattern by repetition and assemblage.

Having set out the general principles governing the explanation of structures we must notice that empirical enquiry can be directed towards two separate kinds of question.

1   By what process is a product produced from a template or from structural elements by the action of an agent?

2   How does the template come into existence prior to the process of production? Is it, for example, generated for the occasion, and by what process? Or, is it preformed, perhaps before the individual which bears it on a particular occasion has come into being? Or does it exist in individuals prior to the occasions on which it is realized? In either case, how does it come to be represented in that individual?

Similarly we can ask how the pieces of social 'jigsaws' come to be produced. It may be that there are elementary templates that are produced like jigsaws out of still more elementary components, and these act as templates for the pieces that go to make up the episodes and institutions with which social psychology is supposed to deal. The latter certainly seems to be the most plausible picture for use in trying to understand where the forms of the individual utterances that are assembled into a conversation come from. For sociologists the patterns of unintended consequences of the interplay of small scale patterns of individual actions assume great importance. In many cases it seems clear that the jigsaw model is the best way to formulate an explanatory hypothesis to account for large-scale social order. These are questions which empirical investigations of the sources of structure will have to answer.

CONTINUITY OF STRUCTURE

To refine this scheme for application to the analysis of social life we shall have to lay down certain conditions for the persistence of a structure over time and through different sorts of transformation, which are more precisely specified than the very general conditions set out above. The most important one for our purpose derives from the distinction between those structures which can tolerate the substitution of materially distinct individuals and preserve their identity, from those which cannot. The preservation of identity will, it is clear, have to be defined in terms of some property or properties of a structure other than the material identity of the individuals which comprise it. An obvious candidate would be the preservation of the relations, and particularly the invariant relations, which enable us to identify the structure in the first place. It is clear that this distinction between substitution-tolerant and -intolerant structures is indifferent to the distinction between internally and externally related structures, for it may be that in substitution, a materially distinct individual takes on the characteristics of the appropriate category by virtue of coming to stand in the new relation. For example, a divorced man, Mr X, acquires a second wife by entering into the relation of marriage, so that a materially distinct woman becomes 'the wife of Mr X'.

PEOPLE STRUCTURES

I turn now to a detailed application of structural concepts to the analysis of the two main kinds of social entity with which social science can be concerned. These are what one might call people-structures, where the products, institutions and societies are relational systems whose elements are individual human beings. Each element is partly constituted as a person by virtue of the many systems of relations, actual and latent in which the person stands, and partly by his or her biological embodiment as an embodied actor having a location or world line in space-time. On the other hand, we will be looking at the activities of human beings, constituted as persons by the collectives to which they belong, which issue in sequential structures of actions. Action-sequences cluster into structured groups, necessary for the performance of social acts, which collectively constitute a continuing and unfolding social life. We shall call these sequences 'episodes'. Since they will be analysed both with respect to public social acts that are brought about in/by their performance, and individual contributions of actions to a co-operatively created sequence, they are to be considered as act-action sequences. We shall suppose, unless we have definite evidence to the contrary, that such sequences are orderly and so we shall approach them with the structural conception of analysis and explanation in mind. We can now apply the distinction between the three kinds of structure genesis developed in the general theory of structure.

Assemblage

An aggregate of individuals can become a collective, that is have an overall invariant structure, deriving from individual properties of the members making up the collective, which constrain their ways of fitting together. For example, the overall structure of a crystal is thought to be the result of the constraints which the structures of individual atoms exert on the assemblage of myriads of atomic units which go to make it up. Assemblage as a mode of structuring would be a natural way of looking at the genesis of some of the properties which very large-scale collectives of human beings might have. For example there are structures which are thought to form patterns of unintended consequences of individual actions directed to small-scale, immediate ends.

Transformation and replication

The structural properties of a collective could be produced by the coming together of material to form the collective on some preexisting template. This can occur, in principle, in two different ways. The template may be incorporated into the product so that though it exists before the product structure is generated, after the product has formed the template is no longer an independent existent. An example of such a process might be that by which the armature of a statue is incorporated in the final product. The armature serves as a template of the final overall form but has become part of the finished statue. Alternatively, the template may continue to exist after the product has been 'peeled off' it. In die-stamping of metal, the die as template is responsible for the structure of the product but die and product remain distinct existences after the process of replication is complete.

Both transformation and replication can be found in the social world. Transformation: In some African states a single family occupies all the official positions. In some cases relationships defined in the family are transformed into relationships between the offices of state. Replication of an ironic and sometimes tragic sort sometimes happens when a radical party, in order to win a revolutionary war, has to adopt the organization of the very social order which it originally set out to combat.

Another kind of replication occurs when the structure of the collective is produced by a projection from some small-scale model, or plan, which is composed of the same kind of elements. For example, in time of war the professional army may be expanded to become a volunteer, or perhaps conscript army, many times its size and many times more complicated, but preserving the same chains of command and the same strategic organization.

In applying these ideas to the understanding of social collectives we must look for the social templates from which social structure is produced, and at the same time propose an empirically testable and plausible causal process by which that production might occur. But a residual question remains to be answered. How are the templates for replication produced, and if they are replicas of earlier templates how do templates come into existence in the first place? A template is a structured object and as such must be some kind of collective, with a relational structure among its elements, incorporating one or more invariants. Either the template is produced by another template (replication) or it is produced by some process of assemblage from elements whose individual properties limit the kind of structures they can form. As far as social explanation goes the regress of templates can be continued for some time. For example historians trace the structure of the modern European state from the structure of the medieval state by successive imperfect replications of action structures. But an historical sociology and social psychology can be called upon eventually to give some kind of account of how the first template came to be. Theoretically a chain of replication could be broken only by a first template generated by assemblage. But of course assumptions of evolutionary gradualism would count against the hypothesis of a first or primal template.

The most famous example of replication relationship between one social collective and another is Marx's theory of the social formation. He believed the apparent social order to be a structural reflection of the social order concealed in the basic economic organization. This would seem to require a hypothesis of some form of replication. But which? In the absence of any plausible causal theory, we can only speculate on what Marx himself would have offered by way of an account had he expressed his theory in these terms. However, it seems clear that the relationship is not as likely to be one of replication as projection since if a social formation is generated according to an ideology, and the ideology is itself a partly false picture of the economic base (on Marx's theory it must be an inaccurate or misleading picture), then the ideology cannot serve as a causal mediator between base and superstructure if the superstructure is supposed to accurately replicate the structural properties of the economic system which forms the base. This difficulty is not resolved by turning to the idea of replication as transformation since it seems very unlikely that Marx would have been prepared to accept the proposal that the structure of the economic system itself is taken up into and becomes the structure of the whole social formation. Indeed, he was very much concerned to distinguish both ontologically and socially between these two aspects of a modern industrial society. These difficulties are really reflections of a deeper difficulty which permeates Marx's whole social thought, namely the problems that it poses for us by the striking absence of a plausible social psychology.

THE GENERAL THEORY OF INSTITUTIONS

The study of institutions seems to me to have been the most satisfactory form of social investigation to have yet been undertaken if we consider only institutions of a reasonably small size. Goffman's *Asylums* (1968) and Hargreaves's (1967) study of the social structure of the secondary school are models of good work. Studies of such larger scale matters as the social class system or the gross economic organization strike me as very much less satisfactory. We shall come to see some necessity in the relation between the largeness of scale and the weakness of the method of study, as we proceed.

How then in the light of the best work are we to see an institution, such as a shop, a school, a local police force, or a football supporters' club? The first point to notice is that an institution is a double relational network of social practices and of people. A post office contains sellings of stamps, frankings and sortings of letters, throwings of parcels, brewings of tea; and postmen and postwomen. Each aspect can be looked at separately to observe how the action-units are inter-related and how the people-units form structured groups, but must then be combined. They cannot be combined arbitrarily by mere conjunction since some activities are open only to some kinds of people.

And these kinds are not usually identifiable in any other way than by convention. A sorter is 'really' no different from a loader, *sub specie humanitas*, yet the difference between them in the Post Office goes far beyond merely loading and sorting, and woe betide the office where one of either kind does the work of the other!

To keep all this clear we need a distinction between personal identity, the basis of the individuality and uniqueness of existence of a single human being, and social identity, the type, kind or category of person the individual appears to be, or the type of role they occupy, or the kind of job they do . . . A single individual can occupy different posts and enjoy different social identities, while the same post can be occupied by different individuals. But could we simply ignore the transposition of individuals, since after all one might argue, what counts socially is what they do as fulfilling these roles? Of course different people may perform more or less well in certain roles but that seems a trivial point. There is, however, a deep reason why we cannot ignore personal identity and difference.

Role-theory, as the theory of internal relations between people as embodiments of social identities, cannot serve as a comprehensive theory of the behaviour of people in and with respect to institutions, since it is continuously modified by the *expressive* aims and activities of the individuals which occupy role-positions. Richard Nixon did not just want to be President but to be Nixon-the-Great President; to stamp the office with the mark of the man. Since expressive aims and activities may have a profound effect on the institution, social psychology must concern itself with personal identity – manifested in the personal stamp placed by some people on the expressive aspect of social life.

We are now in a position to deal with the problem of the criteria for the identity of institutions. These will become important in later discussion when we consider the background of stabilities against which judgements of change would have to be made. An institution was defined as an interlocking double-structure of persons-as-role-holders or office-bearers and the like, and of social practices involving both expressive and practical aims and outcomes. It is not at all easy to define the boundaries of an institution in any general way. In many, the roles and role-holders are limited in number, by criteria of qualification or in some other way. In most there is a subclass of social practices that purport to be the activities by which the official theory of 'the' institution is fulfilled. Thus as an institution a hospital cannot be delimited by identifying sick people and those who purport to cure them, since this would include too much. Nor can it be identified by reference to curative practices of a certain intensive, externally administered kind, since this would include too little of what goes on. Sometimes a set of buildings or physical plant can define a geographical setting within which are accomplished the practices constitutive of the institutions. But this mode of demarcation would be inappropriate to many institution which are not located in particular places. Instead let us shift to an empirical criterion, differently specified for each institution, namely where people constitutive of the institution would draw its bounds. No doubt different categories of members would draw it differently, and locate its 'centre of gravity' in diverse places, but not so differently and not so diversely as to give the impression of total chaos.

It is worth noticing that institutional continuity does not require identity of social practices. For example the City Guilds of London have completely abandoned their practical activities as cloth workers, silver smiths and so on and retained only the expressive practices and moral careers that go with them. Continuity of office and partial but overlapping short-term continuity of practices is sufficient. Thus the continuity of the monarchy through discontinuity of the monarchs is expressed in the formula 'The King is dead, long live the King'. And a discontinuity could be expressed in the formula 'The King is deposed, long live the Revolutionary Council'.

From Goffman's account of institutions we can draw the useful idea of a contrast between the official and the unofficial life of the people in an institution, and the official and unofficial rhetorics in terms of which the institutional activities can be described, and made to seem proper and meaningful. The first directs our attention to the very different criteria of respect and worth held by people in different positions in the institution; the second to the variety of attitudes to apparently the same activities held by differently situated people – drill as a necessary training for the preservation of a soldier's life, and drill as meaningless, and perhaps even sadistic, 'square bashing'.

The reality of an institution consists in the existence of all these facets, this complex of attitudes, forms of speech and many-sided activities, and the people who engage in them. But we have already noticed that any social entity exists not just as its daily manifestations but as the habits, prejudices, beliefs, knowledge and expectations of its constituent members, and of the general public who know of it, and of the officials and functionaries who are related to it. With respect to these matters we can see an institution as not so much ideal as latent. Because of the large degree of latency of any institution compared with any of its current activities, when it is reproduced each day from the stored knowledge and skill of its members, and the expectations of their clients, it is never perfectly replicated. Even with the help of charts and forms, manuals and standing orders, some practices are forgotten and others arise to masquerade as 'proper' features of the institution. We shall be coming back to these apparently minor perturbations in a later section of this study, for they will be found to have as profound consequences for the theory of social change as did the minute thickenings of the beaks of nestling finches in the Galapagos Islands for the theory of biological evolution.

THE BOUNDARIES OF ORDER

The groups which have been at the focus of this chapter have been stable and orderly. From the point of view of social psychology, the salient feature of such groups is that they are created and maintained by people through the use of rules and conventions, normative constraints which take explicit form in accounts. But there are also rabbles and mobs. The importance of rules and conventions in the social psychology of everyday life can be highlighted by looking briefly at those forms of human association in which rules and conventions play a diminished role, or even no role at all. This is the phenomenon of the 'crowd'.

According to Park (1972:7) 'seen from the outside, the crowd is an unorganized multitude composed of heterogeneous elements and lacking structure and specialized parts . . .'. However the proper contrast is not between a group with a common organization and a mere heterogeneous multitude. It is between different ways in which co-ordinated action occurs. The distinction is first roughly adumbrated by Signale (1981). 'Individuals who normally do not rebel against the restrictions of custom and law lose their usual moral stability and self-control under the influence of crowd excitement.' Following this hint Park (1972:78–80) distinguished between 'the crowd' and 'the public'. In the former emotions dominate the formation of intentions, while in the latter, individuals form common, that is similar intentions, by reference to considerations of reason.

The basic idea of a distinctive psychological mechanism for understanding the behaviour of mobs and rabbles, Park's 'crowds', comes from Le Bon (1979). According to Le Bon there are three psychological conditions under which the ephemeral and distinctive 'mob', or 'psychological crowd' comes into being. Each individual has a sense of anonymity. Then there is a kind of contagion of emotions and intentions by something like imitation, that is a process that is independent of the usual normative controls of institutional life. Finally each individual is in a heightened state of suggestibility, not unlike the state induced by hypnosis. In these circumstances 'the sentiments and ideas of all the persons in the gathering take one and the same direction, and their conscious personality vanishes' (Park, 1972:59).

In this way we can identify the boundary between two basic forms of association, the stable form of an institution, and the ephemeral seeming 'formlessness' of a mob. Looking more closely it becomes clear that what distinguishes a mob from an institution psychologically is that the former is a group of people who cease to use existing rules and conventions as the means for coordinating their actions towards common goals. Instead a common purpose emerges '. . . in the suggestive influence exerted by people on each other' (Park). Recently Moscovici has developed the basic Le Bon account of the psychology of crowds by incorporating it in the framework of collective representations (Moscovici, 1985).

3

PEOPLE IN ACTION

ANTICIPATORY SUMMARY

The interactions of everyday life are, more often than not, orderly sequences of meaningful actions. Any such sequence which seems to have some measure of coherence and structure I shall call an 'episode'. It is a fundamental principle of the theory presented in this book that most of the psychological phenomena which define the subject matter of social psychology are properties or features of the interchanges in interactional episodes rather than subjective attributes of individual actors.

In this chapter the idea of social meaning is introduced with which a general account of the identifying criteria for elementary social actions is developed. The meaning of actions are acts. The notion of an 'act' is explicated in conscious generalization of Austin's concept of 'illocutionary force'. Taking people as agents acting together jointly and intentionally to accomplish all kinds of common tasks presupposes that norms and conventions play a leading role in the management of action. Correctness and incorrectness, propriety and impropriety of actions as accomplishing acts, is a fundamental distinction in all cultures.

The more rigid constraints on how episodes should unfold can be expressed as rules and the more fluid as story-lines. An important methodological thesis, to be argued for in this chapter, is that notions of 'rule' and 'story-line', though ideal devices for use by psychologists to express their discoveries about the tacit knowledge of a community, must be taken cautiously in attempts to explain how orderly episodes are produced. Rules and narrative conventions are not causes of human action, not even formal causes. They are amongst the tools or means that people use to create and maintain order in their joint productions.

I shall use a wide variety of examples to illustrate the way the orderly structures of episodes can be analytically revealed. We shall find that the use of the 'linguistic analogy' can be the basis of revealing analyses not only of formal episodes like business meetings, ceremonial events of many kinds, but also such informal encounters as quarrels, picnics and the family meal.

In analysing episodes the structure that can be revealed will depend upon how the elements of the structure are chosen. Scale is an important variant in this matter. Courtship – marriage – divorce form an orderly structure with respect to the relation 'later than', but each unit episode, treated as a social ritual, is itself internally complex. By choosing a scale of analysis corresponding to the simplest social actions, that is actions the components of which are not themselves actions, that internal complexity could be represented as an orderly sequential structure. Furthermore at different degrees of refinement the principles of order are different. In the first case, if the three rituals occur they *must* occur in that order, since 'marriage' *is* the ritual conformation and transformation of a male/female bond as a sociolegal relation, and a 'divorce' *is* the ritual dissolution of that ritually created bond. But it is surely a convention, though a socially significant one, that the groom has precedence over the bride in the making of ritual affirmations.

Structure, then, will be related to the 'grain' of the analysis. J-P. De Waele has pointed out in conversation that important temporal properties of sequents, such as whether they are the only sequent of a kind, or the first, second or third and so on, depends on the time perspective one adopts. Since an actor is living through an episode with continually changing time perspective some of the sequential properties of the elements of the episode are unstable. Until one has succeeded or failed one doesn't know whether what one is doing is or is not an attempt, and until one has tried a second time, that it was a first attempt, and so on. Even when one has a stable vantage point from which to examine the structured sequence of socially distinct elements one has lived through, other perspectives may have the effect of amplifying some elements and even suppressing others. This is evident, for instance, in Schutz's (1972) idea of perspectivity. A segment of one's biography may show different structures and even bring out different interpretations of this matter or that matter, depending on the perspective from which one is then viewing it. This has been nicely illustrated in Ingeborg Helling's (1977) study of life stories told to her by the carpenters of Konstanz. In different parts of their tales they may use the very same episode for illustrating quite different social predicaments, and so as having quite different significance.

A SIMPLE ANALYSIS, USING COMMON-SENSE
SOCIAL CATEGORIES

Contemporary English stranger introduction ritual, involving three
people – the stranger, his sponsor, and the host to whom the introduction is being made – comprises, if carried through in full, the following
phases:

(a) Approach and recognition
(b) Opening formula: *Sponsor*: 'Master, I'd like you
                                    to meet my guest.'
(c) Name exchange: *Sponsor*: 'This is Dr X: Mr Y,
                                    our master.'
(d) Formula of mutual
     recognition as persons: *X*: 'How do you do?'
                                        Y: 'How do you do?'
(e) Physical contact or
     substitute; confirmation
     of recognition: Handshake (if 'done')
     (d and e are usually simultaneous)
(f) Determination of
     Identity: This is a complex phase and
                                    will be analysed below.
(g) Formula of Incorporation: *Y*: 'I'm so glad you
                                           could join us.'
                                      X1: 'It's nice to be here.'
                                      X2: 'I'm very glad to be
                                            here.'
The distribution of 'Glad' (condescending) and 'Nice' (deferential)
depends upon the outcome of (f)

This is a very elaborate form of exchange, though common in many
different variants. Each section deserves commentary, since each
reveals something about the society in which a form of this exchange is
embedded.

The first point to notice is that the stranger, as stranger, has
temporarily high rank, marked in (d) by the fact that his or her name is
mentioned first, and in (a) by the speaking his or her part of the
formula first. But by phase (g) this courtesy is no longer extended,
and the overall status determination of order of speaking becomes
paramount. There are some exceptions to this structural feature we
will discuss below.

The approach and recognition phase is characterized by the use of the glance as a device to communicate intention and to hold attention. Sponsor tries to catch the eye of Y, the host, and having done so glances at the stranger, back to Y again, and so on, holding Y's attention and sweeping the stranger forward. The stranger's gaze is fixed on Y, until Y 'recognizes' the newcomer by looking towards him or her, at which the stranger, showing proper deference, glances aside. Y and the sponsor exchange glances during phases (b) and (c), after which Y and the stranger become eye-locked in ordinary Argyle-type turn taking, until Y, opening the way for the closing formula in (g), looks away markedly to sponsor.

From this example we can introduce two important distinctions, that between social acts and social actions, and that between social syntax and social semantics.

Acts and actions

In the example, a particular, non-literal social meaning is given to the utterance 'How do you do?' Grammatically the utterance is a question, but it would be a mistake to interpret it as an enquiry as to the health of the counterparticipant. Socially considered it is a ritual device for my public acknowledgment that you are to count as a person, that is a being in whose welfare I might take an interest. In the last sentence I have been trying to describe the social *act* I have performed in saying 'How do you do?' in that context. The saying of that ritual formula is the appropriate, but conventionally associated *action* with which in that context and with that kind of person I perform the act. The ceremony as performance is analysed as a sequence of action-types, the doing of tokens of which are performances of instances of act-types, whose sequential order is the ceremony as a socially potent episode.

Social syntax and social semantics

Any sequential structure obtaining among types or categories of things suggests an analogue with the syntactical structure of language – since syntax comprises the formal principles of sequential order of categories of lexical items. 'Horse' and 'galloping' are syntactically related in 'The horse was galloping', as instances of the categories 'noun' and 'participle'. From the syntactical point of view the same relation obtains between the relevant lexical items as tokens of types in 'The water was boiling'. This is so even though no other animal but a horse can be said to be galloping, while even pitch and lead can be said to be boiling. We shall find the social parallels to these further sub-categorial restrictions on language of the greatest importance.

Since the social force of an action seems to be only conventionally associated with the means of its performance, for the most part, and bearing in mind the fact that many linguists have insisted on the arbitrary character of the relation between a sign and what it signifies, there might be some insight to be gained by treating the relation between act and action as parallel to that between meaning and sign. This suggests the idea of a social semantics.

We shall explore both parallels in detail in the sections to come.

The concept of a performative

A performative *use* of a sentence is a use, not primarily to convey information but to carry out a social act, and to bring about certain effects, via the performance of the act. The former involves the illocutionary force of the sentence-as-used; the latter its perlocutionary force. Bruner (1990) has pointed out that standard grammatical form is not a good guide to performative force since small children grasp performative force in the course of day-to-day social practices that is non-co-ordinate with grammatical form. For instance they readily grasp parental use of the interrogative form to give orders, and distinguish it from the use of the form to ask questions. The same distinction goes through into adult life where 'I wonder if you'd mind terribly retyping this?' is performatively equivalent to 'Do it again! It's all wrong!'.

MEANING IN SOCIAL ACTION

My task is to give an account of meaning adequate to the general thesis that in some way a mixing of actor's intentions and interactor's understandings secures the mediation of social performance. At the same time it would be pleasing if this account were to be consonant with the conditions for the use of an analogue of syntactical analysis to reveal the structure of social episodes. The most crucial condition in this context is that we should be able to recognize elementary social actions. To achieve this we need criteria adequate to individuate and identify the components of social episodes in a way which is relevant to their being interpretable as the performance of social acts.

According to what semantic theory should one attempt to explicate what is meant by treating social actions and acts as individuated and identified as 'meanings'? Contemporary semantic theories differ radically in their conception of the elementary semantic relation. In extensional theories the elementary or primary semantic relation obtains between a sign and a referent on condition that the sign and referent are distinct existences. This theory comes in two varieties depending upon whether one thinks the relation to have been established baptismally, that is from sign to referent; or causally, that is from referent to sign. In intentional theories, on the other hand, the primary semantic relation is a complex network in which a semantic element is defined by its location with respect to other semantic elements. Elementary acts are related to the public social world only in systems, referential relations to entities outside the system being established as a secondary property of the sign system.

Empirical work in developmental psycho-linguists – studies of how children acquire language – favours the latter theory, that in which the primary semantic relation is internal to the semantic system.

Acts, actions and meanings

To decide which theory is the appropriate model for formulating a theory of 'social' meaning the relation between elements at the several levels of social analysis must be closely investigated.

Colloquially, one might be inclined to say:

Actions are the meanings of movements and utterances.
Acts are the meanings of actions.

in that at each level the left-hand element involves an interpretation or 'reading' of the right-hand element.

My proposal for a theory of social meaning runs as follows:

Movements, actions and acts should not be treated as distinct existences.
Their distinctness derives from the embedding of the same neutral core existent in three distinct and irreducible relational systems, *RS1*, *RS2*, and *RS3*.

RS1: The core existent, say a pattern of sounds and bodily movement is distinguished as a molecular unity when taken as embedded in a network of physical and physiological relations to other elements of the same sort: for example, an elbow as a bodily joint contacting a rib of another body is 'a nudge'.
RS2: The core existent appears as an action when taken as embedded in a relational network with other actions. These

networks might be conventional sequences such as marriage ceremonies, criminal trials and so on. A movement is an action only if it seems that the actors have intentions, for instance only if someone intends a nudge is flesh meeting flesh, a 'dig in the ribs'.

RS3: The core existent appears as an act when taken as embedded in a relational network comprising a social world. Such a world includes persons, and the collectives in which they are constituted as persons, such as families, institutions and so on, and is manifested in episodes that constitute, change and sustain that world. In this network the core existent of the example is to be read as a conventional indication that an apparently insulting remark is to be interpreted as non-denigrating to a friendship, that is as a socially meaningful act.

On this view, though the three networks of relations are distinct, their common node is a physical happening. This seems to rule out immediately any version of the referential theory of meaning as a way of understanding how a movement, or uttered sound pattern, has social meaning. For example, since a saying and a speech act are not existentially distinct, the one could not refer to the other. No referential theory could explain how a saying can be the performance of a speech act. Happily relational theories are able to offer at least the main outlines of a theory through the above three-layered structure as a generator of meanings. Choosing a certain level of description brings one or other system of relationships into view. Changing the descriptive level does not change the world, but brings into focus different relational systems that are in the world. Describing social interactions at the act level will highlight a different structure from descriptions which pick out actions. For instance the same action may be used to perform different acts in different contexts.

Adapting Saussurean theory

I propose to develop the idea of a social semantics by borrowing from the relational theory of Saussure. For the purposes of this study the key Saussurean analytical concepts are *valeur* and *signifié* since it is in terms of these that Saussure gives an account of what we could loosely term 'meaning in a language' (de Saussure, 1959).

Valeur (linguistic 'value') of an item is the location it has in a network of relations to other items which themselves have *valeur* within the language. As Saussure defines *valeur* it is a composition of

1 'dissimilar things that can be *exchanged* for a thing of which the value is to be determined';
2 'similar things that can be *compared* with the thing of which the value is to be determined'.

To represent *valeur* of an item, one could construct a two-dimensional grid. The horizontal dimension consists of syntagmata, structured linear sequences of items in which the item occurs. In the case of language the syntagmata would be sentences. The vertical dimension consists of sets of contrasting items to the item of interest, either items which are similar in the sense that their substitution for the item in question would leave the meaning unchanged or dissimilar items whose substitution for it would change the meaning of the sentence under consideration (see figure 1).

In this way of representing Saussurean fields, the dimensions are extensionally and non-generatively defined, that is as ordered sets of actual entities. The same structure could be represented generatively in terms of two intersecting rule systems. Sequencing or combinatorial rules could be thought to generate such structured sequences as sentences or ceremonies that are laid along the S-dimension. Given a specific social setting, appropriate persons present and involved, the known and accepted rules generate the forms of social episodes. The P-dimension could be thought of generatively as a set of selection rules, which, by reference to the situations, settings and personas to be presented, generate the appropriate item, movement, action or act,

	Semantic Paradigm	Semantic Paradigm		Semantic Paradigm
	.	.		.
	.	.		.
	.	.		.
	STICK			TEAM
	FLAG			
	SWORD	RACED		
Syntagmatic	PISTOL	REVVED		ARSENAL
→ Take a	GUN; He	GUNNED	the engine; Up the	GUNNERS →
Dimension	BUN	SHUNNED		RUNNERS
	.	.		.
	.	.		.
	Phonetic Paradigm	Phonetic Paradigm		Phonetic Paradigm

Figure 1 A truncated Saussurean grid.

depending on the level of analysis, at the place in the sequence whose general character has been fixed by the sequencing rules.

Signifié is not clearly defined in Saussure's surviving work. For the most part he speaks of the *signifié* of a sign as the concept associated with it. But in an important diagram he juxtaposes a pictorial representation of the sign as 'sound-image' plus concept, with a similar diagram blending concept and object. Whatever its exact determination it involved a relation to an external referent.

For Saussure the establishment of an external referent for a sign was contingent and arbitrary, concerned with how the sign would be applied rather than with the establishment of that sign as meaningful within a language. *Signifié* could be achieved in a great many different ways, for example by reference to a theory of abstract objects or by experience of real things. There is no one primitive way of achieving signification.

The Saussurean approach links syntax (structure) and semantics (meaning) in an essential way. The syntagmatic dimension is essentially an extensional representation of the rules, knowledge of which would enable us to generate a potential infinity of well-formed sentences or in the enlargement of the approach to include social episodes, orderly, structured sequences of actions. The paradigmatic dimension is essentially an extensional representation of a lexicon, ordered by contrastive and associative principles, such as synonymy, antonymy, and by principles of phonological likeness and difference. In the social application the paradigmatic dimension will consist of actions and acts.

Action-explication

Our social semantics will be based upon the proposal that actions can be individuated and identified with an analogue of a representation of *valeur*. Let us try to represent 'Please' and 'please'-phrases as social action elements. A plausible syntagm found during, say, an English children's tea-party would be:

> Sees cake / 'Please may I have a cake?' / Takes cake / 'Thanks' / Eats cake.

All three movements 'sees cake', 'takes cake', and 'eats cake' are performed not only as ingestive but as social actions, that is performed in a style proper to polite society. The item whose social meaning as action we are intent upon representing is 'Please may I have . . . ?' The paradigmatic dimension includes such contrastive items as 'Do you think I could have?', 'interrogative eyebrows and half smile with head cocked on one side'. This last item illustrates the fact that in social interaction gestures sometimes have an equivalent social force to utterances. The phonological dimension includes 'Jeez, may I have . . . ' (torn forth by the sheer munificence of the gastronomical offering, a hearing of the given speech which is excluded by hearing it as 'Please etc.').

Finally, one should notice that the collapsed syntagm

Sees cake / Grabs cake / Eats cake

is barbarous in the strict meaning of that term, that is not social within the conventions of sociality of any society properly so considered since it omits the items by which the humanity of the provider of the feast is acknowledged and their concern for the guests recognized and ritually acknowledged. Action in that syntagma illustrates the perception of the feast as treasure trove.

Syntagmata are individuated by reference respectively to time, place and current personas of the actors and social acts performed. Thus signification for the whole performance is ensured via act-interpretation.

Act-explication

Questions like, 'What does "Please" mean?' are not adequately answered by displaying a Saussurean grid. To complete an account, the significance of the saying as a social act must be described. I should like to argue that descriptions of actions as acts draw upon folk theories of the social world and the place and possible relations of distinctive kinds of people in it.

In the Saussurean grid physically distinct behaviours or movements are collected into sets as 'ways of doing the same action' if they lie along one of the axes in the paradigmatic dimension. But the setting up of paradigmatic axes is dependent upon prior identification of syntagmata as completed action sequences. They are recognized as belonging to this or that social category with respect to the acts their performance is conventionally supposed to achieve. The conception of a social act depends upon a theory of sociality. For example, a ceremony (syntagm type) for incorporating a new member into a social group is able to be understood as the performance of that act with respect to local conceptions of membership, members' ideas as to the nature of their group and perhaps with respect to a theory about how, in general, in that social milieu, the transition from non-membership to membership *really* occurs. Consider for example the act of confirmation into the Anglican Church and the theory as to what occurs both *in* virtue and *by* virtue of the performance of the ceremony of the laying on of hands. One could compare it with the ceremonies required to become a member of a Hell's Angel troupe, or of the local lending library. In the library case there is no theory of the 'reality' of the incorporation corresponding to the descent of the Holy Spirit by virtue of the performance of the ceremony.

A description of act-significance alone would serve to explicate an isolated socially significant item, since it would allow us to begin the construction of a grid based upon that interpretation and our existing understandings of other items. If *valeur* is revealed by showing that the action has a proper place in an orderly sequence of actions, the act-interpretation introduces the other member of the Saussurean pair, *signifié*, since 'act' seems to be exactly the *signifié* of the action of doing a social performance or carrying out a practice.

Suppose we explain 'Please' by reference to the theory that we use it to obtain legitimate possession of something belonging to somebody else, that is it used to bring about a transfer of ownership agreed to by the original owner. The point can be illustrated with the case of a plate of cakes. Even though the cakes are intended for general consumption the effort or expense incurred in providing them for the company (free) can be acknowledged by behaving as if the provider owned them. This can be done by going through a change of ownership ritual or some fragment of it. This theory might even serve to explain the difficulty children seem to have in maintaining the 'Please' and 'Thank you' rituals for such items as food provided in the family. To treat the obtaining of a cake, at home, on a par with change of ownership seems bizarre.

The effect of acknowledging the underlying principle literally rather than symbolically can be catastrophic. The German students who, inspired by ethnomethodology, insisted on paying their professor's wife for the drinks at a Sunday entertainment, brought the Frau Professor to nervous prostration so it is reported.

But most people competent in the use of 'Please' and 'Thank-you', of clenched fists, stabbing fingers, administration of oaths, insults and put downs, consolation and the ritual expression of joy in another's success, do not *deploy* theories, such as the one sketched above, in the genesis of social action. Their ways of drawing on their social resources in the cognitive preparation of action ought not, I believe, to be called 'theorizing', nor should their resources be thought of as theories. No doubt people do, from time to time, construct theories of this sort, and that they can do so is an important fact of human social life, the basis of accounting. It is significant though, that in general, theorizing of this sort is undertaken for the benefit of children and foreigners. If what people know can be represented in a set of overlapping Saussurean grids, and if what they know makes up their cognitive resources it would seem appropriate to think of that knowledge as a system of rules. One must be careful, however, to qualify the concept of 'rule' in this context. It should be thought of as a scientific metaphor rather than taken literally. Day-to-day social practices seem more naturally looked upon as the result of rule-following, where the act seems to be demanded by the situation as interpreted by the actor and all that is at issue is how properly to carry it out, that is what actions are required. 'Rules' determine what is appropriate at both the act-level and the action-level.

Gricean conditions on meaning

I have taken for granted that a social episode is a mutual product to which all those who are party must make their proper contributions at the socially correct place and time. This condition holds whether the episode is 'nice' or 'nasty'; 'cooperative' or 'agnostic'. Lacking the detailed records we can only speculate on these matters but I would guess that social interchanges, even between torturer and victim, are conducted in an orderly well-defined way, and would not turn out to be any different in principle from the ways order is achieved as a day-to-day, minute-by-minute achievement, say on an outing of an old people's social club. Improvisation is the dominant mode of social interaction only in the opening phases of social encounter during which the kind of encounter it is going to be is negotiated. Pattern, convention and rule emerge even in the apparently most inhumane or most casual of social surroundings. The tendency to identify coordinated social action with cooperative altruistic action is a sentimentality.

We can again look to the study of conversation for a clue as to how to deal with the cooperative aspect of meaning creation. Grice (1989) has proposed certain conditions by which meaning is established and sustained in a conversational interaction with another person. They centre on an actor's beliefs about the interactions, interpretations of the actors intentions. They can be summarised:

1 The meaning of your action for me is what I believe you intend by it.
2 The meaning of your action for you is not only what you intend by it but what you believe I will believe you intend by it.

These are important social principles, in that (1) allows for misunderstanding, while (2) allows for hypocrisy, deceit and tact.

If we take this not so much as a theory of meaning but as a statement of the conditions that have to be met for a social action to have a shared meaning, and to be effective by virtue of that shared meaning, the Gricean conditions fit nicely with the Saussurean account. Intentions are prefigurements of acts and rules are taken as the templates of action. Actions are understood as the intended movements, utterings, etc., of contributors to social episodes as represented in our social knowledge. The items on the syntagmatic axis of a Saussurean grid must be the templates of action sequences and hence must be none other than a representation of the conventional devices by which the content of intentions, that is social acts, are achieved. In so far as our Saussurean fields match we can be cognitively co-ordinated in such a way that in the course of our interaction Gricean conditions can be met. That is to say our beliefs about what an action means to the actor can be synchronized with the actor's beliefs about what we believe he or she intends. The inter-personal public *act* is created in the common meaning of an action, just by virtue of the synchronization of belief. And this is possible only if we each draw upon roughly the same corpus of social knowledge. We *can* create a patterned episode of social life by human action. Of course we may fail, even in these favourable conditions, since there is no condition the satisfaction of which would render misunderstanding or hypocrisy impossible.

COMMITMENT AS MEANING

In this section I want to take up the question of the legitimacy of certain semi-colloquial uses of the word 'meaning'. The problem can best be approached through the perception of the importance of two forms of folk understanding of acts. These understandings are essential to acts being effective in creating and maintaining the social world.

Shared expectations

Folk-understanding of the action-sequences locally required for the performance of an act is a feature we have already investigated fairly thoroughly. We have seen that this knowledge (it might be expressed in a local rule) is crucial to the understanding of how the content of an intention to perform a certain act is sufficiently specified to serve as a determinant of the form the appropriate action-sequence takes.

But there must also be folk-knowledge of the constraints upon the future that are generated by the performance of the act. For example, by concluding a contract, parties to the act commit themselves to a certain future action and are entitled to have expectations of each other. There is a colloquial use of the word 'meaning' for the specific determinations of the future consequent upon such acts. It occurs in such phrases as 'the meaning of marriage', 'the meaning of friendship'. I shall be arguing that in these phrases it is not the act but the social relations established in the performing of the act that are implied.

A beginning can be made by noticing that understanding an act involves grasping both the way the performance of an action-sequence changes the social world *and* the fact that certain consequences of the changes wrought by the performance are to be understood as accomplishing a specific act. At first glance one might think that a simple reciprocity of understanding between the parties was all that was required for acts to have consequences. For example, unless you recognize my gesture as a dismissal, have I succeeded in dismissing you? It is clear, I think, that it is no part of the necessary conditions for my act to be socially potent or legally binding for you to have grasped its import. You may not grasp that you have been fired but other people will. Nevertheless, it seems improper to say I have confirmed our friendship, if you do not understand my offer of a drink as having that import. Yet I could, I think, be said to have inadvertently insulted you and be called upon to apologize, even if I did not intend my action as an insult.

There seem to be three classes of cases: (1) those where your understanding the meaning of my actions is a necessary condition of the accomplishment of the act, for example in my confirming our friendship; (2) those where such understanding is not required, for instance in my dismissing you. (3) There are some cases where my intention in acting may be outweighed by the conventional potency of the action as act. In such a case the public reading is dominant, as in the case of an inadvertent insult. Apology must be based on admitting the insult and emphasizing the inadvertence.

In explicating these cases one might be tempted to fall back on the account of meaning proposed by Grice and attempt an explanation of act as meaning in terms of your recognition of my intentions and my beliefs about your recognition of my intentions, and so on. Clearly, something of the sort must be part of the necessary conditions for some actions to be acts, since for my offer of a drink to be effective as confirmation of our friendship, it must be understood for what it is meant to be. There could not be a class of acts never intended but always understood. But that leaves what the action-sequence is meant to be, for instance a confirmation of friendship, unexplicated. Grice offers us, then, at best a necessary condition for an action-sequence to come off as an act. In order to understand how an act can be the meaning of an action-sequence, we must turn to another aspect of acts, that they have consequences.

Austin (1961) broached this matter in his distinction between perlocutionary and illocutionary forces. He saw two points of importance: not every consequence of an action-sequence is relevant to its meaning as an act; the significance of the act has less to do with the actual consequences of the performance of a particular action sequence than with the determination or limitation of possible consequences. An act, one might say, determines in advance the shape or form of a possible course of life for the parties to the act. But in real life such a course might never be realized. Thus the meaning of the act could not be taken to be a summary prediction of certain features of the future as the product of commitments acquired by the parties consequent upon the performance of the appropriate action-sequence, whose meaning it is, since the failure of the future to have those features would not show that the act had not had that meaning.

The effects of a ceremony can be distinguished into two categories. There are the social changes brought about by the completion of the ceremony; for example, the new relationship which exists between two families when a wedding takes place between a member of each. Then there is a category of effect which derives from what the members of the wedding understand as their commitments and take as their legitimate expectations having performed the ceremony. These effects one might call the determinations of a future form of life.

That these are genuinely different categories of effects is shown by the fact that they fail in different and distinct ways. If the ceremony is not adequately or fully performed, if the roles as defined in and for the ceremony are filled by persons who are disqualified in some way or another, then the social change does not occur. For example, it is impossible in England for someone who is already married to one man or woman to be wedded to another, no matter how seriously or fully he or she has taken part in the wedding ceremony. This failure is due to the fact that a married person is legally disqualified as an occupant of the ceremonial role of bride or bridegroom. On the other hand, what the law now calls 'the breakdown of marriage' is a failure of another sort. It is a failure to fulfil the commitments to a form of life, knowledge of which is implicit in the under-takings of those who took part in the original ceremony. I will be arguing that each of these categories of effects serves to define a different aspect of meaning with respect to the marriage ceremony.

The justification of speaking of 'getting wed' as the meaning of the marriage ceremony, that is of the seriously and completely performed action sequence, can be found in the category of effects which I have called social changes. The meaning of the ceremony in that sense *is* the set of social changes which its completion brings about, and in this sense the wedding as a social act is the meaning of the marriage ceremony. In Saussurean terms this is part of the *signifié* of the ceremony, an aspect of the act performed.

The propriety of speaking of the meaning of marriage, of the state which is a product of wedding, that is socially joining two people, derives, I propose, from the idea that explaining or glossing the socio-psychological effects of the ceremonial action-sequences is like defining the married state, perhaps in an ideal form. Performing an act has something in common with agreeing to a plan. But, unlike agreement to a plan, what is expected of the consequential lasting stage is a standardized and usually tacit part of local social knowledge. Just in case there is any doubt about the form the future state is supposed to take, in certain important act performances, a scenario is included, explicating the requirements. This, we shall see, is an important component in the marriage ceremony. Marrying then, as an act, sets in train the scenario by binding the partners to it as their scenario or strategic plan for the future. This act binds the future like strategic planning binds the future. In the case of two friends having a drink, the scenario tacitly included in the concept of friendship has a much less precise form in our culture, though Aristotle thought the details worth discussion. To understand how an act has meaning in this sense, we must understand the way a strategic plan or scenario can control the form of the future.

Expectations as scenarios for the future

Marriage ceremonies, affirmations of friendships, and the like, I have argued, are like acts of commitment to a strategic plan. The language once allowed 'rule' to be used for the scenario to which one committed oneself. The act of joining a religious order committed one, for example, to the Rule of St Benedict. But the Rule of St Benedict was much more like the scenario of family life included in the marriage ceremony than it was like, say, a rule of grammar. This becomes clear if we ask how closely the future is determined by the ceremony of introduction and incorporation of a stranger, a marriage, a farewell, or a friendly drink. Acts of this sort determine the future in a much less determinate way than a rule usually does. It is for this reason that I have called the anticipatory representation of the form of the future that goes along with an act, a 'scenario'.

I shall argue that though acts are not logically related to scenarios (i.e. act-identity could be based upon the social bond produced despite change of scenarios), commission of the act entails agreement to a scenario in such a way that we may speak of *a* scenario as part of the meaning of the act. A scenario I would argue, is part of the associative meaning of the act, following Lyons' terminology, and thus sufficiently strongly related to it to be adduced as part of the meaning. One should notice, at this point, the way a word for an institution regularly subject to qualitative assessment, tends to take on the sense of the good or proper form of the institution, as, for instance, when we speak of what 'marriage really means'.

I have already suggested that it is the scenario as represented in the social knowledge of each person that determines the future. It could be thought of as a structured template working in each of the parties like a rule or its equivalent works as a tool people use in the production of the structural properties of an action-sequence. Preparation for social action involves, I believe, the creation and propagation of preformed structures.

But in order to accomplish this I must show that acts do involve scenarios, and that scenarios are structured objects meet to determine the form of the future.

A good rule in social psychology is to examine formal episodes where there is explicit verbal representation of matters that are tacit in other less formal episodes of social life, and then to utilize the insight so derived to analyse interactive action-sequences that have no formal representation. In this spirit I shall look first of all at marriage to investigate act and scenario, and then try to apply the same analytical framework to the attempt to make sense of the idea that a suicide, as the act accomplished or attempted in the course of the action of killing oneself, has an associated scenario.

Formally-defined scenarios: marriage
The marriage ceremony, as printed in the Prayer Book, includes two distinct classes of prescriptions. There are rules which, if followed, determine the action-sequence that makes it an instance of a marriage ceremony, as, for instance, 'the woman shall answer "I will"'. Other sentences spell out what I have suggested is often called colloquially, but philosophically aptly, 'the meaning of marriage'. For example, '. . . duly considering the causes for which matrimony was ordained, . . . it was ordained for the procreation of children to be brought up in the fear and nurture of the Lord and to praise His holy name . . . It was

ordained for the mutual society, help and comfort that the one ought
to have of the other, both in prosperity and adversity'. And again, in
the oath of marriage, each is required to 'love, comfort, honour in
sickness and in health', to forsake all others, and to keep only to the
person one has married. As if this were not enough, the solemnizing
minister has the option of preaching a sermon 'declaring the duties of
man and wife', or of reading excerpts from St Paul and St Peter on the
duties of husbands and wives. For example, husbands are enjoined to
'love your wives and be not bitter against them', and wives are advised
'not to adorn themselves with gold, but with a meek and quiet spirit'.

   This material addition to the rules for the conduct of the ceremony,
represents, I believe, an attempt to make the 'meaning of marriage'
explicit and is a scenario on my sense.

Informally-known scenarios: suicide
Can we understand a dramatic but informal fragment of social life
along similar lines? Consider the case of suicide. In suicide the scenario
is implicit, just as it is in an act which cements a friendship. A person
performs a suicide as a structured action sequence, according to the
fairly strict conventions of the local ethnography. This action-sequence,
if 'correctly' carried out, serves as the commission of the act, that
which, through an associated scenario, determines the future. 'There
was no note, the victim was a woman, so it cannot be suicide.' Provided
that the death, or more commonly near-death, is interpreted as a
suicide, the action-sequence as act has potency. The interpretive
process, as a gloss on a social 'text', has been carefully explored by
Douglas (1966) and Atkinson (1985). The person intent upon committing suicide, and understanding its meaning in the local culture,
sees the act as having consequences via the readings he or she con-
fidently expects others to give to the death, seen as an act of suicide.
Thus the person depends upon a belief in a shared interpretation of
suicide involving a scenario of the future, including the actions and
feelings of others. 'When they realize it's suicide they'll be sorry they
treated me so badly; by their grief I will punish them,' and so on. So,
for the poor soul driven to this extremity, it is essential that the action-
sequence be interpreted as suicide. If we think along these lines, the
'note' is more properly interpreted as a label than a message, ensuring
that the actions are given the 'correct' interpretation, that is, the
interpretation under which, via the associated scenario, the form of the
future is determined. This determination occurs because the others
involved, knowing the meaning of suicide, have as part of their tacit
knowledge, a representation of the very same scenario drawn upon by
the person committing the act.

INTERPRETATION OR HERMENEUTICAL EXPLICATION

The basic formulae of the analogy of social analysis to semantics have been:

1 Actions are the meanings of movements and utterances;
2 Acts are the meanings of actions;
3 Commitments and expectations are the meanings of acts.

At each stage of the investigation we have seen that the point of introducing the notion of meaning as an explanatory concept has been the same. In each case it directs our attention to the fact that the items we are concerned with achieve their effects not through physical consequences, but through conventional and other non-physical associations. In short, their effects are cognitively mediated and culturally differentiated.

Commitments and expectations are not the only existentially distinct entities conventionally associated with acts. There is another category which I propose to call 'hermeneutical meanings'.

Examples of this last sense of meaning can be found in the Anglican Prayer Book in a discussion of the relationship between marriage and the Church, and in the works of Durkheim, in particular his theory of the way a social institution is represented in or by a religious ceremony.

According to the Anglican Prayer Book the hermeneutical meaning of marriage is given as follows: 'Matrimony . . . signifying unto us the mystical union that is between Christ and his Church . . .' and 'the state of matrimony . . . in it is signified and represented the spiritual marriage and unity betwixt Christ and His Church . . .'. The interpretive framework is carried further into the continuous state of being married, by St Paul in the Epistle to the Ephesians, 'Wives, submit yourselves unto your own husbands, as unto the Lord. For the husband is the head of the wife even as Christ is head of the Church; and He is the Saviour of the body. Therefore, as the Church is subject unto Christ, so let the wives be to the husbands in everything.' It might be remarked that in this last quotation St Paul is not only carrying the interpretative framework further, but using it to give a particular interpretation of the state of marriage.

Durkheim's (1915) conception of the way in which the principles and rites of a religion are to be interpreted as representing social facts has been elegantly summed up by Lukes (1973).

1 Religion represents 'society and social relationships in a cognitive sense, to the mind or intellect'.
2 Religion represents in 'the sense of expressing, symbolizing, or dramatizing social relationships'.

I take Lukes to be saying that Durkheim claims that the religious stories and practices of a society are to be interpreted both as a literal representation of social relations and as a symbolic or expressive representation. So a Durkheimean hermeneutical analysis would operate at two levels, the one literal and the other metaphorical.

Be that as it may, a general definition of hermeneutical meaning can be given in the following principle:

> If the relation which obtains between signifier and signified is representation, then the signifier has hermeneutical meaning.

But since representation is a relation based upon real likenesses and differences, it is part of the theory of natural signs and not analogous to linguistic meaning which must be arbitrary in de Saussure's sense. At this point the notion of meaning has diverged so far from linguistic meaning that its investigation converges on the territory of literary criticism and its further discussion would carry me beyond the limits of this study.

At the heart of the theory of meaning I am proposing is the open character of the quasi-Saussurean grid which represents our grasp of a socially significant item as having a distinct *valeur* or value as a sign. Knowing *valeur* alone we could learn to place the sign correctly in a formalistic kind of way in stretches of social life in which we could recognize sufficiently similar structures to those which we have experienced before. The approval or disapproval or the 'not noticing' by the others involved would enable us to amplify our knowledge at the action level, by extending the axes of our Saussurean grid in the syntagmatic and paradigmatic directions.

Equally, since our grasp of the act-significance of an action is dependent on the sophistication of our theory of our social world and what is required of those who live in it, we may have only a very simplistic or superficial idea of what is or ought to be going on. For example, I may not have grasped the ritual character of many professions of friendship, and be surprised to find that the relationship had been struck up and maintained by the other for some personal advantage. Again, as I come to understand such matters my theoretical grasp of social practices is amplified.

Though the ideal of perfect social knowledge is unrealizable, even for an ethogenically oriented and industrious machiavellian, we can nevertheless have the idea of a disparity between what I do know and recognize as socially distinct, and what I might know in similar circumstances. We can have an idea of how individual social knowledge might grow. One might argue that Weber's idea of *verstehen*, (Weber, 1957) understanding of the intentions of others, could be explained in terms of what one must know to grasp the act/action character of some performance. On this view, *verstehen* as a progressively refinable understanding of the social meanings (and thereby of the intentions and projects of the actors) would be immune to the complaint that understanding has to be a single, unitary act. On the contrary, while degrees of partial understanding could be identified in terms of Saussurean value-grids and folk-theories of the social force of actions their essential incompleteness entails the indefinite improvability of any insight into social life.

Natural meanings

My argument so far has taken no account of the possibility of natural meanings, indeed I have gone to some trouble to emphasize that the relation between social sign and social significance is conventional. This emphasis has been a consequence of the insight that the means of social action are culturally specific, even though they may be used in the performance of social acts that are found necessary by all tribes and associations of human beings in the conduct of their lives.

We need to distinguish between the meaning of say, a smile as it is an outward and public sign of an inner and personal event or state, such as being amused or glad about something, and its meaning as a social sign. A smile seems to be a way of approving, a frown of disapproving of something. But the formulation 'A smile is an expression of approval' is seriously misleading, I would argue, since it suggests that approval is an inner state like contentment, rather than a social act like consent. Sometimes, of course, 'approval' is used to speak of the personal state of approving, but more importantly a smile is the action for performing the public act of approval. But a smile might convey a threat, a warning, a triumph, and many, many other acts depending on its location in an action-sequence, and on whose lips it forms.

What then of the idea of the natural meaning of a smile? At best perhaps we might notice a general and rather weak connection of this grimace with being pleased and amused. But just as 'Spots mean he's got measles' is an incorrigible but shallow truth if that is all one means by 'measles', so 'He's smiling so he's happy' may be equally incorrigible and similarly banal. The concept of measles includes hypotheses as to the cause of the spots; in most cases concepts such as 'happy' or 'content' include the personal state of the smiler. And this allows for the possibility that the smile may be assumed, ironic, subject to an inversion of meaning, and so on. If there are natural meanings one would not be advised to rely on them. There is a parallel with the way one can be misled by grammatical form – but the literal meaning of a speech is to its social meaning, as the natural meaning of a smile is to its social significance, the action by which we perform this or that social act.

Paul Theroux (1988) in his observations on the Chinese uses of laughter, provides an example both of how the action/act distinction should be used, and of a startling cultural difference. Chinese people, as members of the species *homo sapiens* are well equipped with the disposition to laugh. But the uses they make of laughter are diverse. However Theroux claims, and offers many examples to back up his thesis, that Chinese rarely use laughter as an expression of amusement, joy or delight. 'By now' he says

> I was able to differentiate between the various Chinese laughs. There were about twenty. None of them had the slightest suggestion of humour. Some were nervous, some were respectful, many were warnings. The loud hoinking was one sort of Chinese anxiety attack. Another brisk titter meant something had gone badly wrong. Mr Fang's laugh this morning resembled the bark of a seal. It meant *Hold on there!* It stopped me in my tracks. (Theroux, 1988:169.)

And again 'Mr Yang shrieked with laughter. It was the Chinese laugh that means: *On the contrary!*' (*op. cit.* p. 201.) And again (p. 214) 'This grunting, mirthless laugh meant: *I have just made a jackass of myself.*' And (p. 372) 'His face became very thin with the chattering laugh that meant: *You have just asked me a tactless question but I will nevertheless answer it.*' And so on through a catalogue of felicitous observations. What Theroux supplies is the act or illocutionary force of the laugh indexed, so to say, to that very situation.

The upshot of the discussion is the principle that the meanings of social events are created, not given. How are they created? First by the use of certain repertoires of actions and vocabularies of expressions. In this chapter so far we have been looking at language use *in* action. But meaning is also created in accounts of and glosses on the actions we and others have performed. This is a use of language about action. Of course this use of language (and gesture etc.) is itself a kind of action, and subject to the same accountings and glosses as action of the first order. Recently social psychologists have turned their attention to the role of rhetoric in social action (Billig, 1987). I shall reserve the word 'rhetoric' for accounting. In so describing act-action sequences in terms of rhetoric I shall be emphasizing the way we create meanings by ascribing motives to others (and to ourselves), by displaying attitudes of and about the current speaker, and so on. Rhetorical discourse of this sort affects language and other semantically significant systems in use. It does so because it affects the interpretation of actions sequences as acts, that is what actors make of the events of an episode, indeed what events they are able to pay attention to from the myriad of happenings that ebb and flow in any human encounter. I have already drawn attention to Tolstoy's social psychology, in which he uses the device of the novel to show how the fine grain structure of a sequence of episodes comes into being through the superposition of meanings upon what would otherwise be disorderly and chaotic happenings. Disorder threatens us at every turn, not because it might suddenly 'break out', but because we may cease to create order though the rhetorical devices which have been described in these chapters. People do not always produce orderly interactions by following rules and scripts, though they do sometimes. More often they use rules and scripts to find or impose order on the forms of causal encounters. Gossip, I submit, is the commonest and perhaps the most potent form of meaning creation through the use of rhetorics. This takes us back to the central theme of ancient studies of rhetoric (Billig, 1987). Any account of a slice of life is always, in principle, liable to be challenged by another account, in which a different act structure is conjured into being, and different motives are ascribed. Accounts are essentially contestable.

I have already remarked on the importance of following the way accounts are themselves accountable. Rhetorics are hierarchical. There are higher order motive ascriptions, usually adverted to when it is suspected that some lower order motive ascriptions and meaning claims are disingenuous, machiavellian, self-serving, implausible or 'wrong' in some other way. Since these accounts are essentially contestable there can be various second-order rhetorics and the yet higher-order accounts of why this or that was made use of in this or that context. Since social psychological theories, on my interpretation, can be nothing but rhetorics, there can be no final settling of accounts between them.

The social world, comprised of acts jointly created by the members of a community, is never and could never be fully determinate. The levels of rhetorical accounting feed back upon one another. To ascribe a motive to someone, or to declare one's own motives, are also social acts. The social psychology of episodes of human interaction could never be determinate either, since it will largely consist of spelled out rhetorics, in the form of sets of rules or scripts.

Some examples of episode analysis

Rules of sequence

We can begin with some examples in which types of social items are identified and individuated with the help of commonsense social categories. The elements of such sequences can be described in every-day terms, such as 'apology', 'question', 'answer', 'request', 'refusal' and so on. In the first range of examples, the analysis of brief conversations, each speaker's turn can be treated as the performance of an instance of a type of social act. In this analysis the speech is considered for its illocutionary force alone. Each speech-act as a contribution to a conversation, however cognitively complex, would be identified as, say, *a* request, that is asking something of someone who can bestow it but has the right to refuse. The orderliness, if any, of act/action sequences whose elements are individuated at this level of analysis, will reflect principles of order which we might wish to compare to grammatical rules. The comparison will turn out to be somewhat problematic since the combination of the level of social analysis germane to a comparison with grammar has to be discovered in the course of making the comparison.

Pursuing the analogy uncritically for the moment suggests looking for categories and subcategories of social actions. Let us begin with some intuitively obvious unit actions. As a first approximation actions can be categorized with respect to the social acts they are convention-ally taken to perform. For example:

Act	*Action*
Greeting	Kissing, hand-shaking, nodding, etc.
Insult	Finger-raising, tongue-poking, ignoring, etc.

Common experience is enough to provide some plausible examples of order among acts. Thus greetings occur at the beginning of inter-actions, farewells at the end; apologies usually follow protested insults, injuries, etc. These descriptions have the character of empirical generalizations, since they describe the order in a multiplicity of par-ticular action sequences such as 'Hullo, how are you?', 'Fine; how are you?', 'O.K.', 'See you', 'Yea, bye'; 'Hi', 'hi', 'you going out?',

'Later', 'O.K. Cheers', 'Caio'; 'Don't talk to me like that', 'Sorry': 'You bastard', 'What did you say?', 'Nothing'. . . . etc.

Rules for the simulation of socially proper episodes can be formulated for both levels.

1 *For acts*
   Greetings shall occur only at the beginning of an interaction.
   Apology should follow protested insult.
2 *For actions*
   'How do you do?' should accompany handshaking only.
   'Sorry' should follow a failure to notice an acquaintance.

The relations between empirical generalizations derived from recorded conversations and rules formulated for the construction of conversations need to be investigated.

Consider the following conversations:

1 *A*: 'Care for a drink?'
   B1: 'Thanks.'
   B2: 'Don't mind if I do.'
2 *A*: 'Care for a drink?'
   B1: 'Thanks (but)'
   B2: 'I really mustn't have another.'
   B3: 'I'm driving.'

In (1) A is making an offer. B's subsequent contributions are 'Thanks' which acknowledges the making of the offer, while 'I don't mind if I do' accepts the offer. The sequence of acts is something like this:

A1   Offer
B1   Acknowledgment
B2   Acceptance

The three distinct social acts constitute two orderly pairs, that is A1B1, A1B2. I propose to examine only the simplest of these pairs, 'Offer'/ 'Acceptance'. It would be of interest to try to determine whether B1B2 was a third orderly pair. My intuition suggests that it is not, that is a conversation in which acceptance preceded acknowledgment would not pass as civil.

Taking 'Offer' and 'Acceptance' as the names of species of performatives classified by reference to their illocutionary force, we can formulate a rule of sequence, the following of which would generate the pair A1B2 as a proper social episode.

Speaker 'Offer' should be followed by Addressee 'Acceptance', R1.
But sometimes offers are refused. Empirical studies have shown that in Refusal Sequences the rule is more complex than R1 but related to it. It turns out that refusals are 'accountable'. A reason or explanation must follow as a second contribution by the addressee, generating the pair B2B3 of the second conversation reported above. It could be argued that the 'Refusal'/'Reason' rule, R2, is dependent upon the 'Offers'/'Acceptance' rule, since if it is polite to accept an offer, an unqualified refusal is necessarily impolite. Its potential offensiveness must be remedied by the giving of a reason.

In general acceptances are not accountable, that is it is not mandatory to give reasons. The option of giving a reason for acceptance of course remains open, as in 'Thanks, I'd love a drink, I'm terribly thirsty', which might be called for in a special setting, say very hot weather. Accounts in such conditions seem to be socially efficacious as amplifications of 'Thanks', rather than as reasons for the acceptance.

The rules are beginning to display a satisfying systematic character consonant with the mandatory force of the modal verbs in R1 and R2, reflecting norms of politeness. That these rules be followed, or at least that structure be created, whether the psychological mechanism by which it is generated is or is not literally following a rule, is a necessary condition for the interaction to have the social property of politeness. Taking the two rules together we get: Speaker 'Offer' should be followed by Addressee 'Acceptance', and in case it is followed by 'Refusal' that 'Refusal' must be followed by 'Reason', (if politeness is to be achieved and gracious personas presented and sustained, and this is a condition derived from the necessities of the expressive order).

If the sequence A^n: Offer; B^n: Acceptance, is too long prolonged B's $n + k$ acceptance becomes accountable, for instance, 'I really must buy a round but I've left my money in another jacket.' 'Can you lend me a quid?' and so on.

The logical relations obtaining between the locutionary aspects of the speech involved in these reported conversations is not being addressed as an issue at this level of analysis. I am concerned only with the sequencing principles among the social acts 'Offer', 'Acceptance', 'Refusal', 'Reason'. Investigation of the criteria by which illocutionary forces are actually identified as a day-to-day practice could indeed involve consideration of logical relations, for instance whether 'Refusal' is identical with 'Non-Acceptance'. Relations of a more philosophical kind are involved in the rule that 'Offer', 'Acceptance', and 'Refusal' form a sequence only if they each have the same content or putative referent, namely a drink. And there are lots of other logical relations that could be involved too, for instance scope.

Justification of the rules
But if we were to ask, in the spirit of social science, why these sequencing principles seem to be at work, intending our query to direct attention to their social aspects, two further issues can be raised. The sequencing rule (the analogue of a syntactical rule) can be associated with a social principle, that accepting an offer is a way of showing respect to the person who offers. We can ask for a justification of the principle. This might be attempted as follows: a fundamental activity of social life is the presentation of an agreeable persona or social self and the sustaining of the persona presentations of others. To accept an offer is to acknowledge the benevolence of the putative host. It allows the other to be gracious and at the same time, by providing the opportunity for this, one presents oneself in an agreeable light.

The sequencing rule can also be taken as an empirical generalization: in civil society offers are usually followed by acceptances (even when this involves considerable inconvenience for the addressee).

Either or both the associated general statements could be offered in support of the sequencing rule. But is there always a sequencing rule involved in the genesis of action by particular individuals? That is, are we to take 'syntax' as part of a performance theory? Must social knowledge and action be related in this way? In a highly formalist society it is conceivable (and I think indeed often the case) that the sequencing rules would be taught without the associated supporting or explanatory general statements in that social knowledge would be exhausted by more sequencing rules. In such a society it might not be implausible to conceive a naive rule-following model as the icon of a generative mechanism of action, a description of which would be the core of a performance theory. But in contemporary society, great efforts are made to support the sequencing rules with social generalizations of both categories. Consider the 'Please'/Response/'Thanks' sequencing rule. We try to make it intelligible by reference to principles from just the two categories of general statements I have mentioned.

'It's a way of showing that you have noticed and appreciated the trouble someone has taken on your behalf.' This is to make reference to a general principle of social order.

'That's what nice little girls say.' This is clearly offered as an empirical generalization about social behaviour. The reference to 'nice little girls' excludes too easy empirical refutation, since the cost of successfully sustaining oneself as a putative counter-instance would be *a priori* exclusion from a desirable category of persons.

This suggests that a rule-following model is not likely to prove adequate as the core of a performance theory for contemporary society.

Somehow people must 'see the sense of what they are doing'. This, I believe, suggests a more cognitive, problem-solving conception of the individual genesis of co-ordinated action, such as the desire/belief/intention theory sketched in recent studies in the philosophy of action.

It is worth noticing that our lay efforts to support or explain an apparently formalistic sequencing rule to our children involve rudimentary social science. We attempt the exposition of a feature of our local ethnography in terms of a cultural norm and its relation to a more general principle involved in the maintenance of social order, such as the propriety of acknowledging efforts directed towards one's wellbeing by others. It may take the form of the statement of an empirical generalization concerning the orderliness actually present in a class of social interactions. Finally, one could offer theoretical and normative principles of social order in explanation of the existence of the empirical regularity. Ethogenic social psychology depends on the systematic and rigorous pursuit of the same interests, but controlled by continuous empirical testing of hypotheses as to the degree that people actually control action by reference to norms.

Levels of analysis: identifying act-categories
David Clarke (1983) has shown that people recognize social order not just in sequences of particular speech-act instances, that is real and artificial conversations, but also in sequences of common-sense terms for specific performative forces, that is in cases where a conversation between A and B is represented only in a sequence of the names for acts, for instance:

A_1 Greeting B_1 Greeting
A_2 Question B_2 Answer
A_3 Apology   etc.

The importance of Clarke's discovery can hardly be over-emphasized. It demonstrates that people are able to recognize social orderliness in two wholly different modes. In the first mode order is recognized in a representation of their own and other's action-sequences, for example in a transcript of a conversation, in the second in a list of names for the elementary acts generated in action-sequences. People know both that 'Sorry' should follow treading on someone's foot *and* that an 'apology' should follow an 'offence'. It is as if the native speakers not only knew how to talk and were able to recognize proper and improper forms of speech, but were also able routinely to deploy a grammar that expresses abstract knowledge of the structure of proper grammatical forms. But 'noun', 'verb', etc., though part of the language of the educated, are grammarians' terms. They are not part of the vocabulary routinely employed in the speech of daily life. They are part of a theory of that speech. Yet 'insult', 'apology', 'plea', 'excuse', and so on are terms of native speech and are routinely employed as part of the social resources of competent social actors. This discovery highlights a profound asymmetry between social action and the linguistic (as opposed to social) properties of speech. In the realm of social action we possess an explicit 'grammar' and deploy it in our day-to-day practice.

Why this asymmetry? The answer seems to lie in the dual character of human social performance. There is both action and the speech which accounts for the action. Accounts are, in part, continuous commentary upon the social propriety of the acts and action-sequences generated by ourselves and others. We could take social propriety as the social analogue of linguistic wellformedness. Clarke's discovery suggests that people have a more explicit abstract knowledge of the principles of social orderliness than they have of the rules of grammar. Grammarians must rely on native speakers' intuitions whereas we can reasonably ask directly for at least some of the rules of social orderliness.

At least two assumptions are involved in the argument of the preceding section. First, though grammatical categories may reflect ultimate metaphysical categories, sequencing rules are arbitrary. Second, selection and sequencing rules at the level of common-sense categorizations of social acts are not arbitrary. The importance of these assumptions in judging the use of the linguistic analogy in explicating social meaning comes out when we consider the level of orderliness that can be shown to exist in social act-action sequences by comparison with the structure of linguistic performances. I consider first Austin's (1961) scheme for categorizing the social force of speech acts.

Consider the following exchanges:

	Common-sense categories	Austinian categories	
'Stupid bitch!'	Insult	Verdictive	V
'Don't talk to me like that'	Protest	Exercitive	E
'Sorr-*rry*'	Apology	Behabitive	B
'I won't' (as act of defiance)	Defiance	Commissive	C
'Very well, then, you're not going out tonight'.	Threat/Verdict + Sentence	Commissive (or Exercitive & Verdictive)	C
'Alright, *alright*! But it's not fair'	Submission Protest	Commissive Verdictive	C V

Could the Austinian categories form the basis of a social grammar? If every possible combination of Austinian categories is 'well-formed' then the order of sequences of social acts categorized at this level is socially without significance. In fact there seem to be neither selection nor sequencing rules at the level of Austinian categories. It seems to me that any sequence of types of elements identified at the Austinian level could be realized, for instance any of CCCV, VCCC, CVCC, etc. For example:

A_1:	You're lying	V
B_1:	I promise you I'm not	C
A_2:	I'll make you tell me the truth	C
B_2:	I swear I'm not lying	C

I hope the reader shares my intuition that the quoted conversation-fragment represents a perfectly orderly sequence of social acts.

To show conclusively that the Austinian categorial structure of a sequence is irrelevant to social meaningfulness it would suffice to find another realization of each of the Austinian categories which, at the level of common-sense categorization was disorderly. The example above realizes the structure VCCC as the sequence of common-sense categories:

A_1	accusation
B_1	assurance
A_2	threat
B_2	reassurance

If on the basis of our intuitions we judged that another realization of VCCC was disorderly, and that intuition could be sustained by reference to the sequence of acts categorized in the common-sense scheme, then we have shown that the Austinian categories are too weak to serve in the setting out of structure. Disorderly sequences are readily identified at the common-sense level of categorization. For example, VCCC realized as:

A_1	convict
B_1	appeal
A_2	allow
B_2	make restoration

strikes me as clearly disorderly. Consider, for example, the realization of the above structure in:

A_1:   *You* finished the marmalade.
B_1:   No, I didn't.
A_2:   Oh, sorry.
B_2:   I suppose *I'll* have to get you some more then.

(Just as a context *can* be found in which green ideas do sleep furiously, so B_2 can be taken to be orderly on the assumption that B proposes to punish A by 'martyrdom'.)

Failure to reveal order at the level of Austin's categories could have more than one interpretation. The argument so far could be used to suggest that treating orderliness of social acts as analogous to syntax cannot be sustained at the level at which social sequences have been shown to be orderly, namely at the level of specific illocutions, since common-sense categories of social acts do not correspond to grammatical categories.

But taking the parallel to be at the level where order first appears in each realm would involve matching commonsense categories of social acts to grammatical categories. There are some obvious disparities. There are very many more categories of social acts than there are syntactical categories. The ratio might be something of the order of four hundred to seven or eight. The range and interrelations of syntactical categories can be grounded in a rather course-grained general metaphysics of nature. The grounding of the corresponding diversity of illocutionary categories and their permitted combinations in a theory of sociality is a much more daunting task and demands more attention to social detail, so leading towards cultural specificity and thus relativity of explanations. The taxonomy of social acts is messy, contingent and naturalistic, while the taxonomy of syntactical categories is neat, apparently necessary and *a priori*.

Alternatively, the resolution of the apparent failure to match might be found by introducing the idea of sub-categorial rules on the linguistic side of the analogy.

The principles upon which 'Hot brown icicles trade anxiety under two' is recognized as improper are sometimes called sub-categorial rules. They seem to reflect a rather wide range of considerations. Compare:

My dog chewed the cud
My dog chewed the wind
My dog chewed the North Pole

Each of these could be treated in two different ways. The sentence could be taken as well-formed, but each and every use of it would issue in a false statement (provided linguistic and empirical considerations were normal). The sentence could be judged to be ill-formed prior to any putative use, because it violated sub-categorial rules.

But unlike the categorial rules of language which are fully arbitrary in Saussure's sense, the rules according to which each of the above sentences is ill-formed could be justified by reference to contingent empirical considerations such as the masticatory habits of dogs, the lack of a firm texture in the wind as material substance, and the abstract geometrical character of the North Pole.

Since dogs never chew the cud, the wind is always without texture and the North Pole defined as a purely geometrical concept, one could as well absorb these features of the world into the rules for the formation of sentences as reserve them for the inevitable rejection of proposed statements as false.

But to treat the wrongness of the above sentences as stemming from an intuition of rule-violation rather than a judgement of falsehood in every normal putative application is to extend the notion of syntax beyond the limits laid down by Saussure, limits defined by the arbitrariness of the rules. As I have shown, the rules which express the intuitively felt orderliness of social life are non-arbitrary, that is capable of justification with respect to general features of social experience and social theory. In this respect they match the sub-categorial rules of language. Each embeds in its formal principles some pervasive but contingent features of the world to which it is primarily related.

The conversational examples I have analysed have been chosen for their simplicity and brevity. More extended conversations reveal a much more complex structure, but the principles of analysis are the same. Brenner (1978) has shown that the analysis of a longer conversation requires the attribution to the speakers of a hierarchy of intentions, there being a dominant theme, the working out of each member's global intentions or projects, and minor themes brought about by the clash and mesh of momentary intentions. These generate an act-structure which is realized in speech, gesture, and so on through a four-fold rule system which associates actions with acts, and controls their sequencing. The act/action structure so generated consists of a halting progress through loops and nesting inserts towards the realization of the dominant theme. The orderliness of the transitions in a fifteen-minute conversation of a specific social form can be represented by a total of about ninety rules.

Generative transformations

We can hardly touch upon an analogy between social order and linguistic structure without examining the possibility of an analogue of generative transformation as a way of representing members' knowledge of correct order. A very striking example can be found in tracing the source of orderliness of meals. A meal is an orderly sequence of dishes, the template for which is a menu. Cuisines are distinguishable families of menus, and dishes are orderly assemblages of comestibles, the templates for which are recipes.

A plausible case can be made for treating the working out of a menu from which a meal will be prepared and served, along the lines of the transformation of a base-structure according to cuisine-specific rewrite rules. Unlike the use of transformational grammar in linguistics, which is confined to the representation of competence, we might treat the generative 'grammar' of cooks as a quasiperformance theory. Following the Burgundian cuisine:

R1   M (meal) goes into (Salt plus Sweet)
R2   Salt goes into (Beginners plus Main dish)
R3   Sweet goes into (Pudding plus Dessert)
R4   Any main dish goes into (Main element plus two subsidiary elements)
R5   Any subsidiary dish goes into (Main element plus one subsidiary element)
R6   Cheese and (or) salad can be interposed between Salt and Sweet

In current degenerate versions of the Burgundian cuisine one of the subsidiary elements of the menu generated by R4 must be potatoes.

Applying these rules we write a typical Burgundian menu (garnish omitted):

Smoked salmon and brown bread
Tournedos Rossini, baked celery and scalloped potatoes
Ice pudding and sponge fingers
Fruit (grapes and apples)

One could serve a Mersault with the salmon a Macon with the steak, and then a Barsac with the pudding and dessert.

To test the analogy this apparently frivolous example is just what we need. It highlights the differences between syntax and social order. Syntax is a determinant of meaning, or to put this more precisely: order in language is message specific. 'You didn't go' (an accusation), 'Didn't you go?' (a question), differ partly and significantly in syntactical order, while the disorderly 'You go didn't' conveys no message at all.

But the message specificity of meals is coarse-grained. Mary Douglas (1972) distinguishes message specificity only at that degree of analysis which would distinguish 'drinks' from 'formal dinners' from 'family meals', the sequential partaking of which she takes to be ritual markings of passage from stranger to intimate. Why, then, all the fuss about cuisine? After all, beginning with salad and thousand island dressing, then steak and Idaho baked potato, followed by ice cream and chocolate sauce, accompanied by a King-size Coke *is* a meal.

There are, I think, two complementary influences at work, both of which detract from the literalness of the linguistic analogy, as it concerns the treating of sequential orderliness in meals as parallel to syntax. One is aesthetic. A Burgundian dinner is nicer than a drug-store supper. A gastronome like Brillat-Savarin (1970) can explain why it is nicer in a convincing way. He proceeds in much the same way as a musicologist would proceed in explaining to us why a Mahler symphony is a greater work than a symphony by Brahms, that is his 'explanation' would be in part, a pedagogical exercise.

The other influence is more diffuse, but quite as important. Goffman has pointed out the importance of securing an untroubled setting for the mutual actions of social life (1972). Mere orderliness in the *Umwelt* is sufficient to reassure against the possibility of threat. The *mere* orderliness of a meal, the standardization of its sequencing, allows the accompanying social interaction to proceed unimpeded by doubts, fears of digestive upsets, or by social uncertainty, as dish follows dish in accordance with some recognized cuisine. The identification of this influence owes nothing to the specifically linguistic source of the syntactical analogy.

THE BOUNDARIES OF MEANING

In this chapter the concept of social meaning has been explicated in terms of the ideas of social acts and actions. Acts have been defined as the meanings of actions, and the whole structure has been based on the idea of meaning as rule conforming use. Without evoking the magic name of Ludwig Wittgenstein explicitly it ought to have been evident that the idea of rules as tools for the creation and maintenance of meaning in this sense is basic to the treatment of social conduct. But what of anomalies? What of actions for which no act force can be found? It seems to me that the boundaries of the intelligible and the warrantable are defined for us by two procedures.

One of these, common in the practices of contemporary societies, is to invoke the notion of 'madness'. In this context the concept of 'madness' is tied up with concepts such as 'unmotivated', 'random', 'irrational' and the like. The boundary of this familiar domain was explored by R.D. Laing (1969) in his attempt to find meaning in the meaningless, that is in the discourses of those suffering from schizophrenia. I suppose it is now generally conceded that Laing failed in this project. I shall not pursue this issue further here, other than to remark that it seems to me that the failure of Laing's project leaves much unfinished business, offering interesting opportunities for social psychological research focussed on the relevant discursive practices.

The other procedure, or rather cluster of procedures, is less central in modern Western cultures than in the European past, or in some contemporary societies, still somewhat independent of Western influences. It is what one might call the 'management of meaning'. I owe to N.C. Much notice that some of these procedures have been thoroughly analyzed by Mary Douglas (1966). What is to be done with the anomalous, be it an anomolous action, one without act-force, or an anomalous object, one without a place in the accepted taxonomy of the tribe?

Broadly speaking there are three strategies by which we manage meaning in the face of anomalies. We can and do simply ignore the meaningless action or the categoriless thing, or if action is taken it is simply to delete it from the world, to discard it and even to deny that it ever existed. A second strategy is to celebrate it as the very exemplification of the obscene, the polluted, the vile. In the popular press one can find all sorts of examples of the move from meaningless to evil. Mary Douglas, and other students of the boundary that marks off the sacred from the profane, have interpreted the role of the monster as affirming the propriety of the good and the correct. A similar account has been given of the fascination of 'rary' shows, the exhibition of such anomalous beings as the 'Elephant man'. A third strategy is to assimilate the anomaly to the category of the sacred. Its meaninglessness and lack of place in the order of society and nature can be treated as a mark of its special status.

From the point of view of this study, the key point is that nowhere in social reality *can* the truly anomalous have a place. Actions and things either have a meaning or they do not exist. Once again we can turn to Wittgenstein (1969) for a deeper illumination of the nature of this boundary. The borders of the human forms of life can be expressed by certain very distinctive propositions. The frame or boundary of a form of life is defined by statements and practices which seem incontrovertible. 'Persons are beings who can be held responsible for their actions' looks at first sight like a necessary truth, a kind of definition. It would then follow that the negation of this statement,

'Persons are not beings who can be held responsible for their actions' would be necessarily false. But that, according to Wittgenstein, would be a mistake. It allows that the negated statement is meaningful, but just happens to be false. It makes it seem rather like 'All the tea in my caddy is from Assam'. The negation of this statement, that 'All the tea in my caddy is not from Assam' is false, but it is quite meaningful and there are conditions under which it could be true. The negation of a statement which marks the boundary of a form of life is not false. It is meaningless. The point of a monster is that it has no place in the order of the world.

PART II

Methods for Social Psychology

INTRODUCTION: METHODS FOR SOCIAL PSYCHOLOGY

The central thesis of social constructionism is the claim that most psychological phenomena are created in and have their primal being in social encounters. Social encounters are processes of interaction. They have a dynamics. The structures of social encounters are like melodies in that they come into existence sequentially. If we are to understand how attitudes, memories, personalities, status hierarchies and so on are created in the sequential development of structured sequences of act-actions, we must understand the dynamics of social episodes. In Part Two I address the question of how a systematic method is to be developed for revealing such structures. Drawing on the discussions of basic principles in Part One I develop a methodological framework, based on the position/act-action/story-line triad, and the analogy of social life to one of its manifestations, conversation. The finer-grain methodological frameworks to be developed in this part are best looked on as specifications of that triad at different levels of analytical stringency.

I shall show, very briefly, how the traditional 'experimental' methodology fails as a technique for revealing the act-action structures of the episodes of everyday life. (A useful survey of the issues can be found in Greenwood, 1991). Nor is it capable of revealing the tacit conventions by which people jointly create orderly interactions and render them as explicit rule-systems. Suitable methodologies for respectable empirical studies do exist and I shall sketch four of them.

One great contrast between old paradigm social psychology and the new is the extent to which the complexity of social life is taken into account. One dimension of complexity which I have drawn attention to from time to time is the multiplicity of distinct episodes that may be occurring simultaneously on the basis of just one sequence of actions. The relation between acts and the actions by which they are publicly manifested is frequently many-one. The most usual situation, I believe, is the simultaneous existence of at least two *levels of dynamic structure* with respect to the underlying duality of practical and expressive orders. At each level of dynamic structure both the practical and expressive orders are being created, maintained and reproduced in the episodes of everyday life. Our methodology will borrow heavily from that of the physical sciences at this point. But that borrowing will not be from the fanciful picture of 'science' that most psychologists have unknowingly inherited from logical positivism. It will be from the methods actually in use in those almost miraculous research programmes. The technique we shall be borrowing is that of descriptive (analytical) and explanatory modelling.

A model, as physicists and chemists understand the term, is an analogue or simulation of some real structure or process. The occasions for inventing models have become more and more common as these sciences have progressed. It is because the reality nowadays in question is usually inacessible to observation and indescribable with the resources available in the current discourses of these fields, that models of reality are devised. An analogue is above all a representation. Models are used in two main ways.

They are used analytically to create a simplified or highlighted version of a reality too complex or too ephemeral to handle or even to describe in any adequate way.

They are used explanatorily to create intelligible and observable or imaginable versions of what is often unintelligible and unobservable, namely the structures and processes by which the phenomena represented by analytical models come about.

The discourse of physicists and chemists is not about reality – how could it be? It is about models of reality. Experimental set ups are virtual worlds, models of the real world, while theories describe the way the world is imagined to be, a conceptual model of that real world, which it is the ultimate project of science to understand. As Etchemendy has put it (1988: 95) 'Models are just abstract representations of the world as it *is*, and as it *might have been* [or *could be*].' The key question on the answer to which the long run plausibility of a science depends is 'how similar are the models and the realities they represent?' When models are used analytically the answer is already known in outline, since an analytical model is created by analogy from some real process or structure according to certain criteria of abstraction and idealization. In constructing the Newtonian model of the universe, physicists knew that they were setting aside at least some of the aspects of the world they were trying to represent. But when models are used in explanatory schemata the question of their fit with that which they represent may remain open for generations, since it must wait upon the development of a technology that will open up new realms to human experience. Even then the answers may be problematic.

However, in our construction of the virtual world of a model for some aspect of human psychology the 'resemblance' question, which is at the heart of the methodology of model use in physics, may be fatally misleading. It may lead back to the very picture of individual human beings as information-processing devices that one wishes at all costs to avoid. The role-rule model that will emerge from the use of a model-building methodology for the description and explanation of the structure of episodes represents tacit knowledge of norms of conduct. It is not a pictorial sketch of a mental mechanism. It presents the content of a skill, a knowing how.

However there is another dimension to models. We could call this the 'as if' dimension. In creating a model of a complex phenomenon such as a social episode of a certain kind we can proceed by using a set of concepts derived from some other kind of episode, treating the former as if it were of the same kind as the latter. In physics there are many examples of this kind of procedure. Boyle treated the air trapped in his bent tube as if it were an air spring. The models to be described in the coming chapters are all 'as if' models. We shall be seeking a clear view of the structures of complex episodes by treating them as if they were procedures for solving problems, as if they were the stagings of dramas, as if they were productive processes in the world of work.

The upshot of the use of these 'as if' models will be another 'as if' super model. We shall be expressing the results of using the lower-order models analytically as sets of rules, representing the normative constraints on the production of intelligible and warrantable act-action sequences. Now comes the moment of greatest danger. These sets of rules are drawn from a picture of social life, as if it were created by people following rules. How are we to use the role-rule models explanatorily? Should we say that there is a computational process occurring 'behind' the overt process of social interaction, of which that interaction is the upshot? Is there a 'computation' of which the rules with which we have presented the normative order are the 'programme'? That is the temptation we wish to resist. The explanatory use of rules is itself a category of social episode, through which what we do is rendered intelligible and warrantable. We can exercise our social skills, our know how, in doing things and in displaying those things as the correct things to do or to have done in the circumstances. Nothing is hidden. There are no information processing mechanisms behind what we are doing, doing these things for us! Rules and scripts are not the causes of actions. They are what we use to present our actions as correct or incorrect. The metaphor of causation is out of place. It leads to the fantasy of hidden processors that we are only to ready to entertain, mesmerized as we are by the Hertzian ideal of physics, though we may never have heard of him. The only causes of actions are persons.

One still finds resurgences of the Humean reductive conception of causality as mere regularity of sequence. Social psychologists of the old school are particularly prone to think that in discovering the conditions under which a certain kind of act is performed, they have found its causes. This is so serious a misunderstanding of the concept of causality that it would be best to interpet it as a distinct concept, another way of talking of the conditions and antecedents of action. One must be careful not to read into this use any implications from the generative sense of the word 'cause' which is central to its usual uses and particularly to its use in the physical sciences. In the context of social psychology causal power resides in people, not in any of the tools they use to accomplish their ends nor the conditions under which they use them, however systematic these may be.

Yet another way of presenting models and their sources and subjects is as types under a common supertype. Taking 'dramatic performance' as a common supertype we have among its subtypes 'staged drama' and 'everyday episodes'. By putting everyday episodes under the same supertype as staged dramas we highlight such similarities between staged dramas and everyday episodes as are to be found represented in the generic supertype. Differences between staged dramas and everyday experiences emerge only at the sub-type level.

The analytic schema

Human social activity consists of two main kinds of performance.

1　Performance 1 is the doings of actions and thus the performing of acts in socially recognized episodes.
2　Performance 2 is the speaking of accounts, both to ensure that the act/action performances are given a certain meaning, and that they can be seen as the doings of rational beings.

The fundamental principle of new paradign research is the belief that both kinds of performance stem from one and only one system of social knowledge and social skill, from which come our rules of action and interpretative principles. On the basis of this hypothesis one can use the results of the analysis of action and of accounting to attribute knowledge and skill to a competent actor, or more usually to a group of actors.

To use this as a real empirical method we need analytical models for performances of kind 1 and analytical concepts for performances of kind 2. I propose two main models in this work. This does not exclude the possibility that others may be required as social studies progress.

1   *The problem-solving model.* This includes the treatment of act/ action episodes as solving practical and social problems by the use of standard techniques, shading off into cases where the techniques are improvised. It also includes the treatment of accounts as solutions to a range of metaproblems raised by the possibility of misunderstandings of the meaning and legitimacy of actions.

2   *The dramaturgical model.* This includes the analysis of episodes according to the overall scene, action, actor schema, and the treatment of accounts as presentational activities, as part of the performance by which we show what sort of person we are. In most Western and Western-influenced cultures, we are required to show that we are rational beings.

The explanation schema

Having attributed knowledge and skill to competent members of a well-identified collective by the use of the methods outlined above, we have now to explain how they produce their actions on particular occasions. The outline schema for explanation runs as follows:

Social knowledge is drawn upon by an actor to formulate intentions to perform appropriate acts. Action to realize intentions draws further on the rules and conventions as to how those acts are to be performed in cultures and within situations and settings in which actors finds themselves. Contrary to recent attempts to develop this in a Humean mode I argue that the fulfilling of the conditions for action implicit in this scheme is neither sufficient nor necessary for action to occur. Empirical considerations force us to introduce the pure agent or person who acts in accordance with these conditions, but not because of them. Intentions control the content of an actor's performance as to the acts he or she is trying to perform and the rules and conventions of the society control the way intentions are realized. Neither singly nor jointly could these conditions produce action.

At the 'task' level the problem of making social acts and positions determinate is solved, up to a certain degree of specificity, by structuring the acts of an unfolding encounter in certain ways. To bring out this level of structure I will be describing, developing and applying the problem-solving model. This is an analytical model, the purpose of which is to reveal the structures through which certain basic features of the respective social orders are created, particularly the human being as worker and the human being as person.

At the 'act' level the social scientist's project must be to try to bring out the structures of act-actions, positions and story-lines in the unfolding of which social psychological phenomena like attitudes, motives, friendships, personas and so on are created. For this purpose I shall be developing the dramaturgical model in some depth. Again it is to be emphasized that this is an analytical model, the purpose of which is to reveal the dynamic structure of those encounters in which psychological phenomena of a multitude of different kinds are engendered.

4

METHODS OF RESEARCH: ALTERNATIVES TO THE EXPERIMENT

INTRODUCTION

In the preceding chapters I have presented a general view of the nature of social life. We have come to see human association in terms of structures and meanings, rather than causes and effects. We have added the all-important distinction between static social relations and dynamic social interactions to our analytic scheme. Underlying this view of how we manage to live together in associations is a metaphysical thesis: that human beings are active agents and that they are intent on the joint production of orderly social artifacts, such as institutions and evolving 'conversational' episodes. It can hardly be too strongly emphasized that scientific methods, the techniques of enquiry appropriate to some class of phenomena, are intimately related to the metaphysical assumptions that investigators bring to their task. There is no such thing as *the* scientific method. It is now quite clear that to be a scientist is to commit oneself to a certain kind of morality (Polanyi, 1962) rather than to adopt this or that technique. Investigative techniques are determined by metaphysical commitments not by professional affiliations.

The methodology to be presented in this chapter should be understood not only in relation to the metaphysical scheme presented in the preceding chapters, but also in contrast to five important alternative clusters of investigative techniques. There is the naive laboratory experiment, as practised by, say, Duval and Wicklund (1972) or Zajonc (1968) which is coupled with the use of statistical 'packages' to analyze data. Then there is phenomenological analysis of experience. The third cluster of techniques involves the study of the neurology of social interactions, for instance the work of Plutchik (1980) on the neurochemistry of those bodily agitations that are the somatic grounding of many human emotions. Cognitive science offers a fourth way, based on the theorizing techniques used by physicists and chemists, that is on the construction of models of the unobservable generative processes that supposedly produce the behaviour in question. This technique has been used by Schank and Abelson (1977). Finally there is the idea of human ethology, investigating human social interactions by the recording of interactive displays as ethograms, the methodological side of sociobiology, as practised for instance by Blurton-Jones (1972).

SOME PROBLEMS WITH THE CLASSICAL PSYCHOLOGICAL EXPERIMENT

There are a number of difficulties that have troubled the use of the traditional laboratory 'experiment' as a means of gathering data in social psychology. I shall discuss these at two levels. There are 'superficial problems', difficulties that have long been pointed out with the method. Then are the 'fundamental' problems, which really amount to untenable metaphysical principles that have animated old paradigm social psychology, and belief in which accounts for sensible people following a wrong-headed set of data-gathering procedures.

Among the many superficial difficulties I single out four.

1   The meaning problem: this has two aspects. How can the experimenter ensure that the situation or 'set of stimuli' he or she creates in the laboratory has the same meaning for all the participants? And how can the experimenter ensure that the stimuli have the same meaning for the participants as he or she intended? If the participants give a variety of interpretations to the laboratory situation, as they did in the Milgram experiment, then there is more than one experiment going on at the same time. This may be concealed by the use of statistics. If participants give a different meaning to the situation from that intended by the experimenter, as also ocurred in the Milgram experiment, than the experiment that is going on is not the experiment that was intended. All this was elegantly demonstrated by Mixon (1971) who recreated each of the sub-experiments by manipulating the meanings of the situation in Milgram's laboratory.

2   The partitioning problem: the participants in an experiment are confronted with a situation or a 'stimulus' which is meant to be an abstraction from the complex situations they would encounter in everyday life. In order to ensure a sufficiently simple 'independent

variable' experimenters frequently have to partition complex situations into elements, which turn out to be below the level at which their meaning is relevant to the experiment in hand. For instance Zajonc's (1968) abstraction of 'pure frequency' from the complex situations of human encounters in which people get to like or dislike one another, or Tajfel's (1972) abstraction of 'pure group difference' from the complex situations in which groups of people interact with one another exemplify the partitioning problem. The 'independent variables' they based their experiments on are patently not relevant to human liking or disliking, prejudice or anything else. Replications of the Zajonc's 'experiment' have shown that the relative frequency of the presentation of a stimulus is correlated with a relative increment in *any* pro-attribute, even brightness! Similar replications have not been attempted with the Tajfel 'experiments in a vacuum' but I daresay the same sort of result would emerge. The problem arises simply from the failure of the experimenter to maintain a level of partitioning of the many aspects of a situation at or above that at which the meaning of the stimulus situation remains stable.

3   The sociality of the laboratory problem: an experiment is a social event, an episode, and so subject to the normative constraints appropriate for an episode of that sort. But of what sort? One obvious and interesting answer is 'a psychological experiment'. The results of an experiment should then simply reflect the normative constraints appropriate for experiments and could be reinterpreted in terms of the role-rule model. A less obvious but equally interesting answer would be 'a meeting between strangers'. The results, such as those obtained by Argyle (1976) in his experimental studies of gaze, reveal codes or standards of public politeness. But as they used to say in the Goon Show 'I don't wish to know that!'

4   The loss of data problem. It has become customary, even mandatory, to use a large number of participants in an experimental study, and to analyze the data statistically in search of central tendencies in the behaviour of participants in response to the stimuli. Individual differences in responses to the stimulus situation created in the experiment are deleted, so it is thought, by statistical analysis. All sorts of statistical fallacies befog the literature of social psychology. The commonest is to treat a statistical distribution as equivalent to a probability assignment to each member of the reference class, which is taken to be a measure of a tendency or likelihood. This elementary error is so widespread as to deserve the name the social psychologists' fallacy. But the most important effect of adopting this methodology, technically the 'extensive design', is the artifactual simplification of the phenomena that follows. In the extensive design an intension for the

class of participants is abstracted from the results obtained for all of them. All that survives the process of abstraction is what they have in common. In the intensive design an individual is chosen to typify the class and is subjected to detailed observational or experimental scrutiny. The extension of the class is then created by collecting all those individuals who are sufficiently similar to the one chosen as typical. It is a theorem of logic that the intension of a class varies inversely as its extension. The larger the class the less that can be known about any of its members. In the use of statistical methods for analyzing mass data, if the extensive design has been adopted, there necessarily follows a loss of data. This has a mathematical expression in DuMas's theorem. But it is obvious to commonsense. The physical sciences almost always use the intensive design. Error theory is not the statistics of aggregates! An interesting history of this aberration can be found in Danziger (1991).

These problems and difficulties with the use of the experimental method for data collection and of statistical techniques for its analysis are very well known. They have been pointed out for a quarter of a century. Alternative empirical methods, which are mostly based on naturalistic data collection and involve discursive analysis, have been available for at least as long. The question that haunts one is why the experimental method has continued to be used despite the many theoretical and practical demonstrations of its futility. Why have observational-analytical methods not prevailed? There is no lack of important empirical studies in which the advantages of the use of analytical methods have been amply demonstrated. At first, in reflecting on these matters, I was inclined to blame structural features of the communities of academic psychologists, and even intellectual and moral shortcomings of some of the practitioners. There is some truth in these diagnoses. But why does a clever fellow like R.B. Zajoncs, secure in his career, transparently honest in his dealings, persist in using the experimental methodology, when most of his projects would be more fittingly carried out analytically? The diagnosis of the malaise must go much deeper.

Diagnoses: the ontological fallacies

When a methodology goes awry it is a good rule to look at the metaphysics behind it. This is as true in psychology as it is in physics. There is one pervasive metaphysical assumption, thoroughly examined by Ryle and by Wittgenstein, the holding of which seems to me to explain much of the methodological conservatism of social psychologists. I think it is widely believed that behind the overt processes of discursive thinking, the displaying of emotions, the evincing of attitudes, the ratification of recollections as genuine memories, and so on there are invisible processes, the pure subject matter of psychology. There are assumed to be processing mechanisms, operating at a high level of abstraction, on material provided by low level or concrete psychological phenomena. I have drawn attention to this widespread metaphysical assumption in the introduction to this book, with a wonderfully clear quotation from Shweder. I shall borrow his phrase, the 'central processing mechanism' (hereafter 'c.p.m.') to refer to the mythical machinery to the discovery and understanding of which so many of the efforts of our colleagues seem to be directed. I can find no convincing evidence for the existence of any such mechanism. Wittgenstein thought that the conceptual confusions that he discerned in psychology, of which belief in the existence of the c.p.m. was one, came about in part through the mistaken borrowing of the explanatory tactics of physics as a model for explanatory methods in psychology. He thought that another source of confusion was the use of overly simplified grammatical models for interpreting psychological concepts like 'thinking', 'reading', 'expecting' and so on. These models encouraged belief in the existence of entities such as 'thoughts' and 'expectations'.

In physics one imagines an unobservable mechanism the operations of which appear to observers as physical phenomena. Experimentation consists in attempting to explore the nature of the hidden mechanisms by indirect manipulation. It works well for molecules, not so well for quarks, and not well at all for thoughts. There is no need to postulate a c.p.m. Equally ontologically excessive is the idea that there are mental states doubling up every perceptual and discursive activity. That idea too emerges from mistakes about the grammar of perception talk, of memory declarations and so on. If you do something to offend me, and I get cross wtih you, and display my annoyance, why do we need something other than neurophysiology and discursive conventions to link what is already semantically adjacent? The discursive methodologies to be expounded in the rest of this chapter are based on the idea that there is discursive activity and there is physiological activity, and there is nothing else. Cognitive science ought to be about the former, since that is where the mind is. There is no such thing as information processing, there are no mental modules. There are no mental states. There are neurochemical and neurophysiological changes, and there are public and private discourses, not all the symbols of which are verbal.

Looked at in the light of the problem-solving model, social episodes seem to involve the resolution of two kinds or levels of problems.

There are those I shall call generic human problems. Typically these involve questions as to the humanity of the actors (and the sociality of the episode) and questions as to the relative status of the actors, and the relations of deference, respect and condescension that would serve as a structural frame for the further development of an encounter. Then there are those I shall call specific or local problems for which there are local methods of solution. At an intersection with fourway stop signs priorities can be determined by minute variations in time of arrival at the stop line, by waving on gestures, and so on. Service lines or queues are made orderly according to a variety of locally distinctive procedures, including whether or not it is considered proper for someone already in the queue to hold a place for a friend, whether one can ask someone to 'hold my place please' (and which people have this right), and so on. The implicit contrast, at each point in the unfolding of an episode, lies in the possibility of a unilateral solution of the lower or local level of problems by force. It is possible to get through a door first by shoving the others out of the way, and it is possible to make a living by robbery with violence. It is possible to get across an intersection by aggressive and noisy acceleration. It is important to see that the exclusion of the forceful alternative is predetermined by the way the problem of recognition of persons, of sociality in general, is already solved. If one's victims can be 'demonstrated' to be non-persons the range of solutions any problems they may pose is drastically changed. For instance it was important to the Nazis to establish the generic non-Aryan status of Jews, Gypsies and other 'undesirables' before the local solution to ridding the nation of these minorities by killing them was possible. Within a framework of pre-established sociality solutions would have taken the form of exile or deportation.

Phenomenology seems to me to fall short through its inattention to the uses of language and its failure to pay attention to the all-important normative aspects of human social action. Neuroscience is an essential component of any serious social psychology, as I have argued in many places. The skills that are essential to almost every activity in which human beings engage can only be what they are because they are grounded in enduring states of the nervous system. The mistake is to treat this grounding reductively as if an emotion were nothing but a bodily agitation. The cognitive science approach, once advocated by Secord and myself in our role-rule model, is on the right track, I believe, in its emphasis on scripts, rules and the like. However I share the scepticism of Shweder (1990) and Coulter (1992) about the scientific propriety of injecting rules and other such discursive devices into the heads of social actors as the software of diaphanous and abstract computing machines. There is a continuous production of psychological phenomena in the course of social interaction, in particular that part we can pick out as conversing in some form. There are no *mental* processes or states behind conversing. Conversational interactions *are* the mental processes we are looking for. The methodology of an adequate social psychology must be aimed at recording and analyzing these processes and at trying to understand how skillful people are able jointly to produce them.

In the course of a shift in methodology terminology too changes. One term which will be dropped entirely is 'variable'. Not only has it been used incorrectly by psychologists, confusing it with 'parameter', but it has also been contaminated with implications from the cause-effect metaphysics. The terminology for units of analysis, in what follows, will reflect the analytical scheme developed in chapters two and three. The terms 'act' and 'action' will replace 'variable' throughout for describing classes of elementary units of social behaviour. Psychologists rarely use the mathematical correlative of 'variable', namely 'function', that is an algebraic relation between variables. It will also be absent from our terminology, since it too is touched by implications of cause and effect. Instead we shall be talking of synchronic and diachronic 'structures', the correlative term to 'act' and 'action'. We shall have few occasions to use the expressions 'cause' or 'effect', even metaphorically. Instead I shall use such expressions as 'genesis' and 'production', and refer to 'templates' and 'forms' as the origins of the structured products of human action.

AN OUTLINE OF THE MAIN METHODS FOR SOCIAL PSYCHOLOGY

The metaphysical foundation of the methodology to be described in what follows, I remind the reader, is the principle that social behaviour is the structured product of the joint actions of intelligent and knowledgeable agents acting to further some end or other. It is not the effects of causes. The agentive metaphysics does not imply that people are consciously aware of what they are bringing about or have explicit knowledge of the conventions and rules that express what is normatively maintained in their local moral order. The task of social psychology is, above all, to make explicit all that is tacit in a form of life. The objections to this metaphysics raised by Nisbett and Ross and by Zajonc are beside the point. Both took for granted that the claim that social agents follow rules amounted to the theory that people act by attending to the relevant rule. This reading is to confuse 'rule-following' as the source model for the agentive theory with an explanatory model in use in theory. 'Rule-following' is a metaphor! Its power and its limits had been explored long ago by Wittgenstein (1953:201ff.).

The methodology of social psychology must include a static phase in which the resources available for the discursive creation of social reality are explored. It must also include a dynamic phase in which the processes by which those resources are put to work in the discursive production of social reality are discovered. This distinction matches the old competence/performance distinction with which Chomsky (1965) introduced his methodology for general linguistics.

We shall need to recruit the services of analytical philosophers for the first phase. Philosophical analysis will reveal the interrelations and conceptual structure of the vocabularies with which the members of a loosely bounded community act and with which they repair and comment upon action. The fine grain of local conceptual resources, down to individual versions of these, can be revealed by the use of repertory grids. Neither of these interlocking methods will reveal how people put these resources to work in the moment-by-moment joint production of social episodes.

To reveal the normative constraints on the discursive processes of the public production of social reality we shall need to draw on the techniques of discourse analysis, pioneered by the ethnomethodologists and communication theorists. We shall also need to use account analysis, since it is only in accounts that we see the explicit formulation of a version of some of the local norms of correct action.

The final step will be to sketch the method of dramaturgical replication in which the knowledge made explicit in the studies reported above can be put to work in a simulation of the social world which can be created by its explicit use as a script for action.

Method I: conceptual analysis

Outline of the procedures
Conceptual analysis is directed towards the discovery of those structures of ordinary language that are at work in the way people manage those of their activities that are roughly comprehended under the rubric 'psychological'. By that I mean such activities as 'deciding on a course of action', 'displaying hurt at having been humiliated', 'manifesting an attitude towards some topic', 'remembering' and so on. The method is identical with that practised by Wittgenstein and by the philosophers of the classical 'Oxford' tradition, namely a description of

how this or that word is used. The aim, of course, is different. In using this method in psychology we are not trying to resolve intellectual puzzlements or dispel illusions, though that may from time to time be a bonus.

Conceptual analysis is also directed towards setting out the normative principles of the relevant discourses; what are the correct and incorrect ways of using the appropriate vocabulary. This aspect of analytical methodology has been called 'psychologic' by Smedslund (1988), and is the basis of the technique Stearns and Stearns (1987) have called 'emotionology'. In these studies we are partly concerned with the local conditions under which people make use of the conceptual connections embedded in their linguistic resources.

The technique of language analysis

The first step is to assemble the vocabulary with which we ordinarily create some psychological phenomenon, such as deciding or remembering. This vocabulary will involve both first and second order expressions. By that I mean that it will include expressions such as 'the other day I . . .' and the expressions by which we comment upon and repair the uses of the first order expressions, for instance words and phrases involving the word 'remember'. An 'emotionology', as Stearns and Stearns have defined it, is the second order conceptual system by which people manage the first order system. Compare the way we use such an expression as 'you clumsy oaf!' with the way we use expressions like 'angry'. The first is a way of creating an anger display, the second for commenting upon it. Only the second belongs to an emotionology.

As Wittgenstein so often warns us, we must suspend any preconceptions or theories we may have picked up about a certain vocabulary. His own supremely elegant and powerful investigations of concepts like 'reading' and 'thinking' are wonderfully free of preconceived ideas about what the structured use of these concepts might be. Above all we are to beware picking on one use and trying to make all the others conform to it. This leads to the second phase of the method: the assembly of instances of the use of the vocabulary in question, from which one makes various attempts to formulate a 'grammar', that is an account of the norms which these examples exemplify. One must also look for counter-examples to the norms one has proposed. This is not for the purpose of applying a falsificationist methodology, but to map out the boundaries of the use of a word. If 'deciding' is conceptually related to 'thinking' what are we to make of the use of a phrase like 'Macinroe decided to play a drop shot' when the situation seems to be such as to preclude an interval of reflection?

The technique of 'psychologic'

The method through which a psychologic is displayed involves two main principles.

First, the internal structure of the system of a fragment of psychologic, say that around the concept of 'action', will manifest itself in necessary or conceptual truths. A working sign of a conceptual truth is that everyone, in the local language community, will assent to it. This is, of course, only a necessary and not a sufficient condition for that logical status. Further analytical work must be done (Parrott and Harré, 1992). For example everyone might assent to the proposition that 'an acton is what someone intends'. Only as embedded in a whole network of such propositions could it be shown conclusively that this is not an empirical generalization. The point is an important one. In a recent controversy around this very pair of concepts Coulter (1992) shows Bimmel to be simply wrong in taking 'intending' to be a mental state, just correlated with acting. But to do so Coulter assembles a range of uses.

The second principle ties conceptual structures to what people do. People organize their cognitive activities, their actions and their emotions in accordance with these conceptual truths. They are not only operative in the organization of accounts, but also, tacitly for the most part, they are at work in the organized production of action and of other psychological phenomena.

The methodology involves two steps. People will assent both to conceptual truths and to broad empirical generalizations. By the use of a simple Q-sort technique people are asked to identify which statements, from a repertoire, they think are always true, sometimes true and never true. This is the *test of universal assent*. But only some of those statements universally assented to will be conceptual truths and so be part of the network of concepts that constitutes a psychologic. The investigators must work with the candidate generalizations to try to construct an organized system. That is the second step. Factual truths will lie outside such a system. This is the *test of logical coherence*.

Only if both tests are passed do we have grounds for announcing the outlines of a fragment of a psychologic.

Illustration: towards a psychological of embarrassment

I shall draw on the work of several psychologists in sketching the method of psychologic at work in this example. However I shall mainly be using my own investigation, carried out with J. Parrott and published in our paper of 1992. We can begin with an informal or rough analysis of the concept of 'embarrassment', before we turn to the fine details of a psychologic exploration.

There are several other emotions of social control, prominent among them are chagrin and shame. Chagrin is displayed, for instance, when we realize that we have failed in the execution of a project to the success of which we have publicly committed ourselves. It is a kind of disappointment, but one which involves our public reputation. Shame is akin to embarrassment, in that it is both 'cognitive', we show we know what we did was morally wrong; and 'expressive', it serves as a public act of contrition. Embarrassment is appropriate in moments of public failure, but the failure is not a moral fault. In many cases embarrassment serves to display our realization that we have broken or ignored a social convention or rule of good manners.

It seems that there are two main ways we can fail in an embarrassing way. Our conduct can be improper or unconventional, with respect either to social action or to bodily presentation. Or our conduct can be inept or incompetent, with respect either to social action or bodily presentation. So far as I know (and I am indebted to Dan Robinson for the observation) only the latter form of failure was distinguished in classical Greece, by the name '*amechania*'.

Young Americans assent to a number of statements involving the concept of embarrassment that they take to be generally true. For instance both 'Realizing one's public behaviour is offensive can be an occasion for embarrassment' and 'Receiving public praise can be embarrassing'. Behind these lies the deeper principle that occasions for embarrassment arise when one believes one's behaviour, appearance etc. is the subject of appraisal by others. Is this an empirical generalization or an axiom or theorem of a psychologic? Again the informants in our study assented without exception to the following pairs of statements: 'If one believes that others are aware that one has committed a moral fault one would be ashamed' and 'If one believes that others are aware that one has behaved ineptly one would be embarrassed'. Are these empirical generalizations or axioms or theorems of a psychologic?

The answer to these questions can come only from the result of an attempt to construct a psychologic. We believe we have succeeded in organizing some of the inner conceptual structure of at least part of the field of the emotions of ineptitude and moral fault in the following:

Axiom 1: P can react with signs of confusion if, on any occasion, P believes that P or P's conduct is properly an object of comment by others, Q, R, and so forth with whom P is socially interacting.

Axiom 2: P can react with signs of confusion if, for any reason, P believes that P or P's conduct is a proper subject of moral disapproval by others, Q, R, and so forth with whom P is socially interacting.

Definition 1: (a) P is socially interacting with some Q, if P believes that Q is aware of P; (b) P is socially interacting with some Q, if P and Q share some standards of correct conduct (including the presentation of bodily appearances).

(Note: Definitions 1a and 1b express two of the necessary conditions for an interaction to be counted as a social interaction.)

Definition 2: (a) Being disapproved of is a mode of personal assessment; (b) Being approved of is a mode of personal assessment.

Axioms 1 and 2 express the most general conditions in which embarrassment and shame are to be expected. Yet they seem to miss the core psychological content of the concept. What is it about how we believe we look that occasions embarrassment rather than any other possible emotion? We need an axiom that ties our reactions to real or imagined comments on how we look or what we have done to an implicit valuation of persons.

Axiom 3: P is said to be embarrassed when P displays signs of confusion in reaction to real or imagined comments on P's appearance or conduct that would imply that P is inept, ignorant, or foolish.

Axiom 4: P is said to be ashamed when P displays signs of confusion in reaction to real or imagined comments on P's appearance or conduct that imply that P is evil, indisposed, or otherwise morally defective.

Axiom 5: Some offensive conduct is an occasion for disapproval.

Axiom 6: Some praiseworthy conduct is an occasion for approval.

(Note: Axioms 5 and 6 express necessary truths about the concepts of conduct and its assessment, not about the concept of embarrassment. They are drawn from another fragment of PL.)

Theorem 1: Some offensive conduct is an occasion for embarrassment. (This theorem follows from Axioms 1, 2, and 5 together with the relevant definitions.)

Theorem 2: Some praiseworthy conduct is an occasion for embarrassment. (This theorem follows from Axioms 1, 2, and 6 together with the relevant definitions.)

Further theorems developing the 'shame' concept can easily be proved.

It follows that the generally accepted statements of the paragraph above are conceptual truths, and so serve to display the inner structure of the concept of embarrassment, in relation to other similar concepts. Of course there are also a number of statements which attract general assent that tell us what kinds of conduct and what situations and predicaments our informants found embarrassing. These we take to be empirical generalizations.

In relation to the larger project of founding a social psychology on the principles of the discursive approach, what have we found out in these investigations? Linguistic analysis and psychologic explorations begin to reveal the discursive resources or conceptual repertoires with which competent social actors jointly create evolving social realities. The work of analysis is essentially static. It reveals a system which is locally and momentarily stable, and on the joint use of which the possibility of managing a social episode depends.

Method II: repertory grid analysis

Outline of the procedure

There are many excellent manuals explaining the details of the techniques of repertory grid analysis, for instance Fransella and Bannister (1977). Computer programs are available for ready and rapid analysis of the data. I shall give only a sketch of the procedures without going into detail – just enough, I hope, to make clear why this is an essential tool for a psychology based on the discursive idea. The literature of personality psychology is rich in 'instruments', that is scales and checklists for ascertaining the effect of certain 'treatments' on the subjects of an experimental procedure. Leaving aside the objections to the cause-effect metaphysics on which this kind of procedure is based, there is a pair of insurmountable problems in taking any of the answers seriously.

What guarantee is there that the participants understand the vocabulary of the checklists in the same manner as the experimenter does, and in the same manner as each other. Consistency is no guarantee of either! The Milgram experiment is a startling example of a conceptual gap between the understandings of the participants and that of the experimenter. For Milgram the leading concept of his psychologic was 'obedience', but it is easy to show that the psychologic shared by most of the participants in their understandings of what was said by the experimenters was 'trust'.

The second insurmountable problem concerns the question of whether the participants in an investigation would have used the vocabulary of the 'instrument' were they free to comment 'in their own words'. So called 'pretesting' of an instrument is no guarantee! In my judgement these problems render a huge proportion of the published studies in social and personality psychology worthless. These 'instruments' are works of the Devil.

George Kelly (1955) invented the repertory grid technique partly to overcome this set of problems. He had the idea that people make their way in the material and social world much as scientists do in their studies. They develop concepts for tackling the particular job in hand. 'Man the scientist' joins the repertoire of images of humanity alongside '*homo sapiens*' and '*homo ludens*' and many others. While I find Kelly's slogan unconvincing, his technique has proved to be remarkably powerful.

A sketch of repertory grid technique
The components of a grid are a set of elements, predetermined by the investigator, such as people or situations, and a set of constructs, created by the participants, each for his or her own grid. A construct is pair of polarized concepts, such as 'rich . . . poor'. Each construct can be taken as a scale, with absolute or relative intermediate values, that is as a representation of a rating or of a ranking of elements. In the most sophisticated development of this kind of analysis constructs themselves can become elements in further grids. Analysis of each grid reveals the structure of the resources used by its creator for the classificatory task in hand. Comparison between grids reveals changes over time, if the grids are made by the same person at intervals; or similarities and differences between the conceptual resources of participants, if some assumptions about common meanings of key terms can be justified by the application of the analytical techniques of Method I.

Construct elicitation can be achieved in a wide variety of ways. The handiest is simply to take the elements proposed for a study in threes. One asks oneself 'in what way are the first and second alike and different from the third?' Then one takes the first and third against the second and the second and third against the first; and so on through the whole set of elements. Schematically a grid will begin to look like figure 2.

Once the grid is complete the participant then ranks all the elements with respect to all the constructs, using whatever numerical scaling system is appropriate.

Elements	e_1	e_2	e_3	etc.

Constructs

$C_{1a} \ldots C_{1n}$
$C_{2a} \ldots C_{2n}$
etc.

Figure 2.

Analysis is aimed at finding out (a) which concept-pairs or constructs are consistently used for the same sets of elements and which are more widely deployed; (b) which elements are taken to be alike and in what ways. A fully analyzed repertory grid could be interpreted as a display of the internal structure of a semantic field.

The question remains though as to why some sets of constructs are consistently used for the same element or set of elements. Are the constructs merely lexical variants of the same concept-pair, or are they internally related as they would be in a psychologic? Method II, repertory grid analysis, needs to be combined with Method I, linguistic analysis and psychologic, to give a fully detailed and methodologically adequate answer to the question originally posed: what are the resources available to someone for the discursive production (with others) of a strip, fragment or aspect of local social reality? The next stage of an investigation will require somewhat different techniques, since we need to have a way of understanding how the resources available are put to use in the production of social life.

Method III: discourse analysis

Functions and structures of discourse
The research programme of new paradigm social psychology is built around a very general notion of 'discourse'. Almost any intentional use of language is to be counted as a part of discourse. Since the analytic methods now to be described are aimed at the understanding of the dynamics of social life they must be extended to cover not only linguistic exchanges but also the use of any mode of communicative exchange, including gestures, dress and so on that plays a part in the discursive construction of psychological phenomena.

A discourse, in the special sense given to this rather loosely used term in new paradigm social psychology, is a sequence of jointly produced acts. The object of discourse analysis is two-fold:

1   The analysis is aimed at revealing the act-action structure of a sequence of actions constitutive of an episode of human interaction. This includes the special case of reflexive interactions when the other is oneself.

2   The analysis is also aimed at identifying the psychological phenomena which are brought into being in the course of the unfolding episode and understanding how they are discursively constructed.

These will include emotions, cognitions of various sorts such as inferences and decisions, personas, selves, memories, genders, health and illness and many, many more. It must be emphasized that it does not mean to say there are no material conditions, such as the shapes and functions of bodily parts, the state of the nervous system, bacterial and viral infections and so on, on which the discursive edifices that we experience as psychological states and processes are built.

In discourse analysis we are interested in revealing the structures of such edifices and how they are built. How do we decide what actions to include within a discourse? The criterion must be based on an assessment of function. A simple version could be whether the actions under scrutiny are taken to have illocutionary force, that is whether they are involved in the joint accomplishment of social acts. The research topic, so to say, of discourse analysis is how the structures and the functions of discursive exchanges are related. The active uses of discourse include not only the creation of psychological entities and states, but also certain classes of social relations. For instance there are discursive practices by which people are assigned certain speaking parts and roles ('voices') in the development of an episode. Such 'positions' can be defined in terms of one's rights, duties and obligations as a speaker. For example in some recent studies of the joint construction of memories, Middleton and Edwards (1990) showed that the women members of the group were positioned differently from the men, in that their rights to correct tentative memory proposals were weaker than those of the men.

The functions of discourse are manifold. It is in and through discourse that we construct the forms of personal experience, sometimes called 'subjectivity', for instance by Hollway (1985). This includes such structures as the self. This aspect of human life is the topic of *Personal being*. But it is also in and through discourse that we construct our social being and the episodes in which it is made manifest. This aspect of human life is the topic of this work.

Discourse analysis and account analysis
An account is a discourse in which the intelligibility and propriety of some other discourse is made clear, challenged or repaired. Potter and

Wetherell (1987) include account analysis under the general umbrella
of discourse analysis. Of course the giving of accounts is a discursive
activity. But I think it important to distinguish two kinds of discourse.
There is that with which social acts are accomplished and there is that
with which we comment upon and theorize about those social acts.
Accounts are discourses of the second kind. It is true and important
that we realize that in giving accounts we are, *inter alia* performing
social acts. So any study of accounts must involve consideration of the
account as a first order performance. However methodologically we
shall find it essential to distinguish between discursive activities which
are wholly first order and those which are both first and second order.
Some of the norms of social action are made explicit in accounts,
though for all sorts of reasons. In first order discourse the norms of
action are implicit. I shall treat the analysis of first and second order
discourses as distinct analytical tasks.

The structure and elements of a discourse
Episodes, as has been emphasized in chapters 2 and 3, can be arranged
in a spectrum with respect to the degree to which the sequence of
act-actions constitutive of the episode is controlled by a preexisting
structured template such as a formal protocol for the carrying through
of a ceremony. To understand the more formal episodes we need
concepts like role and rule. To understand the less formal we can
make use of the three interrelated concepts of position (or voice),
illocutionary or act-force (or social significance), already introduced
above, together with the idea of local narrative conventions (or story-
lines). In analyzing a record of some social interaction as discourse, a
record obtained through video or audio technology or even by the old-
fashioned medium of note taking, the analysis can be initiated by
trying to identify these three features: 'position', 'act-force' and 'story-
line'. These are the discursive concepts by means of which we hope to
reveal the dynamics of social episodes.

As an episode unfolds it is possible that some of the action will
include acts of repositioning. Once the actors are repositioned the
significance of their actions as social acts may change while the story-
line that is being lived out can modulate into a different set of narrative
conventions.

When analyzing records of discursive interactions it is vital to bear
in mind that a person's actions, their intended behaviour, may be seen
by other interlocutors in many different ways. It is not unusual for the
public act-force of what someone is taken to have done not to be what
they intended. From the point of view of social psychology it is the
force that an action has in the public sphere that matters. A remark
may be meant as a piece of advice by a speaker but it is taken by

another participant in the conversation as an act of condescension, while another takes it up as the speaker intended. It follows that a discourse analysis of an interactional episode may reveal more than one conversation occurring simultaneously on the basis of a single flow of utterances. From the point of view of the social psychologist it is the conversations that are or should be the focus of study, since it is through them that social status is created, attitudes displayed, memories authenticated and so on. How can we tell how many and what conversations are occurring? Only by attending to the subsequent actions of the participants, and the act-forces we take them to display. Each act structure constitutes a social psychological reality.

The concept of position or voice brings out the important qualification that 'speaker' or 'actor' ought not to be identified with the named or indexed person. The unit of analysis is 'actor' not 'person'. The analysis of an episode from the discursive point of view is quite likely to disclose that the match between 'actor' or 'speaker' and 'person' is complex, with some people appearing as more than one actor and others as less than one. There are very interesting cases in which a person's contributions to a conversation are always supplemented (and sometimes corrected) by one of the others. So the illocutionary or act-force of the first person's utterances is created by the contributions of the second person.

The act-actions created by mutual intention and uptake among the participants in social interactions form structures, usually strongly sequential, though there may be other forms of order too. What does discourse analysis reveal about these structures? There are three main structural forms, which I shall distinguish as the formal, the narratological and the minimal.

In a formal structure positions are roles, and there are well-defined 'accomplishment points' in the sequence of act-actions. In the course of a trial there is the moment of giving the verdict, and then there is the moment of pronouncing sentence and so on. Story-lines give way to ceremonial protocols. However formal episodes, such as judicial trials, include other classes of episodes within their role-rule structure. There are nested informal and minimal episodes embedded within the formal framework.

There are any number of questions which discourse analysis can answer. For instance, how is order maintained in a court of law or in a parliament? In these institutions recourse is had to the protocol in which the proper order of act-action types is laid down. There are formal devices for ensuring its hegemony (Atkinson, 1985), and these too are structured by recourse to further protocols. How are people able to participate in such episodes? In general they are knowledgable about where to find a script or some other representation of the protocol constitutive of the episode in question as being of a certain kind, or they are reminded of their next moves by someone to whom that role is assigned. This too is generally bound by protocol into a further formal episode. More often than not yet another formal step is undertaken through which the actors are committed publicly to respect the protocols. This may take all sorts of forms.

I distinguish episodes as 'minimal' if they serve to accomplish a bare acknowledgment of personhood, and at the same time, a minimal structure of rights, a primitive moral order. For instance the simple discursive exchanges between motorist and pedestrian at a stop sign establish a personal relation between the protagonists, and assign differential rights to proceed. In a discursive analysis of these brief encounters we should be able to identify a local lexicon of actions whose act-force is mutually understood, some conventions of sequence defining a minimal structure (a zero-level story-line) and two or more simple positions, one with the right to go, the other with the obligation to give way. The exchanges between beggars and their 'clients' form another class of minimal episodes whose position/act-action/story-line structure would be worth serious study. It is often the case that a discursive analysis of a more complex episode reveals that it opens with a minimal episode in which a bare acknowledgment of the personhood of the other is accomplished.

To illustrate the use of discourse analysis at its most subtle, namely in the analysis of the structures of informal episodes in which psychological phenomena are routinely brought into existence, I shall use the position/act-action/story-line triad to uncover the structure of an episode transcribed by Deborah Tannen (1986:82). The conversation ran as follows:

(9) Deborah: 'Yeah?'
(10)　　Peter: Before that . . . I read The French Lieutenant's Woman?
　　　　　　　⌐Have you ⌐read that?⌐
(11) Deborah:　　　　　　⌊Oh yeah?⌋ No. Whó wrote that?
(12)　　Peter: John Fowles.
(13) Deborah: Yeah I've heárd that he's good.
(14)　　Peter: 'He's a ⌄gréat writer. 'Í think he's one of the ⌄bést writers.⌐
　　　　Deborah:⌊hm
(15) Deborah: /?/
(16)　　Peter: 'He's really, goòd.
(17) Deborah: /?/

(18)   Peter: But Í get very bùsy. . . . ⌈Y'know?
                                      ⌊Yeah.   I- . . hàrdly   eýer
(19) Deborah: reàd.

. . . .

(20)   Peter: What I've been dòing is cutting down on my sléep.
(21) Deborah: Oy!⌉ [sighs]
(22)   Peter: ⌊And I've been [Steve *laughts*] . . . .
                  and I ⌈ s
(23) Deborah: ⌊Í do that tòo
              but it's páinful. ⌉
(24)   Peter: ⌊Yeah. Fi:ve, six hours a 'nîght,
              and ⌉
(25) Deborah: ⌊Oh Gód, hòw can you dó it. You survíve?

. . . .

(26)   Peter: Yeah làte afternoon méetings are hàrd. . . . . But
              outside
                               Deborah: ∟mmm⌐
              of thát I can keep gòing⌈pretty well
(27) Deborah: ⌊Not sleeping enough is
              térrible . . . I'd múch rather not eàt than not sleèp.
                                          p
                                [Sally *laughs*]
(28)   Peter: I próbably should not èat so much, it would . . it
              would uh . . . sáve a lot of tîme.

From (9) to (17) there is one story-line being followed, while from (18) to (28) there is another. The shift in positions takes place at (18) in the remark ascribed to Peter. The first episode displays Deborah and Peter positioned as the complementary pair, 'teacher' and 'learner'. The story-line is 'instruction' and the speech-actions of the positioned interlocutors accomplish the relevant acts. But at (18) Peter repositions himself as 'martyr' and this move is confirmed by Deborah who herself takes up the complementary position of 'friend'. A new story-line unfolds in which Peter tells a strip of his life with the narrative conventions of 'hard times'. Again the speech-acts shift to create the story. There are a sequence of statements, overtly describing a way of life, which have the performative force of complaints. But these complaints are also displays of personhood, as one who continues despite difficulties, a supervenient story-line, 'hero triumphing over the odds', in which the 'hard times' story-line becomes an sustaining element. Deborah's remarks are a continuous stream of confirmations of the double line – how hard your life is and how heroically you overcome it.

This is a mere sketch. Much more would be required to complete an analysis. The choice of vocabulary, pronouns and so on are crucial elements in the way the effect is achieved. I need only enough detail to point out two significant features of the example. Neither story-lines nor positions are freely constructed. The conversation has a *familiar* air. It reflects narrative forms already existing in the culture, which are part of the repertoire of competent members, who, like Peter and Deborah, can jointly construct a sequence of position/act-action/story-line triads. What psychological phenomena are these two jointly creating? At least Peter's personality – or rather, one should say, the one on show in this conversation. They are also creating a relationship, maybe a friendship, for the accomplishment of which this kind of joint work is a necessary ritual part. And so on.

Method IV: account analysis

Accounts as texts
Accounts have a key role in both social action and social psychology. Social psychological texts are accounts and must be analyzed as such. All accounts are texts, since accounting is a discursive practice, almost always accomplished directly with words. (Sometimes there are gestural accounts, but I shall concentrate in this discussion only on those which are spoken or written.) But what are accounts directed towards? The answer is to other texts, those of which discourse analyses in the manner of Method III can be given. This use of the term 'text' is a common contemporary extension of the usual meaning, of a written or printed discourse. A conversation, indeed any episode to which the concept of 'meaning' can be usefully applied, is, in this extended sense, a text.

What does accounting accomplish? In general it is the act by which a text is made relatively determinate with respect to its *intelligibility* and its *warrantability*. Let us call the texts to which accounts are directed 'primary' and the accounts 'secondary'. It should be clear by now that it is always possible for accounts to be taken as primary texts and further accounts be constructed as secondary texts relative to them. To undertake accounting at all, the intelligibility and warrantability of the last level of account must be taken for granted. As Wittgenstein reminded us, the giving of rules must end somewhere – at a certain point he says 'my spade is turned'. There is rock bottom. Accounts at that level are constitutive of a form of life.

Searching accounts

An account is a secondary text. As such it can be subjected to the three methods of analysis which I have outlined, namely conceptual analysis, repertory grid analysis and discourse analysis. But the point of distinguishing account analysis from the other three analytical methods, is the task to which this kind of analysis is directed. At each level accounts *describe* norms and conventions. The principle upon which account analysis works is simple to state but not so easy to establish. It is this: the norms described (that is, made explicit) in an account as a secondary text are among the norms implicit in the primary text. The secondary text as an account, is directed to displaying the intelligibility and warrantability of the primary text. Methodologically account analysis could hardly be simpler – just search the account for explicit statements of rules and conventions, meanings and norms. These can be assembled according to a variety of schemes. One of the most fruitful is to classify the rule/convention material relevant to defining what is meaningful and proper action by reference to the distinctive kinds of episodes in which action of that kind would be appropriate. Along with this goes material describing the norms of self-presentation, to accord with the unfolding act-action structure.

Occasions for accounting

How and when to elicit accounts? There are four main kinds of occasion in which people tend to provide accounts. Von Cranach (1981) and others have shown that accounts are routinely offered when the smooth flow of coordinated joint action breaks down. To the implicit question 'What shall we do next?' the answer is often an account. We could call this, following Goffman, the 'repair function'. Then there are breakdowns in intelligibility of what is being done. It may be that the action is clear enough but the act is indeterminate. 'I meant to . . .' followed by an explicit performative verb such as 'congratulate', is the kind of opening that signals an account the function of which is to make an act determinate. But there may also be breakdowns with respect to the action level – is the actor doing whatever it is intentionally? Thirdly there are breakdowns in the warrantability of what is being done. Accounts here function to show that what was done, as act-action, is correct, proper and so on or not correct etc. Here norms of structure are made explicit. 'In these circumstances I would have [meaning "you should have"] done so and so . . .'. An account may look like advice. This raises the issue of accounts of accounts, and of the analysis of accounts within the framework of Methods I to III. For instance we may need to invoke the position/act-action/story-line triad to understand the illocutionary force of a statement as an account. Finally there is the situation of social instruction, in which a knowledgable member of a cultural group gives overt instruction in the norms of intelligibility and warrantability to an untutored or ignorant novice. It is worth remarking that much of the instructional activity through which new members are incorporated into a culture, psychologically, is by psychological symbiosis, in which inadequate contributions offered by junior member are routinely supplemented by the senior to complete proper performances. By far the commonest occasions for accounting are breakdowns in the intelligibility and warrantability of actions.

What does account analysis contribute to the analytical task? We must remember that the psychological theory underlying the whole of the discursive programme is that human action is a skilled performance by active agents realizing projects according to local norms. Account analysis enables us to add yet more material to our description of the resources that must be available to the competent and skilled actor. We must, however, beware falling into the trap that has ensnared so many would-be scientific psychologists, the error of putting these resources into the heads of the individual actors. Most of the norms of those forms of human action in which psychological phenomena are created are immanent in the routine social practices of a culture, rather than available for discursive presentation. It can hardly be emphasized enough that the discursive presentation of the norms of a culture is a second order activity, the work of psychologists, grammarians, sociologists and the like. Of course people do give and receive accounts. But most are indirect and many are embedded in higher order account givings. That is why we cannot rely on Method IV alone but must *progressively* develop our understanding through the systematic and sequential use of the four methods of analysis of discourse.

Concluding remarks

An enormous advantage of the discursive methodology over other ways of trying to elicit the norms of human action is that it can reveal (disclose) the constructive aspects of other forms of life. Unlike the experimental method or the main devices of so-called cross-cultural psychology, it is morally and metaphysically neutral. The traditional methods of academic psychology embody specific ontologies and local moral orders. A beautiful example of the use of the methods described in this chapter can be found in Lutz's (1988) marvellous study of the emotions of the Italuk. So far we have said nothing about the way to analyze, classify and explain the story-lines and formal 'scripts' that are our way of expressing the orderliness of social interactions.

For that step we need to turn, at last, to the physical sciences for guidance – to the methodology of models. This is a problem for psychologists because of their idiosyncratic use of the word 'model'. In the next few chapters the uses of three major models will be explored: the problem-solving model, the dramaturgical model and the labour/ work model. In what follows, the term 'model' will be used as it is in the philosophy of the physical sciences.

5

THE USES OF MODELS I: SOCIAL
ACTION AS PROBLEM SOLVING

ANTICIPATORY SUMMARY

I shall try to show that many social episodes are made up of multiple 'layers' of problem-solving procedures. In performing the rituals for the introduction of a stranger to a social group we must establish that the being in question is a person to whom and by whom general duties of the maintenance of sociality are owed. In the same episode there are other, more specific problems to be solved, such as the question of the relative social status of the stranger once he or she is admitted to our group. The way problems of this kind are solved has important psychological consequences, for instance in how the constructive processes of memory formation will turn out in any actual case.

But there is a second dimension of generic problems, a dimension which is ever present in social interactions. At any moment we may need to solve the problem of whether and how what is going on is intelligible and warrantable as social action at all. Generally speaking this class of problem is solved by the giving and receiving of accounts. Examples of both dimensions of problem solving are examined in this chapter.

However there is still the issue of the ultimate boundaries of sociality. Even in social psychology the question of 'power' cannot be avoided (Parker, 1987). I address that issue in two ways. 'Power' as 'force' delineates the boundary of 'the social', that is a solution to an everyday interpersonal problem achieved by physical coercion is an asocial solution. But what of the threat of physical coercion? Doesn't the social status, assumed character and so on of the one who threatens, relative to the one who is threatened, enter into the episode? It seems to me that threats of force are indeed part of a certain class of social solutions, so that for me they do not lie outside the boundary of the social.

They are proper material for social psychological investigations, of the forms advocated in this book.

The main question, for the kind of 'power' that is exercised within the bounds of sociality, becomes 'How is power of one person over another established and maintained discursively?' I shall call instances of this phenomenon the 'Rasputin effect'. The role of 'power' as a sociological concept in describing how one group can have hegemony over another raises other kinds of questions, not to be addressed here. Power in this sense is not to be explicated as the summation of a myriad instances of the Rasputin effect.

ACT/ACTION SEQUENCES
AS RITUALIZED SOLUTION TECHNIQUES

Introduction

The great Japanese novelist Mishima once pointed out that we have to show both to ourselves and to others that we 'willed' our actions. There seem to be two aspects to such an achievement. For one, social actors have to achieve recognition by the others around them that they are indeed social actors. Some categories of people, for example children, can find this recognition hard to achieve. Then, too, an actor has also to make what he or she says and does intelligible, meaningful to the others present, those whom the actions and speech affect and who realize that that person was the author of them. Each of these aspects supports the other. To recognize someone as an actor is to see their actions as informed by their intentions and that person as actor, realizing them in actions. The recognition of speech and movements as meaningful, that is, as actions, is to see them as informed by intentions.

In accordance with the theory of the meaning of social actions developed in earlier chapters, the problems of intelligibility are solved as a continuous day-to-day achievement by the use of two main techniques. We attain intelligibility most readily if we draw upon standardized solutions to the specific social problems our social and physical environment presents us. These solutions involve a standardized, integrated personal style appropriate to each type of problem-situation. There is a local typology of personas available to draw upon. We recognize, by reference to cues not yet fully investigated, stylistic unities of action and the appropriate heraldic regalia of such as policeman, nurse, bank clerk, leftish ecologically-oriented mother of two, and so on. A detailed study of these organized styles, their aetiology and the processes by which they come to be widely enough known to be a social resource for the achievement of intelligibility would be a useful contribution. Style, and regalia associated with specific role-places in football fan groups, have been closely studied by Marsh (1977).

The solutions to standard problem situations that are available under each persona are, it seems, learned in a standardized form in each socially distinct locality. The use of ritual and ceremonial forms for the production of an action-sequence appropriate to some recognized social task guarantees the intelligibility and effectiveness of what has been done. The ritualization of apology, for example, allows each of us to maintain our dignity as actors when one of us inadvertently bursts into the other's space or time.

Wide though the scope of these ritualized ceremonies may be in solving socially problematic situations, there is a penumbra of uncertainty remaining. Empirical studies are beginning to show that improvisation of solutions draws upon the same repertoire of actions which serve as components, that is as parts of the 'vocabulary' of standardized solutions available in a local culture (Williams, 1976).

Human beings have a further resource for achieving the intelligibility required of their actions, namely accounting. Accounting is speech which precedes, accompanies and follows action. Actors give accounts to ensure the twin goals of intelligibility and warrantability, that is, the meaningfulness and propriety of their actions. Empirical studies have shown that accounts involve, among other items, statements of rules, implicit or explicit exposition of meanings, and stories and anecdotes, the social meaning of which may need some interpretation. Accounts may draw on the rhetoric of causality but are not to be taken as unproblematic, introspective causal explanations. Rather, accounts reveal the sources of the structural properties of action in the resources of individuals, and allow us to develop hypotheses of ideal social competence for a given society against which the actual resources of any individual can be matched. Whatever one may think of the merits of introspective investigations of alleged cognitive causal processes is quite irrelevant to account analysis since it is not aimed at that goal. The study of the efficient causes of human action may not be possible, at least in the immediate future, because the stimulating causes of the socially identical actions of different people may be quite idiosyncratic. The commonalities of social life are structures which pre-exist action and speech and it is to the study of these that accounting theory is directed.

If we regard the day-to-day social world as a cooperative achievement, what sort of achievement is it? From the standpoint of this model we can view it as the successful and continuous attainment of solutions to a myriad of problems of action and understanding, modulating from one set of conventions to another. Clearcut gaps seldom develop in the flow of interaction. We modulate smoothly through sequences: attending a meeting, breaking up, walking down the corridor, and having a drink in the bar. In the course of these sequences the very same topics may be under discussion but action proceeds according to distinctly different conventions of behaviour and self-presentation, but maintaining a socially coherent and continuously interacting group. To keep each stage going and to make smooth transitions from one to the next, all kinds of small problems must be solved.

Theoretically, we can draw a distinction between problems which have socially constructive solutions which bring people together into a fragment of the orderly, meaningful action sequences which constitute social life, and problems which have socially maintaining solutions where threats to existing orderliness are dealt with in a ritual fashion. In detailing the importance of the socially maintaining solutions, I am not claiming that existing forms of order should be maintained; only that as a matter of fact they are preserved. Those who wish to change the social order had best know how it is achieved.

Problems and solutions

The sources of problems

Problems arise through the interplay of the following contingencies:

1   Contingencies in the physical environment, the social meaning of which requires interpretation. The first and most obvious contingency is the presence of human beings or their social animals, such as dogs. Though its significance may be problematic, this would pose no problem if the physical environment did not have features which force propinquity and interaction. These qualities could be spatial, such as the narrowness of a path or corridor. They might involve depletion of resources requiring the setting up of agreed practices for sharing or conservation.

2   Contingencies in the social environment. The appropriateness of a solution will depend upon the state of the other people, for instance their attitudes (hostile or friendly), their projects and their traditions of response to the situation, such as their formalized obligations of hospitality, politeness, and so on.

3   Contingencies in the actors. There are fluctuations of attitudes, projects and so on in the actor's make up which are among the

conditions which create the problematic character of the situation. If the actor were not determined to ascend by the narrow path, the descending goat-herd would not constitute a problem.

Types of problems
Out of these contingencies arise three distinct types of problems:

1 With what category of person are we dealing?
2 What are their current attitudes?
3 How am I as initiator of the action to secure agreement to the practical details of the solution I propose while remaining within the boundaries of the social?

Types of solutions
Of all the ways open to the actor at this point we must distinguish the social from the non-social as basic categories of solution. Clearly, to bash or shoot the descending goat-herd and throw him off the path is not a social solution, just as lashing out when someone bumps into one in a crowded public place is not a social solution to the problem of maintaining a social space. Compare these with greeting the goat-herd, squeezing back against the rock wall and ushering him past with a smile, or dealing with the bump by taking the blame oneself and opening with 'I'm very sorry' and getting the return, 'No, no, my fault', achieving (as Goffman calls it) the maintenance of civility. The distinction between these categories is intuitively obvious, but we must look more closely into the differentia.

Each category of solution depends upon an initial ontological casting of the interactor by the actor. The non-social solution clearly involves treating the goat-herd as being in the same category as an awkwardly placed boulder, a thing-like impediment to be merely disposed of. To attempt the social solution involves an attribution of cognitive status and of autonomy to the interactor, that is, he is cast as a person. In that category he can now be expected to behave as such. Social psychologists have yet to address the problem of how personhood is achieved against the ever-present threat of being cast as a thing. The study of alter-casting is a beginning (Weinstein & Deutschberger, 1964).

Further, each type of solution draws upon a technique of effective action. The non-social solution depends upon the techniques involving physical causality. The social solution calls upon techniques of revealing intentions through speech and action, and the recognition of the force of speech-acts such as pleas and apologies upon which their effectiveness depends. And the actor's knowledge must include an

ethnography, a representation of the general form of these achievements, for instance the rule for achieving polite ushering. Much of
this knowledge may be tacit or reduced to habit. It may be known
explicitly only to machiavellians.

These distinctions of ontological status and action technique are not
new. They are central distinctions of Kant's (1961) theory of human
interaction. Moral action is identified by the degree to which we treat
others as ends rather than means. And they are also implicit in everyday practice. For example, we occasionally cast a doubtful dog into the
role of social actor by treating him as such, assigning him to that
category by such civil attributions as, 'There's a *good dog*', 'Down
boy', and so on.

The three problems of the social actor are solved by the techniques
of civility. The upshot of greeting is the casting of the other into
the role of a person, requiring intelligibility and warrantability to be
sustained in their action sequences. The second problem is solved by
the demeanour of the other person, their formalized style of self-
presentation which ought to reflect and respond to the way the actor
has opened the encounter with a civil greeting. How far problems
of the second type can be solved independently of local cultural conventions is unknown. Finally, a solution to the technical problem is
achieved by the mutual production of a standardized (or improvised)
ritual action-sequence, which provides a conventional solution to the
problem, preserving the dignity of each individual as a person, and
characterized by a style expressive of civility.

Sometimes the local solution to the technical aspect of a social
problem is itself covertly social, for example it may reflect a local social
hierarchy. In some New Guinea tribes each member of the community
had a right to a certain part of a kill depending upon his or her social
placement. The division of the meat was regulated not by reference to
the dietetic needs of various members of the community but by their
social standing (Brown, 1973).

Standardization of solutions

Occasions for standardization

I have already touched on the standardization of the form of some
of the action-sequences available for social problem-solving. These
generally occur either when the act to be performed is socially important (consider for instance name-giving rituals such as baptisms); or
when the problem situation occurs very frequently (dealing with the
presence of a stranger at a social gathering). An introduction of a

stranger by a sponsor to a host can be seen as a device to solve in standardized form the following problems:

1 What is the stranger's name?
2 What is their relative status?
3 Can he or she be 'one of us'?

These questions are answered in one way or another in the course of our familiar introduction-rituals. Detailed studies have shown the complexity of even such commonplace action sequences as introductions. Several kinds of knowledge and several different levels of self-management are required for successful accomplishment. Analysis suggests that the linguistic distinction between semantics and syntax can be used in analysing such complex sequences. There are questions about the meaning of component elements of the ritual (semantics) as well as uncertainties about the sequential structure (syntax) of the sequence. Both the semantics of elements of the ritual and the syntactic structure determine its overall significance. For instance, the syntactical property of relative order of speech by host, sponsor and stranger reflects and expresses the relative status each allows the other. Initially, unless the host is manifestly more socially important than the stranger, the stranger has notional high status. This is reflected in many subtle features of the interaction including the ordering of speech-turns. However, in the course of the introduction, if a microsequence occurs in which status uncertainty is resolved, there may be a formal recognition of the stranger's inferior standing, which is expressed in his losing temporal precedence in speech and action. The introduction of a stranger thus involves both the creation and the maintenance of social orderliness. It extends orderliness to include the stranger, and it serves to maintain the existing order surrounding the host by minimizing the threat the stranger, as unknown, may pose.

Standardization of agonistic sequences
Action-sequences are standardized in form even when the outcome or act performed is problematic. For example, a formalized resolution of a status uncertainty involves a non-problematic and shared conception of status. But since, logically, only one of a pair of status contestants can occupy the upper position, the determination of which person achieves this status is problematic. I shall call those action-sequences, or components of action-sequences, that accomplish the resolution of such problems, *within a framework of orderliness*, agonistic sequences.

Level of improvisation
The idea of a non-standard action sequence can be applied at two
levels of generality. There are sequences which are non-standard relative to the social techniques generally available in a community but
which are the standard sequences for some isolated group of people.
The private rituals of individual families are non-standard in this
sense. There are also sequences that are non-standard in that they are
improvised for a particular occasion, for the solution of a problem
for which a ritual solution does not exist in the local ethnography.
Examples of improvisation can be seen at many semi-formal social
gatherings.

It is worth noticing that the improvisations of non-standard solutions
may still open out into an 'agonistic abyss' even though they are within
traditions of civility. The improvisations may bring the standard components under challenge. This may even extend to pretended in-
comprehension of another's words. When even the intelligibility of
speech is conventionally denied the possibility of improvising a civil
encounter is gone. Some unfortunate people may forever feel as if they
are on the edge of an agonistic abyss. There are people who, for one
reason or another, find it very difficult to make themselves understood,
perhaps because they do not use language or action in the standard
ways. Improvisation, unless in the hands of genius, cannot extend to
the basic semantic system.

Negotiation of initial social conditions
Finally, I would like to emphasize the role of interactive social
processes as essential preliminaries in the improvisation of a solution
to a socially defined problem. Standard solutions work because they
are applied in recognized situations and involve recognized styles of
person presentation: personas appropriate to those situations. With
situation and persona settled, action can proceed smoothly to the
accomplishment of the act, be it friendly or hostile. Correspondingly
but problematically, a non-standard solution requires a definition of
the situation within scene and relative to setting, and a negotiation of
social identities or personas. These proceedings may have standard
forms, but again they may be improvised for the occasion, opening up
once again the possibility of an indefinitely prolonged challenge to the
successful completion of the task. Some people regularly open
proceedings with a stranger by adopting a probing, challenging, testing
kind of stance, the effect of which is to force the other either into a
display of coolness or counter-provocation or into a demeaning display

of annoyance, fear, aggression and so on. These encounters are not well documented and could do with much more detailed study.

Method of study of problem-solving rituals

So far we have looked at action-sequences from only one point of view, that of the microsociologist, questioning neither their mode of genesis nor their relation to larger structural properties of society. We must now look at problem-solving rituals according to the structure/ template scheme sketched in Part I. The schema for study of the genesis of action-sequences takes the following form:

The preformed templates of the structure or pattern of standard action-sequences are to be called *rules*. They must pre-exist the action and must be known, though not necessarily explicitly, to all for whom the action-pattern is socially potent as a ceremony accomplishing an act. Our hypothesis is that in general the rules are learned, that is, pre-exist individuals.

The potent templates or formal causes of non-standard action-patterns I propose to call *plans*. They may be modulated to rules through such processes as Miller, Galanter and Pribram (1960) hypothesized in their T O T E hierarchies. They must pre-exist the action but perhaps as part of the resources of only one of the inter-actors who has the problem of making his or her actions intelligible and warrantable to the others not privy to the plan. Plans are con-structed; they are among the achievements of individuals.

The cognitive resources which are the basis of social competence are revealed as representations in some medium of knowledge of the local rule system, the immediate resource for competent social performance; knowledge of the general principles of action, laws of nature etc., the resource for the competent formation of plans, for testing them by imaginative rehearsal, for negotiating them with others in the course of the action. These resources can be hypothetically attributed to people on the basis of their observed success in encounters, that is, as social actors, because success constitutes an overt proof of competence. But how do we proceed to test the correctness of these hypothetical attributions? This takes us to account analysis. I shall now deploy the methodology sketched in the last chapter.

ACCOUNTING AS A TECHNIQUE
OF PROBLEM SOLVING

The nature of an account

In accounting we interpret and explain the action-sequences we perform and the acts we thereby accomplish. We shall have occasion to distinguish implicit interpretations and theories from explicit interpretation and explanation in the speech that deals with action. We shall credit the cognitive achievement of accounting to both implicit and explicit interpretation and explanation, provided of course that the implications are understood. Understanding may be no more explicit than the accounting, and may have to be inferred from the smooth, unbroken, unchallenged flow of action.

To forestall a common misinterpretation to which accounting theory is particularly prone, I want to emphasize again that an account is not to be interpreted as an introspective causal explanation although some accounts, *inter alia*, do have that character. Accounts are generated by ordinary people in the ordinary course of social action, primarily to make actions intelligible and warrantable by interpreting them as proper parts of the structure of interaction sequences.

The dual purpose of accounts

As I argued in the general introduction, accounting seems to involve the performance of two main tasks: the explication of action and the justification of action. Satisfactory performances of the tasks may be linked one with another.

Explication as accounting may be explicit or implicit. A common form of explicit explication is the simple, 'Sorry, I didn't mean to . . .', making available an interpretation which suspends meaning altogether and hence suspends the question of warrantability. Less common, but more committing is the formula, 'Well, what I meant was . . .' It is of considerable importance to grasp the fact that the production of an account can do no more than make available a justification or explication. Mere production of the account cannot ensure that the interpretation offered will be accepted. This brings out the negotiable quality of the meanings and explanations that are going to survive in public space, so to speak, as mutual achievements.

Implicit accounting is more complex. We have already had occasion to notice the distinction between *actions*, the meaningful components of action-sequences identified through their meanings, and *acts*, the social upshot of the performance of a particular pattern sequence.

Cocking a snook is an action, the resulting insult is an act; saying 'Guilty' is an action, the resulting verdict is an act, and so on.

Broadly speaking, the descriptive vocabulary available to a speaker, intent on accounting, allows three stages of description in two of which meaning is imposed.

'He bumped into her' describes mere body contact. The explanation of the contact calls upon neither private intention nor shared social convention. Another example: 'Her fourth finger went through a ring held by him'.

'He pushed her' is a redescription by which the contact becomes invested with the possibility of meaning since it is represented as an action, namely something somebody intended. The meaning is grasped when we know the place of the action in some recognized fragment of social life. The explanation of the happening as now described calls for intentions and perhaps social conventions as well. Another example: 'He put a ring on her fourth finger'.

'He tried to murder her' is a further redescription in which the action is seen as the commission of a socially defined act – attempted murder – that is, attempted unlawful killing. Another example: 'He married her'. In these examples, the act not only is a meaning, but has a meaning itself. It has its special social potency in an obvious way. For example, defining the killing as a murder rather than as an accident leads to a commitment by the state and its officers to accomplish the man's arrest, trial and conviction, all of which are themselves social acts at the second level of meaning. Clearly, the social psychological investigation of the potency of actions as acts to produce all kinds of effects in a society must take its start from the interpretation of behaviour as action. But it must also take account of the accounting, implicit in social custom or explicit in a court of law, by which an action is treated as the performance of an act.

The effect of successive reinterpretation is profound. We can perhaps grasp the theoretical possibilities by supposing that even when we proceed to act-interpretations as we usually do, we have reached them by the successive interpretations I have separated above. First, there is a change in relational structures as we go from behaviour and speech to act. Behaviours are related, probably through physiological mechanisms, and these relations may be largely irrelevant to their social significance. Actions are related in semantic fields and syntactically into action patterns, but requiring knowledge of the act and its local conventions to be fully disambiguated for meaning. Acts relate to the social structure at large. Not only are the behaviours, actions and acts in non-isomorphic relational structures, but the relations of the people involved are different under each stage of the attribution of meaning. If they are merely *behaving* they are related by physical causality. When they are interacting in this way a speech made by one of them may be too piercing but it cannot be too insulting. But if people are performing the *action* of getting married, they are performing the ceremony together, are required to understand one another, and relate to each other within the terms of the role system for that ceremony. On the other hand, when they are performing the *act* of getting married they are generating a fragment of the relatively permanent social order, a fragment which involves anticipation of the future, and another ceremonial act to annul, change or undo.

Transition from one descriptive system to another involves transition from one justificatory and warranting system to another. The rules specifying the variety of actions are usually personcentred and culturally specific. We would naturally treat them as social conventions. It is a social convention that defines the action of giving of a ring as part of the act of marriage. Acts on the other hand come up for judgement under moral and legal rules.

The techniques of warranting by redescription, that is of justifying actions and acts by how we categorize them, deserve careful analysis. They involve subtle relations between the presentation of the person and the presentation of their actions and acts. A person's primary move may be a recategorization. One may produce an account in which one identifies oneself as a mere thing, an object. The events to be accounted for are correspondingly described in the mere-happenings vocabulary, translated neither into actions nor acts. There may be explicit attention in such accounting to causality. One claims as a thing to be subject to physical causality, a form of determination which involves both efficient and material causes and by claiming which one repudiates the normal assumptions of self-management. The prime linguistic mode for achieving such recategorization separates the speaker into an 'I' and a 'me', the former an astonished spectator of the behaviour of the latter. This implies the breaking of control of the 'I' over the 'me', and by categorizing the 'me' as a 'thing', suggests either a physical cause of behaviour or, at best, an automatism. The putative action is treated as a mere effect of happenings within the 'me'. Transcripts of defendants' evidence in murder trials are a rich source of examples of the use of this technique. 'I blacked out, but when I came to I found myself with the knife in my hand and I saw him lying on the floor'. Should the court accept the implication, the actions of the speaker (I) as killer could be classified not as the commission of an act of murder, but as mere behaviour, the effects of automatic processes within the 'me'. As behaviour they escape questions as to their warrantability.

However, the preservation of dignity and selfhood is incompatible with the primary mode of recategorization. It is not surprising that this mode occurs most often in moral emergencies. More common, and indeed an everyday technique, is the recategorization of what the actor did. The original impetus to the study of this technique came from Austin's famous distinction between excuses and justifications, in the context of warranting an action (Austin, 1961). Again we will see an interplay between the categorization of the behaviour and the claim to a special status or situation for the person. Austin proposed that we treat as excuses those speeches in which we admit the moral quality of the act, allowing it to be offensive, insulting, and the like, but disclaim freedom of action. There is a corresponding technique of modest disclaimer of virtue when we accept praise for the products of our activity but disclaim primary responsibility as the agent of the production. 'I'm only the representative of a team, you know . . .' An excuse addresses the warrantability of what has occurred in such formulae as 'I'm terribly sorry I'm late. I got caught in the rush-hour traffic'. The first phase of the excuse serves the joint task of apology and admission that lateness is an offence, while the second phase disclaims agenthood *vis à vis* that occurrence.

A justification, on the other hand, denies the moral quality of the act and claims free agenthood. This often takes the general form, 'I did it, but it was not wrong, obscure, cruel . . . etc.' An extreme form of justification is to be found in the speech of a participant in a psychological study project who, when chided with being late, turned on the critic and made a slashing attack on the institution of punctuality, arguing that it was not a matter of respect between persons but a neurotic symptom.

Austin's investigations were both incomplete and purely conceptual. Backman (1977) carried out an empirical study of the speech produced by people who set out to warrant their actions. He found that justifications formed a complex category in need of subdivisions. An extremely common form involves the use of the technique he calls 'conventionalization'. From the point of view of accounting, conventionalization is a redescription of the act. The action is conserved, 'Oh yes, I took the money', but the description of this action as the act of theft is rebutted, 'but I was only borrowing it . . .' Utilizing the Gricean conditions for intelligibility the speaker proceeds to '. . . I intended to put it back next week . . .' Finally, there is the technique of 'normalizing', again revealed in Backman's study. This technique may apply to action or act and involves the claim that what the actor did is normal or commonplace and hence does not in general come up for special accounting. Normalizing can be achieved either in terms of frequency ('It happens all the time') or generality ('Everybody does it'). Normalizing conserves the standing of the actor as agent and the imputed quality of the act but repudiates the demand for an account as justification.

The content of accounts

So far we have followed Austin and Backman in examining accounts for their social function. The next step is to proceed to the analysis of the content of accounts, in search of the cognitive resources available to an individual as a member of a community. Account analysis starts always with the particular and the local. It begins idiographically and proceeds only after the comparison of the cognitive resources of a great many people of apparently similar skills and social habits to claim a limited generality for the structures it reveals. We assume there is a commonality in the use and understanding of ordinary language between analyst and accounter, but recognize this too as an assumption that may be questionable in specific cases (as an example analyst and accounter may not use the same range of grammatical forms in giving instances of the category of rule). But in general, unless some commonality is assumed as a working hypothesis analysis cannot begin.

Local v. universal accounting systems

The analysis of the accounts of individuals reveals the cognitive groundings of their individual social competence, and from these a hypothetical grounding for an ideal competence in that particular social milieu can be abstracted. I shall refer to the former as 'cognitive resources' and to the latter as 'the local ethnography'. The capacity for achievement, in the ethnomethodologists's sense, that is acting rightly in the appropriate situation, is rooted in the individual's cognitive resources, in so far as these are representations of the local ethnography. Looked at from the point of view of the person producing an account, it has the status of a socio-psychological theory which that person makes available when required as an explanation of the actions and acts that need to justified. But merely making the account available is no guarantee that it will be accepted by the listener. This brings up an interesting class of social events, the negotiation of accounts. Negotiations are action-sequences in the coursé of which accounting acts are performed, for instance acts of excuse and justification, which are themselves accountable. Our problem as social psychologists is to reveal a match between our imputations of cognitive resources to an individual on the basis of what we, by reference to *our* accounting system, take to be the structure and meaning of these performances, and those resources as indicated in the account. Difficulties abound, particularly those posed by self-deception, false consciousness and unconscious motives.

The step from the local ethnography to a universal human action-centred system cannot be made at this time. The nomothetic transition from individual to local society is problematic enough and not yet clearly established. I am certainly not prepared to propose that the formal structural properties of the cognitive resources of the individuals we have studied so far should be taken as universal even within contemporary Western society. We are still smarting under the consequences of the absurd assumption that sophomore psychology students are typical human beings. The greater power of the new paradigm empirical methods ought not to tempt us to make the same mistake again. The empirical work reported in this chapter is to be understood as strictly of *local* significance. But we may have reason to think that though the content of accounts is strictly local, the form accounts take may have some universal properties.

Furthermore, as Gergen (1973) has pointed out in a paper of considerable significance, what little evidence exists concerning the temporal stability of social formations and practices, personality-types and so on, points to their remarkably ephemeral character. We are quite unjustified in supposing that the forms of microsocial action, and even perhaps the way individuals are related to these forms, that is their social psychology, are constant over time. All the evidence we have, slender though it is, suggests that social forms and individual cognitions of these forms are highly unstable and in rapid flux. We expect stability and are alarmed and outraged by social change, but contrary to our social mythology, social forms have a very short life. I believe that this has always been true. Where detailed records exist, for example ancient Greece or pre-Columbian America, a picture of rapid change emerges. Indirect indicators point to the same conclusion; the flux and re-flux of fashion in clothes, hairstyles, furniture and so on, were apparently as rapid in Pharaonic Egypt as they have been in Western Europe.

The fact that certain artifacts, particularly tools and utensils, have a long and unbroken history in a region, shows nothing about the accompanying social forms. Few major changes in basic artifacts occurred between 1300 and 1750 in Western Europe, a period which saw enormous social and linguistic changes.

The anthropological study of 'primitive' people outside Europe reveals the forms of life current when they were examined. Linguists have long since abandoned the idea that 'primitive' societies have preserved earlier forms of language. We should abandon the corresponding assumptions for other phenomena. I propose to start with the hypothesis that human social practices are unstable. Since 'primitive' societies lack any kind of historical record, we must take their rhetoric of 'ancient ways' with considerable scepticism.

It may yet turn out that social science can present us only with a method for understanding each social formation, its practices, and the relation of competent people to it, one by one, and that no social universals may be revealed. At present, we have neither an adequate cross-cultural social psychology by which we can proceed from idiographic to nomothetic assertions, nor an adequate theory of social change. Marxist theory is too localized and Darwinian theory as yet too biological to serve as the basis for a diachronic theory of society. But perhaps some development which fuses these limited but powerful theories into some kind of synthesis will serve.

The material revealed by account analysis

Accounts reveal the social semantic system of individuals. As we have seen, that system involves social knowledge, for example of the kinds of situations we encounter and the action sequences proper to each of them. But accounting is not only a method for revealing the meanings of one's actions but also for warranting or justifying what one does. The cognitive resources required for successfully warranting an action overlap the resources required for explanation of meanings, since a knowledge of the situations that are regarded as socially distinct in the culture and of the form of action sequences appropriate in those situations is required for both.

Two further items are revealed by account analysis. The public presentation of the self as a distinct persona occurs in the way the action sequences required for the performance of social acts are carried out, that is, in their style. Distinct situations call for distinct styles of performance, and hence present the self under distinct personas. Many people have explicit knowledge of the style of actions required in distinct situations, but though they are perfectly adequate performers at the stylistic level, they are not aware of how they appear to others. Nevertheless they do know, at the 'knowing-how' level. This knowledge can be revealed indirectly by picking up the basis of critical judgements of style in their accounts, as well as by assembling explicit fragments of tacit knowledge by forcing a participant to contemplate actions and style previously taken for granted as natural. E. Rosser and I have shown that some adolescents have very detailed and explicit knowledge of style and its relation to impression management (Rosser & Harré, 1976).

Account analysis reveals a further structure-linked resource. The T O T E (test unit) hierarchies, discussed by Miller, Galanter and Pribram, are run, for certain important bits of social action, in advance of the realization of the action sequences in real life. The T O T E hierarchies of social life are partly pretests run in the imagination. In some cases competence is acquired through rehearsal. Judgement of our actions by other people is replaced in these rehearsals by an imagined judgement of an imagined other, which realizes a store of intuitions of proper and improper actions, not as rules, but as the imagined approval of disapproval of some specific person. At present our knowledge of these resources grows out of studies of violent school children, murderers and rubber fetishists, a rather atypical profile of human beings. In each case, the representation by the actor of the knowledge of how actions will be judged has been as a representation of the imagined responses of a concrete individual, the mother the dominant member of a peer group, the spouse, and so on. Which individual's reactions are imagined is highly situation specific. T. Mischel (1964) has proposed that the clash of these empirical findings with the theoretical concept of 'generalized other', proposed by G.H. Mead for a similar role, could be resolved by the hypothesis, as yet untested, that 'ordinary' people utilize a generalized arbiter of action for each and every situation in the course of imaginative rehearsal. They may not have the reactions of a specific person in mind when they consider how their actions will be viewed by others.

Control and rehearsal of action in situations is represented in accounts by normative material one could summarily call 'the rules'. Again, empirical studies of accounting reveal the very situation-specific character of rule-systems. A study of the rules adverted to by pupils in a secondary school where traditional 'order' has broken down, revealed a twelve-fold system, based upon twelve distinguishable situations, in each of which a different rule-system operated (Rosser & Harré, 1976).

There is some evidence that there may be deficits in an individual's cognitive resources. It seems likely that the capacity to recognize situations as socially distinct may be well developed without a corresponding development of knowledge of the appropriate style of self-presentation or of the rules for successful action. The deficit of style may be the more damaging to competence because its implicit character makes it less readily available to contemplation and correction by self-monitoring and self-control.

The structure revealed by the analysis of accounts represents an ideal social competence for that society, that is, represents the local ethnography in ideal form. I propose that this structure also represents the ideal cognitive resources of individuals competent in that society and, coupled with known deficits, the actual resources of real individuals. The structure of social action is matched by the templates of social action, that is, the cognitive resources upon which competence is based.

Accounting as part of the action

Not all accounting is offered as retrospective explanation in the attempt to make actions, which would otherwise be anomic or bizarre, intelligible and warrantable. In real life accounting becomes a social technique in its own right and not a mere ancillary of action. I would like to illustrate this with some examples taken from empirical studies.

Accounting in advance of the action

Marks and Gelder (1967) have shown that fetishists may prepare for their perverse action in advance by developing an account that makes their action intelligible and warrantable under some explanatory scheme other than fetishism. These people often provide in advance a context of interpretation in which the action has a predetermined and commonplace meaning and is warrantable under the rule system for that kind of situation. For instance, a rubber fetishist, preparing to don his gear on Saturday will devote much of his talk in the preceding week to developing a definition of his dressing up as 'keeping clean while unstopping the drains'. He may even include some drain cleaning to sharpen the situational definition and ground the warranting in empirical reality.

Another form of accounting in advance of the action is pre-emptive accounting. This occurs in agonistic situations and involves B using a form of expression which traps A, the interlocutor, so that all accountings left open are personally discreditable. An example revealed in empirical study of talk is the 'Do you mind' manoeuvre. Here is how one instance proceeds.

1 A is asked by B to do something (x) and forgets to do it.
2 B (much later) 'Do you mind doing x?'

As pre-emptive accounting this works in the following way:
Implication 1: A had an ulterior motive for not doing x, that is, 'minded'.
Implication 2: The query offers A the mock-possibility of saying he or she does mind doing x, suggesting that even if A did not have a covert reason for not doing x they might have. The mere contempla-

tion of a covert reason for not doing x may be denigrating to the social relationship between A and B.

So A is trapped. If A takes the question literally and says 'I do (or don't) mind', they are discreditable, for either they have a covert reason or they did not but might have had. If A challenges the literal meaning then he or she is discreditable, for that challenge is itself a denigration of B. A thereby suggests that B did indeed set up a 'Do you mind?' trap for A.

Acting in advance of the accounting
Again, there are cases where action occurs in advance of the accounting but is aimed at predetermining the form that accounting can take. A simple example is the case of a woman who repeatedly found reasons for not accompanying her husband to the theatre or restaurants. She thus accumulated evidence for an accounting of her continued remaining at home as discreditable to her husband, expressed in the accusation, 'You never take me out!'. I have chosen an example of an agonistic relationship but the pre-empting of accounting also occurs in non-agonistic contexts, as when someone does something exciting or dangerous, keeping in mind the subsequent anecdote they can tell their friends. In all these cases the form either of the action or of the account is pre-empted by an initial move which constrains the possible accountings or possible actions.

Non-verbal accounting
Accountings need not necessarily be achieved by verbal means. The desirable sought-after properties of intelligibility and warrantability can also be attained in various non-verbal ways. Empirical studies reveal the following:

1   Situational discounting: an action which would be accounted as discreditable, offensive (unwarranted) or meaningless in one kind of situation is transformed by a non-verbal act directing attention to the scene, with respect to which the action under enquiry acquires meaning and propriety. For instance, bodily contact which would be offensive in an open context is accounted for by the putative offender glancing about to indicate the press of the crowd, and shrugging his shoulders to indicate his helplessness in the situation. This sequence of action can be seen in underground trains (subways), football crowds and other tightly packed people-places.

2   Goffman has drawn attention to the phenomenon of body gloss, the using of an exaggerated form of the usual gestural accompaniment of an action to make a public action intelligible and warrantable. For

example, a person making a sudden turn-about in a public place accompanies the change of trajectory by an exaggerated form of the 'I've just remembered' gesture, often a finger flick followed by a sharp downward movement of the hand. Situational discounting of this sort can be seen from a vantage point in deserted plazas.

By all of these techniques we solve the problems of ordinary social life, and lay to rest some of the doubts our interactions with others can raise. At the same time we achieve the most important thing of all – the expressive advantage of showing ourselves to be reasonable and so worthy people.

THE EXERCISE OF POWER IN EPISODES OF EVERYDAY LIFE

We cannot begin to discuss this problem without a prior analysis of the concept of 'power', as it might be applied in common contexts. The contexts for which the concept is required are set in this chapter by the overall theme of problem solving. Whose solution prevails and how is it imposed? This question immediately raises the issue of power.

The first step must be to set aside the concept of 'power' as naked force, as simply irrelevant to our enquiries, though its existence as a method of coercion can hardly be denied. However it is not irrelevant to enquire into the accounting procedures by which naked force as intended action is discursively presented as a socially meaningful act.

As I see it the central question for social psychology is the problem of how hegemonic relationships are created amongst the members of small groups, the Rasputin effect. How is it that a smelly, half crazed monk can come to exercise day-to-day control over the thoughts and actions of the Russian imperial family? It seems to me that Milgram (1974) came close to addressing the problem, but was led astray by the prevailing ideas about empirical methods of his time. Leadership studies in social psychology seem to me to be largely beside the point, focussing on static characteristics of the phenomenon, and trying to correlate dubious personality traits of leader and follower. As I see it power of the Rasputin type is created and maintained in the discursive dynamics of the unfolding of the episodes in which the dominant person gets their way. There is a dearth of research into power engendering episodes.

How do tyrants like Hitler and Stalin (Bullock, 1962; 1992) achieve their remarkable hold over their immediate followers? There have been studies of charismatic leaders, but these have focussed on the character traits of the leader rather than on the discursive processes by which these traits are publicly displayed (and perhaps even created). What is it that leads to some people being placated and others ignored? My observations suggest it is in large measure due to the ways that they dominate discourse. Among the techniques one observes are the repeating of the last few words and the raising of the voice when a dominant person is challenged for the floor (Tannen, 1986). Another is the random distribution of favours, even such intangible favours as attention. Here we come close to the discoveries about reinforcement schedules that form the best part of radical behaviourism. It is a commonplace but worth repeating that official role is no guarantee of discursive power. Weak kings and feeble chairpersons abound. So far as I know only Torode (1976) has studied the way power is discursively constituted, in such a way as to distinguish the strategies that create power and those that lack it. As he showed, such a seemingly simple matter as the ways that pronouns are used by different speakers can lead to the augmentation of personal power or to its dimunition.

6

THE USES OF MODELS II: SOCIAL ACTION AS DRAMA AND AS WORK

ANTICIPATORY SUMMARY

The theatrical performance is among the oldest sources of models for social episodes. It was much favoured in the sixteenth and seventeenth centuries. In Ben Jonson's *New Inn* the psychological complexities of taking a dramaturgical stance to the events of everyday life are explored not just by locating a play within a play, a common Elizabethan device, but by imagining that the innkeeper has asked his guests (who are themselves a company of players) to perform the play. They must take up the roles of performers in amateur theatricals as a professional act, and that twice over.

The revival of the theatrical model for the analysis of social episodes must be credited to Goffman (1969). However his innovations derive, in part, from the works of Burke (1945). I shall begin this chapter with a brief sketch of Burke's 'Pentad'. This is a scheme of five inter-determining theatrical concepts, which in the manner argued throughout this work, have dual application. They are analytical tools for the description of complex social phenomena, and they are discursive tools for the accounting procedures by which actors can render their actions intelligible and warrantable. In this way and by the use of these concepts actors can present their actions as acts.

Social psychologists of the old paradigm school, have and indeed still do neglect or ignore the settings of the social episodes they analyze. To remedy this I have devoted the bulk of this chapter to a detailed presentation of scene analysis. As Burke makes very clear neither of the complementary concepts, 'actor' or 'action', can be adequately specified for any actual occasions without attending to the scenes in which they have their place.

Can the dramaturgical model be exploited in the explanatory mode as well as the analytic-descriptive? There is no simple answer to this question. Once the myth of the information processing engine is set aside the question still remains of how the social actor's everyday skills are to be compared with those of the stage actor. Again Goffman (1974) addressed the question. As a preliminary to further studies of the matter, I draw on his metaphor of 'key-change' to approach the question of how a pair of qualitatively identical actions are experienced one in a stage play and the other in an episode of everyday life each of which fall under the same episode-type. We shall see that the ideas of seriousness and of commitment loom large in any account of the distinction.

Burke's 'Pentad'

The analytical use of dramaturgical concepts owes a great deal to the work of Kenneth Burke (1945). I shall briefly describe his famous 'pentad' through which the basic structure of the dramaturgical conceptual scheme is expressed. According to Burke the five basic terms of 'dramatism' are Act, Scene, Agent, Agency and Purpose. Taken in pairs they pick out aspects of social interaction that mutually determine one another. These mutual determinations Burke calls 'ratios'. So there is a 'Scene-Agent' ratio, a 'Scene-Action' ratio and so on. For example a gesture, such as holding up the hand palm outward, has one kind of act-meaning and purpose when performed by the celebrant at the Mass and quite another when made by a diner to a server approaching with a pot of coffee to proffer a refill. Burke calls these ratios a 'grammar' in much the same sense as Wittgenstein used the word, that is as a name for the open totality of normative constraints on the proper unfolding of a class of language games.

But the Pentad has another role. It also determines the content of accounts, that is of stories about episodes in which the partitioning of the episode into constitutive events is displayed and in which a story about motives is constructed.

> . . . in any rounded statement about motives, you must have some word that names the *act* (names what took place, in thought or deed), and another that names the *scene* (the background of the act, the situation in which it occurred); also you must indicate what person or kind of person (*agent*) performed the act, what means or instruments he used (*agency*), and the *purpose*. (Burke, 1945)

However much disagreement there may be about an episode amongst participants and spectators Burke asserted that 'any complete statement about motives will offer *some kind of answers to these five questions: what was done (act), when or where it was done (scene), who did it (agent), how he did it (agency), and why it was done (purpose)'.* It should be obvious that in Burke's view a motive story is not a hypothesis about the putative antecedent causes of behaviour.

It is not only possible to use the concepts of dramatism analytically, to study episoides that have already been given and are recorded in some fashion. It is also possible to use that very same conceptual system to fabricate episodes in such a way as to reveal how much a typical member of a participant group knows of the locally valid scripts or role-rule models, story-lines and positions etc, that constitute the grammar in Burke's sense. (For an excellent overview of Burke's social psychology see Overington, 1977).

THE DRAMATURGICAL MODEL

This is perhaps the oldest analytical model of all. We see and hear a simulacrum of life on the stage. Perhaps the way that simulacrum is created and the illusion sustained can be a guide to our understanding of how real life is created. There are obvious differences between real life and stage drama, and it would be as well, to prevent mis-understanding, to notice them now. Stage drama selects from, simplifies and heightens the act/action sequences and personal presentations of real life. Time is foreshortened. Only a few of the many threads of everyday life are followed. Resolutions are frequently achieved in contrast to the endless postponements of the daily round. Issues are faced rather than dodged; lies are discovered and so on. Furthermore a more clearly developed and fully articulated aesthetic frame controls the presentations of the people and the unfolding of their affairs. Life, too, is partly managed in accordance with aesthetic standards, which parallel those of the stage quite closely, but they are rarely dominant.

Despite all the differences the likenesses are worth exploiting. At the very least, as Goffman has observed, the way an actor shows they are a certain kind of person must parallel the way anyone would show, in a certain social milieu, that they are that kind of person. Without some such matching the actor's performance would not 'work' and the audience would not know what was being done or what kind of person the actor was supposed to be. The parallel is not perfect since actors and audiences may share certain conventions about the expression of these matters that once reflected everyday life but have long since ceased to do so. For instance we have no trouble recognizing the villain in a melodrama despite the fact that no one behaves that way any longer, if indeed they ever did carry on quite like that.

What then can we draw from the model? Primarily it is an analytical scheme, coupled with a specially watchful kind of consciousness – at once the consciousness of the actor, the producer, the audience and the critic. To adopt the model is to take a certain kind of stance to the unfolding of everyday life and to the performances of the people who live it. It could be described as an ironic stance, a viewpoint from which life goes forward, becomes visible. For the means of action are not usually attended to, so much do we concentrate on the aims and outcomes of our activities.

As a source-model for developing analyses of everyday activities the dramaturgical model leads to two interlocking conceptual systems. Looking ironically at the performance we can begin to analyse it according to the scheme proposed by Burke. We can look for the way the kind of scene we are to be in is indicated. Scenes are complex objects including both the setting, the physical surrounding, stage props, and so on; and the situation, the human predicament which the unfolding of the drama will, we hope, resolve. The drama unfolds through the performances of the actors, playing parts, in styles we must be able to recognize. The action of the play is usually determined by a script, though actors and producers place their own interpretations on it. In improvised and experimental theatre the script may be reduced to a bare scenario, suggesting the predicament, the persons and the resolution, but leaving the performance and sometimes even the resolution to be created in the course of the action.

Interlocking with all this is the interpretative activity of the producer, who proposes a reading, though the success of the reading depends on how far the audience can be persuaded to share it. By taking something of the position of both audience and producer, critics provide informed commentary upon the action, upon the players and their performance, upon the scene and the scenario. And this too can be looked at dramaturgically. It is a performance by people playing the parts of critics in the unfolding of yet another scenario.

As people living our own lives we are among the actors performing our parts in well or ill-defined scenes, sometimes fully scripted, sometimes improvising. As producers, audience and critics, we appear as social scientists commenting upon the drama. But as people playing the parts of social scientists in appropriate scenes we are performers in yet another drama.

Scene analysis

Setting

All our actions are carried out against a structured background. The physical settings are not neutral. They contribute to the action. Settings broadcast messages of reassurance and threat. Until recently the messages from the background, social musak so to speak, were taken for granted as part of the common-sense world. However, the structure of settings and their manner of working on human social feelings was much discussed in the past. In the Renaissance various general theories were proposed: from Albertus Magnus to Kepler a variety of theories were broached (Yates, 1966). But it is only very recently that sociologists and social psychologists have turned their attention to analysing and understanding settings. The 'scene' has several components. The physical scene can be considered first as to its overall spatio-temporal structure, and then as to the meaning of the various things with which it is furnished, including smells, colours, the state of the weather, and so on. In this section I shall be concerned only with the former, and shall speak of it, with a small measure of licence, as the *Umwelt*. Just as each species of animal has its own spatial environment, in every given area each category of people, professions and sexes, families and age groups, have different spaces within which they freely move, all, for example, within the one city. Each has some spaces proper to itself alone.

We must first take a stand on the central matter of the nature of the environment of social action, whether we should follow Skinner or Kant; whether we should regard the environment as external to the action, or identify at least some of the properties of the environment of action as human products. I have argued in an earlier section for a generally Kantian outlook, which seems to me so utterly indisputable that I can find little to debate about with the other side. That a traffic light is what it is as part of the environment of social action by a social endowment of 'red', 'green', etc. with meanings, and those meanings embedded and maintained within a system of rules, seems to me so obvious that the idea that it is redness as a physical stimulus that brings me to brake can scarcely be taken seriously. Furthermore, it is also clear that the Skinnerian view must be wrong if applied to the institutional environment since that is clearly a product of knowledge and understanding. I hope that as our analysis of the *Umwelt* unfolds we shall see that much the same is true of the 'physical' environment.

The socially significant environment includes many non-structural features. In countries with very variable weather the moods of the inhabitants can be much influenced by these changes. The significance of such moods may be great and read back into nature as a kind of social meteorology. I shall not be concerned with a detailed analysis of these features of the environment in this section, but only with the interrelated structures we impose on space and time, and the structures we build with things and events within space and time.

The socially meaningful physical environment within which we live seems to have two degrees of structure, two levels of granularity. The coarse-grained structure consists of distinct and separated areas in space and periods in time, distinguished as the places and times of socially distinct activities. For instance, the social activities of the street are quite distinct from those inside a bank adjoining that street, and opening off it. This is one of those obvious truths that should yet surprise us. How do I know that I am in the counting hall of a bank and that I should behave reverently therein? Part of the answers to these questions are to be found by *looking* at the décor of the banking hall. Our first task will be to examine some of the ways in which socially distinct areas and volumes of space and periods of time are demarcated and maintained. In this way the coarse-grained structure of the *Umwelt* will be revealed.

But each area and volume, and each period of time, and each thing within an area and each pattern of action within a time, has a structure which differentiates if from other things and makes it thereby a potential vehicle of significance or meaning. These are the fine-grained structures of the *Umwelt*. How are these structures socially significant? I shall try to establish, with a wide range of examples, that we create and maintain such structures and endow them with meaning as a kind of permanent or semi-permanent bill-board or hoarding upon which certain socially important messages can be 'written'. The very fact of order, when recognized by human beings, is, *in itself*, the source of a message that all is well. Orderliness of the physical environment broadcasts a kind of continuous social musak whose message is reassurance. But, as we shall see, the fine structuring of the *Umwelt* allows us to give and receive much more specific messages, public statements of how we wish to be taken as social beings. I will try to show, in broad outline, how these more specific messages are achieved.

If we define the *Umwelt* of a human being as he or she is a person of a certain social category, we could express this in a formula:
Umwelt = Physical Environment × Social meanings.
This formula could be taken literally as a Boolean product. Thus if someone were to be found to be using two interpretative schemata, A and B, then $U = P \times (A \lor B)$ leads to $U = (P \times A) \lor (P \times B)$; in short that person lives in two *Umwelten*.

As we pass through space and time we are continually adjusting ourselves to a complex social topography. Some regions are closed to us, some open. For some various keys or magic passwords are required, such as 'Oh yes, I'm a member here'. Looking at this social psychologically we must ask how these barriers are established and promulgated, how they are maintained, how legitimately crossed, how their accidental violation is remedied. This will reveal what the social structure of the topography thus established might be.

As an introductory illustration, consider the time barrier that separates the period before a school lesson from the lesson itself. It may be created by the ringing of a bell which separates two socially distinct regions. In the period before the lesson the social structure of the class is a complex network of microsocial groupings, one of which, usually the most socially powerful, may include the teacher. The whole interaction pattern is organized as 'chat'. After the lesson starts the social order simplifies into a one-many hierarchy, with the children oriented to the teacher, and an almost complete disappearance of the 'chatting' style of speech which characterized the previous period.

Spatial boundaries, like fences or white lines on the ground, demarcate socially distinct areas. Such social topographies may reflect the polarity between a safe and a dangerous area. But the boundaries may be invisible. Urban Americans are all too familiar with the feeling of relief and relaxation as one passes beyond Such and Such Street, into a 'safe' area.

The structures created by boundaries and associated barriers, the physical markers of boundaries, like fences in space and silences in time, can be very differently related to deliberate human effort. The English Channel is *there*, as is the moment of death, and both have to be coped with, whereas taking a stick and scratching a line on the sand, 'That's your team's home base' or beginning by 'O.K. let's get started', are more or less free creations. They can be challenged and are subject to negotiation in ways that death and geography cannot be. But some human constructions are geographical features, such as permanent architectural or agricultural arrangements. Time is structured permanently by such artifacts as clocks and calendars. Just as our only social response to such entities as the English Channel or the coming of spring can be semantic attributions of meaning, expressed in such famous aphorisms as 'Wogs start at Calais', or 'Oh to be in England now that Spring is here', so we may negotiate the meaning of an hour or of the Great Pyramid. Finally, in contrast to these permanent structurings are the wholly ephemeral, such as the lane changes in 'tidal flow' traffic schemes, and the agreement on the structure of times by which the order of speakers at a meeting is decided by the chairman. Most of the boundaries and barriers we will be examining in detail are neither so unresponsive to human renegotiation as the solar year or the Atlantic Ocean, nor as ephemeral as the chalked grid for street hop-scotch, or the intervention, 'I wish you'd shut up and let A have a chance to say something'.

Time structure and its marking

I shall call the boundaries of conventionally marked, socially distinct time-periods, 'openings' and 'closings' following Schegloff and Sacks (1974). A prime social differentium is whether opening and closing is done for or achieved by the participant. We must also ask whether the openings and closings are natural or contrived.

Close observation of the way beginnings and ends of activities were managed in a kindergarten shows that the initial and final moves in the sequence of an activity are separated from the rest of the activity by being performed in a particularly flamboyant and exaggerated way. Their natural role as beginnings and endings is stylistically enhanced to demarcate the boundaries of distinctive times.

Social closings are notoriously more difficult to achieve than openings. One can, in desperation, just start. However, as a general rule things do not just start, they are opened by the recital of a ritual formula or the performance of a symbolic action: 'Oyez, Oyez, Oyez, as it pleases the Queen, Her Gracious Majesty . . .', cutting the ribbon to open the road, and so on. The variety and sources of such formulae would no doubt repay close study.

The closing of conversations as socially distinct intervals of time has been much illuminated by the studies of Sacks and Schegloff. The problem is created by the fact that the normal ending of an utterance is not a sign of the ending of a conversation, rather it is the signal for next speaker. How is this transition relevance suspended?

Schegloff and Sacks found that there are two ways of generating a terminal section. A speaker can insert a preclosing phrase such as 'Well, O.K. . . .' to mark the end of a topic in such a way that a terminal sequence can politely be introduced. Alternatively one can pick up a topic at the beginning of an interaction to allow for a warrantable lead in the closing section.

The problem of natural openings and closings arises as a separate issue. We have already noticed the technique by which natural initial and terminal parts of a sequence can be stylistically elevated to become openings and closings. Some natural events could find no other place in the sequence than as beginnings and endings. Such for example, are spring and autumn, birth and death. They are not, therefore, available for stylistic heightening *as* openings and closings, they *are* openings and closings. But their importance is too great for them to merely pass by, unattended and unstressed. They become surrounded by ceremony. In general this network of natural openings and closings forms a closed system of metaphors, each binary opposition serving as a metaphor for the others.

Spatial structure and its marking
The boundaries of spaces may be marked by relatively insurmountable barriers, such as high walls, or wide waterways. Such barriers enter social reality only when they are given a meaning by a participant. Does the prison wall keep the prisoner in, or the unpredictable and threatening forces of society out? Is a prison a cage or a refuge? Does its wall show its sheer face inwards or outwards? Clearly the sense of the wall, its vectorial significance, is a function of the way the areas within and without are socially conceived.

Other boundaries are marked by physically surmountable barriers, visible like low walls and white lines, invisible like the high and low status areas of a schoolroom, or the volume of private space around a person. Most boundaries tend to close up on themselves, enclosing areas. Social areas have portals, visible or invisible. These portals are generally valve-like. Passage out is easier than passage in, so that while not all who aspire are admitted, all who have been admitted eventually come out. In public buildings there is often a ceremonial performance involved in achieving entry but a mere valedictory nod marks acceptable leaving of the enclosed volume or area.

Invisible boundaries must be maintained through shared knowledge. They are usually generated by some potent or sanctified dangerous object at their centre. Goffman (1972b) and others have noticed that the area around a 'with', a group who are bound together by social ties and who let it be seen that they are so, moves with the 'with'. Contrary walkers skirt around it. Similarly a person may leave a potent trace such as a pair of sunglasses and a towel upon a crowded beach, creating an unencroachable boundary. A participant has reported that around the door of a school staff-room there is an arc of inviolability, beyond which the pupils will not normally go. If forced to do so they exhibit signs of considerable uneasiness and distress.

The social texture of space and time
The original idea of a social texture to space and time comes from Lewin (1935) who proposed a kind of vector analysis to represent the power of attributions of meaning to different features of an environment. This is particularly easy to illustrate in the behaviour of men involved in the trench warfare of the war of 1914–1918, where the terrain was textured by its potential as a source of danger and of protection from hostile action.

So far we have taken the physical topography as a datum, and seen how it can be endowed with meaning. But the microstructure of the *Umwelt* may be organized as a social topography. A concept like 'social distance' could be introduced to express the rarity and

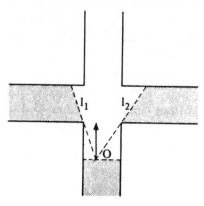

Figure 3 L_1 and L_2 are 'lurk lines' and the shaded and unshaded areas represent the structure of the texture of threat. As O moves forward the structural properties of the space change.

difficulty of a transition from one socially marked space to another.

Goffman's analysis of the texture of threat in an urban *Umwelt* illustrates a space organized along one dimension of social meaning. In a dangerous section of a city the grid pattern of streets is replaced by a modulating structure of clear and dubious areas, areas in which someone might be lurking, the possibility constituting the threat. The boundary between the space that can be seen to be empty and the space that is obscured Goffman calls a 'lurk line'. The threat texture of a grid pattern of streets, from a momentary vantage point in the passage of O, our man on Michigan Avenue, as he passes through the street corner, would look something like figure 3.

A pleasanter illustration of social topography can be found in the social map of a kindergarten. The map is plotted in two dimensions, staff sanctity v. child sanctity and comfort v. threat. The geographical map of the kindergarten (including play area) looks like figure 4.

Plotting these areas on the social map we get a topography such as in figure 5.

(5) and (4), though geographically adjacent, and from a spatial point of view therefore easy of mutual access, are socially very distant, and passage from one to the other is very difficult for a child. Entry to (4) is a special occasion and under close supervision, occurring only for those whose job it is to wash the cups, or for a 'cooking' group who prepare something for a playmate's birthday. (2), (6) and (7) are completely mutually open and the children and staff pass freely from one to the other, without social portals, that is rituals of passage like

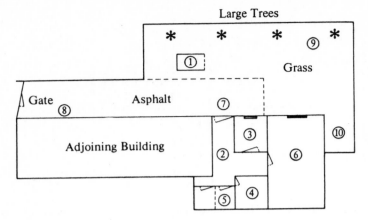

Figure 4
Key (1) Wendy house, (2) Lobby, (3) Staffroom, (4) Kitchen, (5) Lavatories, (6) Play room, (7) Near play area, (8) Far play area, (9) Distant grass, (10) Unobserved areas.

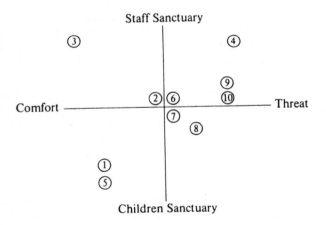

Figure 5

knocking or asking. But there are portals to be passed in making the passage from (2), (6) and (7) into (3), the teachers' room, whose door is ordinarily closed. The staff assert that the toilets are a child sanctuary which they do not enter, but observation shows that their sanctity is seldom taken seriously.

Message-specific structures

The procedures and rituals we have examined so far serve to divide or bound socially distinct spaces and times. Within those areas and periods there are spatial and temporal structures, the arrangement of furniture in a room, or the complex orderliness of a meal. Viewed dramaturgically, these entities are the props which further define the scene, and which together with the *Umwelt* make up the setting. Such structures have a social meaning. But before examining some examples in detail we must ask how a physically structured feature of an environment can have meaning. Social meanings are also given to and read off qualitative properties, such as colours, for example red flags, brown shirts, black skins and so on. These do occur in the *Umwelt*, but as separable items, so I shall not pursue the question of their semantics here, but deal only with entities differentiated by their structural properties. A semantic unit is a structure and is embedded within a structure or structures. The internal structure presents no particular problems provided we recognize that the structure of the unit may be extended in space, in which case we shall look for its synchronic form, or extended in time, in which case we shall look for its diachronic layout. Provided entities are structurally differentiated they can bear distinctive meanings. In the traffic code a triangle has one meaning and a circle another, while in dog-handling the melodic differences between one whistle and another, structurally differentiated in time, are distinct signals. In general the semantic field of an item includes relations of exclusion, such as that between a circle and a triangle, whose meanings exclude each other; and inclusive relations such as that between a triangle and its red colour, relations that range from synonymy through metaphor to metonymy. To express a meaning, then, we must lay out as much of the semantic field as is required to distinguish this entity as meaningful from other items within their possible common contexts.

If we examine a permanent arrangement of furniture in an office we are studying a structure that is physical, laid out in space. Each distinct layout can be assigned a social meaning. Studies have shown that the way furniture is arranged in an office is not just a matter of convenience but is a symbolic representation of the standing of the occupant (Joiner, 1971).

In general the principles seem to be the following: the desk parallel to a wall is of lower status than at an angle to a wall; the desk against a wall is of lower status than freestanding; sitting on the side exposed to the door is of lower status than sitting on the side away from the door.

Applying these rules together we find that the person whose desk is freestanding, at an angle to the wall, and who sits behind the desk facing the door, is of the highest category admitted by that organization, a fact expressed in the furniture for all to see. A person whose desk is up against the wall, who works with their back to the door on the exposed side, is the lowest. Whatever airs they may give themselves furniture shows social position for all to see. How far this code is general among bureaucratic humanity is uncertain, but the study reported covered both English Civil Servants and Swedish Executives, so it has some measure of generality as a sign system. An explanation of the etymology of the semantics is readily forth-coming from Goffman's theory of front and backstage divisions of personal territory. The person of low status is totally exposed, he or she has hardly any backstage area. Their whole official life is enacted frontstage. They are under perpetual threat of supervision. But a simple visualizing of the plan of the office of the highest grade shows that tucked away behind the angled desk, a person has the greatest amount of private space (of backstage) of any of the possible arrangements. Equally, and probably complementarily, the topology would admit of a Durkheimian account in terms of the protection of and at the same time the exhibition of the sanctity or inviolability of the highest status person, whose body is surrounded by a large protective area, freeing them from the possibility of profanation. There must surely be an element of truth in both accounts, and further study could probably elicit their balance in the way the furniture arrangement is read by the various individuals who act within it as their *Umwelt*.

The physical structure of a setting may function as a meaning-bearing entity, that is as a significant icon of the content of certain propositions within the cosmology of a people. A detailed and well documented example is P. Bourdieu's analysis of the microcosmic organization and meaning of the Berber house (Bourdieu, 1973). I will not discuss those individual items which have a social or cosmological significance in themselves, but only the way messages are conveyed by various structural properties of the house. According to Bourdieu, these properties match and hence represent some central structural properties of the Berber cosmology, that is of the content of certain of their important beliefs, expressed in proverbs and sayings.

Once again we find the two dimensions of scene analysis, the structure of the entity, in this case the house, and the structure of the larger entity into which the house fits. And, of course, certain differentiated elements within the structure of the house are themselves structurally differentiated, and some qualitatively, as, for example, light and dark, or fresh and preserved. The appearance of both structurally differentiated elements, for example forked and straight, shows that we are dealing with basic semantic units, the higher-order structure having the character of syntax.

Our problem is *how* does the house as a structure, as a social or cosmological microcosm, express the macrocosm? There seem to be two distinct ways. In one the representation is established by isomorphism of structure, in the other by conventional assignment of meaning to generate a symbol. An etymology for the symbol can be reconstructed from the folk sayings, in terms of which the particular assignment of meaning makes sense. It is as a symbol, not as structured isomorph, that the fire is conceived by the Berber as the representation of the female principle in the house.

It seems from Bourdieu's account that structural properties of the house represent at two levels of sophistication. The ridge pole rests in the fork of the central wooden pillar, and this is read as an icon of the male/female relationship. Here the structural isomorphism is exceedingly simple. A considerable amount of social meaning is taken to be vested in this conjunction, and a good many of the rituals associated with procreation are related to it. Furthermore, the ridge pole and supporting pillar are the central metaphors in a large number of sayings and expressions by which the Berber social organization of the male/female dichotomy is described (and no doubt promulgated as rules and norms).

But Bourdieu has shown that the structure of the house is a microcosm in much more subtle ways. The division of the house into a light part and a dark part matches the division of social time into night and day. The openness of the light part is in contrast to the closedness of the dark part, matching the division between public (male) life and private (female) life. But these simple homologies are only the basis for more elaborate structures. 'The opposition between the world of female life and the world of the city of man is based upon the same principles as the two systems of opposition that it opposes.' In short, private life is not just female life, but as the procreative part of life is female/male. So the fact that the light part is in some sense the preserve of the women, where cooking and weaving are done, leads to the inner homology that the light part: dark part *as* public: private *as* male; female *as* female/female; female/male. Thus in general

$$a: b \; as \; b1; b2$$

Finally, the house can be considered in its geographical isomorphisms. The door is related to the compass points of geographical space. Going out one faces the East, the direction of worship, with the warm South on one's right. But the door is also related to a kind of inner geography. Coming in one faces the wall of the loom, which being illuminated by the door is treated as bright, honourable and so on, in short as the 'East' of the inner space. On one's right on entry is the wall with the fire, the 'South' of the interior. Thus the door is the point of logical inversion through which one passes from macrocosm and back, always in the same relation to the social and cosmological significance of these structured spaces.

Situations

My basic thesis is that in most times and most historical conditions expressive motivations dominate practical. Practical aspects of activities will usually have some part to play, but from the dramaturgical perspective they fade into relative unimportance. Situations will arise mostly from expressive contradictions.

In a general way one can see that there can be only two kinds of situations – those in which people are related to the setting, and those in which they are related to each other. I shall try to show how each naturally provides the opportunity for expressive tensions. There are many, many ways in which expressive tension can be created, and the cases I shall describe are meant only to illustrate the kind of thing I have in mind and not to masquerade as an exhaustive catalogue.

People in relation to setting

The simplest relation a person can have to a setting is to be occupying some part of its space and/or its time. And that occupancy seems to create in most people a sense of proprietorship. The sense of possession does seem to be close to universal. Mary Douglas (1966) has amplified our understanding of the sense of proprietorship or 'ownership' of spaces and times with the idea that we invest those for which we feel this relation with some measure of sanctity. In consequence we tend to treat the intrusion of others as a profanation, a defilement of some *thing* close enough to us to be almost part of ourselves. Lyman has remarked on the way people will decorate whatever space they take to be theirs, emphasizing their proprietorship, even if the last territory for the dispossessed is their own bodies. If all this is in some measure sound, then one's dignity and worth would be seriously threatened by other people making free with those regions of space and time one felt proprietorial towards. And this provides our first source of social tension. It arises in the situation created by an actual, immanent or virtual violation of one's personal spaces and times. We shall see how this tension is dealt with in the section on action.

People in relation to one another

Of the innumerable variety of possible cases I shall sketch only two, as illustrative of rather different forms of tension.

Social tension can arise, and what I have called a situation come into being, when it is apparent to two or more people that a relationship already exists between them, but it has not been publicly proclaimed or ritually ratified. A couple may have reached the point of establishing a very formal and apparently stable relationship which has to be transformed into a socially ratified bonding, either into the informal 'They are going out together' or the formal 'They are engaged'. This is the tension of the implicit about to be transformed into the explicit, the potential about to become actual. The scenes to be discussed in detail below concern the ritual transformation of a privately or personally experienced mutual liking into a publicly acknowledged friendship.

But social tensions can also arise in cases where it is uncertain what relation is going to come to exist between people. A perennial problem is posed by the appearance of a stranger, whose place in our network of social relations and reputations has yet to be determined. We could look at introduction ceremonials as minor dramatic resolutions of this kind of problem.

There are a huge number of such tension-situations, which life dramas resolve. There is the discovery that someone is not what they seem. There is the realization that a relation which has been certified officially has no further foundation in personal feeling – how is it to be terminated? There is the challenge to established reputation for one who aspires to the mantle. There is the sudden realization that one is getting old and the bitter discovery of the uselessness of one's life in the eyes of others, and so on, and so on. The expressive aspect of action, the dominant aspect, I claim, can be understood from the partial point of view provided by the dramaturgical model as a resolution of these and other 'dramatic' situations.

ACTION ANALYSIS

Introduction

Of course, a great deal of action in a great many scenes from kitchens to carpenters' shops, from space-modules to cow-byres, is practical.

The actions undertaken by the folk legitimately on the scene are explicable in terms of the practical aims of the undertaking and the practically or scientifically sanctioned means of bringing these about. But it is the argument of this work that for most people, in most historical conditions, expressive motivations dominate practical aims in the energy and even in the time expended on co-ordinated social activities. In many cases too the prime motivation of the practical activities is to be found in their expressive value – space flight, scientific research and cooking are obvious examples. I shall devote no space to a discussion of the practical activities of mankind since I believe that they bear only tangentially on social life during most of human history. With the exception of the nineteenth century in Western Europe and in certain countries whose 'nineteenth century' is still to come, practical motivations are and will be secondary.

Paying most attention, then, to expressive aspects of action, I propose a threefold division of dramatic scenarios – remedies, resolutions and monodramas. Each has to do with the management of a situation of tension, in such a way that the social order, though it may be changed, is maintained in some form or other. Remedies are action-sequences which serve to restore lost dignity or honour; resolutions are action-sequences which resolve a growing tension between expressive and practical activity by formally or ritually redefining relationships on another plane, for example friendship stages, marriages and so on; while monodramas are action-sequences in which an actor achieves his or her personal expressive projects while continuing to have the good will and respect of those who have to subordinate their aims and wills. Doubtless there are very many more kinds of scenarios played out against the background of well defined social scenes. These are offered as illustrations.

Remedies

If the major human preoccupation in the complex interweaving of practical and expressive activities is the presentation of an acceptable persona, appropriate to the scene and the part in the action (the social collective component) associated with a sense of worth and dignity (the psychological/individual component), then since the possibility of loss of dignity, of humiliation and expressive failure exists, we would expect an elaboration of remedial activities for their restoration.

The existence of boundaries creates the possibility of their violation, and violations require remedies. The general form of remedial exchanges has been analysed by Goffman (1972) and I shall follow his treatment closely. The first point to notice is that for a remedial interchange, say an apology, to be required, there must be someone who has proprietorial rights on that space or time. It must in some sense be *their* space or *their* time. For instance, a lesson is a teacher's time, and a party is the time of the hostess, just as my office is my space, and the kitchen, the cook's. If the space or time is 'owned' by no one, there can be no occasion for remedy, so if I miss the train and thus exclude myself from that period of time, that is train-journey time, I cannot apologize for my lateness, for there is nobody whose time it is, except of course mine. It is the guard's train but not his journey-time.

Goffman's analysis depends upon an underlying distinction between virtual and actual offence. To arrive late is to commit an actual offence, and the person whose time it is must be apologized to in the proper ritual form. But the generality of Goffman's analysis is made possible by the extension of the notion of offence to virtual violations, which are remedied in advance, so to speak. In order to get the water-jug I must violate your table territory which I remedy in advance by asking politely, that is in proper ritual form: 'Would you mind passing the water-jug please?' which allows, but never admits, the response, 'Yes, I would mind'.

The general form, then, of remedial exchange is as follows:
A: Remedy: I'm terribly sorry I'm late.
B: Relief: That's O.K.

There are two further elaborations of this basic form. Frequently the Remedy-Relief interchange, whose referent is the actual or virtual violation of someone's space or time, is supplemented by a second interchange whose referent is the first interchange. Thus

A1:   Remedy: I'm sorry I'm late.
B1:   Relief: That's O.K.
A2:   Appreciation: Gee, I'm glad I didn't upset things too much.
B2:   No, no, it was O.K.

where A2 in the second bracket expresses appreciation for B's granting of relief, and in B2, B minimizes the extent of his condescension, thus restoring to A his status as a person in equal moral standing with B.

But particularly where time is concerned there is another form of remedial interchange, the counter-apology. So far as I can see the final product, that is maintenance of the boundary and equilibration of the moral standing of the people involved is just the same as in the Goffman ritual. Consider the following:

A1:   Remedy: I'm awfully sorry I'm late.
B1:   Relief: That's O.K.
B2:   Counter-apology: I'm afraid we had to start without you.
A2:   Counter-relief: Gosh, I should hope so.

Goffman's remedial exchanges allow for the management of the defilement of sacred or proper territory, and for the violation of spatial and temporal boundaries. But *how* is being late or early a violation of a time boundary? If early you are present in a socially distinct period which, for example, may be a preparatory period for the action to come, and a great deal of back-stage equipment may still litter the scene (the cooking utensils or the baby's toys have not yet been put away). The style of the action may be inappropriate to the presence of a stranger. Under these conditions a remedial interchange is required to maintain the social order. The equilibration of civility may even require the early arrival to join the home team, and pay the penalty by tidying up the sitting room. In short, times as well as spaces may be distinguished as front and back stage.

To be late is equally the breaching of a boundary, since you were not there for some temporal sections of the action, though expected, and you did not arrive through the time portal provided just before the beginning of the action. A remedial interchange is required. We need no special theory to account for the fact that late arrivals are very much more common than early. Of course late arrival may be part of a presentational sequence, susceptible of dramaturgical analysis, as when someone conspicuously arrives late in order to be noticed.

Another important category of plots concerns the scenarios for the preservation or restoration of social identity and dignity in the face of actual or potential threats. I instance here, for illustrative purposes, one such plot, which may take somewhat different forms in an actual production – the plot Goffman (1972) has called 'face-work'. He defines 'face' as 'the positive social value a person effectively claims for himself by the lines others assume he has taken during a particular contact', for example, he may have been supposed to have knowledge and experience of mountaineering. Since it is usually demeaning to everyone in the group if any one member, previously in good standing, loses face by some contradiction to his right to take the line emerging, it is in each person's interest to support every other person's line. By saving the face of others, each person saves his own and vice versa. Goffman calls activities directed to this end 'face-work'.

The sequence of the actions by which actual and potential loss of face can be dealt with are sufficiently standardized for them to be treated as ritual. The sequence begins with a challenge in which the actual or potential offence is 'noticed'. The offender is then given the chance to re-establish the expressive order either by redefining the action as of another social-type, 'not this act but that', or by making some form of compensation, or by punishment with a 'silly me!', or something of the sort. The offering is then usually accepted and the offender's gratitude made known in a terminal move. Though these actions are conventionally called for as expressions of ritually correct social attitudes and relations, they serve to illustrate the sensibility and personhood of the actor.

A more subtle form of ritual remedies can be found during 'trouble in school'. The point of 'trouble' is reached by a growing feeling in some schoolchildren that the school system and the school teachers do not value them. They experience the efforts to make them study pointless subjects ('getting at me') as well as abandonment of those very efforts ('writing me off') as degrading. A gap opens up between how they would like to be evaluated, the dignity they would like to have ritually ratified, and how they interpret themselves as presently conceived by others. Children create systematic remedial exchanges in which dignity between teachers as represent*ations* (as opposed to represent*atives*) of the educational system and pupils as persons supposedly in good standing, is equilibrated.

To understand these cycles of remedial exchange two categories of insult have to be distinguished. There are the results which preserve dignity such as a teacher swearing at a child or even hitting it. At least in principle, the child is noticed as someone of consequence as the recipient of that act. Insults of that sort are reciprocated in kind. But children distinguish another category of insults – those that demean. Demeaning insults include two main sub-categories. Failing to know a child's name or treating it like a sibling are construed as wounding to personal esteem. They indicate both a lack of care from the teacher and a lack of reputation for the child. But worse, according to the childish interpretation, is some form of 'writing off'. This is illustrated most vividly for them by their discovering that some of their teachers are both weak and frightened. 'If we were being taken seriously'. they reason, 'we would not be given such feeble teachers.'

How to restore the dignity they have lost? Many such children have devised a double cycle of retribution to balance the dignity equation. The first cycle tests the teacher by 'playing up' or 'dossing about'. If the teacher is strong and seriously concerned with them this will be shown in firmness and there is no disequilibrium in the equation to balance. The balance is already there. But if the teacher fails, this is read as an insult, a demeaning not of the teacher but of the class itself, and each member of it. An imbalance exists. The second phase of the cycle involves a retesting of the teacher aimed at reducing him or her to a condition of indignity – breakdown or retreat. When that has been achieved the pupils withdraw, amplifying their own dignity by completely ignoring the impotent rage and posturing of their official mentor. But, we have found, if the teacher tries to break the cycle by an attempt at strength and fails a second time, the results are likely to be violent. Physical punishment of the teacher may be meted out, so high a state of excitement is reached.

Resolutions

My second category of examples of scenarios are resolutions. Situations arise where private and personal attitudes shadow forth or anticipate a relationship not yet publicly or socially ratified. I take friendship and its complement as examples. (Since there is no word for 'enemyship' in English, I shall distinguish the formally ratified states as *Bruderschaft* and *Feindschaft*, borrowing a convenient German distinction.) I take it that the individuals who proceed to these ritual ratifications whose scenarios I will describe are psychologically prepared for transformation, and are aware of each others' attitudes, though misreadings may show up in the unfolding of the scenarios.

We can look at the action sequences which one might have to carry out for the creation or maintenance of a friendship or a state of enmity as the performing of a ritual, a *Bruderschaft* ceremony in the first case and a *Feindschaft* ceremony in the latter.

It seems to me that there are two quite separate aspects that can be studied. There are ways of speaking to friends, styles of speech manifestly regardless of content. I notice myself adopting a peculiar half-jocular style of speech with friends. I certainly use such a style for indicating and maintaining friendship. The emergence of this style could be explained by seeing it as a kind of test. If one uses language which if it were taken literally by someone would be insulting, and then make it jocular, this could be a test of friendship of the other person. As a friend he does not take offence at being called an 'old bastard' or whatever happens to be the local expression. There are uses of speech and action which are strictly ceremonial in character. Alan Cook has pointed out to me, for example, the reference to fighting as a *Bruderschaft* ritual in the works of D. H. Lawrence. I have outlined earlier Mary Douglas's idea that some ritual resolutions and markings of social relations can be done with food and drink. Peter Marsh has noticed that in working-class communities, except for close relatives, there is not much inviting of people to meals. Intimacy may be politely ratified by 'going out' together. We need another project, complementary to Mary Douglas's, to look at how intimacy is 'done' amongst cultures other than the British professional classes. Inversion is frequent, I believe, in anomic communities. People who are not very intimate tend to invite each other to a meal. Mary Douglas's hypothesis that passage through more structured rituals, in passing a person through degrees of greater intimacy, needs two further dimensions. When a relation goes beyond a certain degree of intimacy, then ratification rituals become less and less structured. When one wishes to express a purely formal relation, though a close one, the rhetoric of friendship may be used metaphorically and without irony.

The maintenance of hostility among intimates involves verbal rituals I shall call 'needlings'. An apparently harmless opening pair of remarks are made by A and B. But B's remark contains two aspects: it has a literal, primary sense, but it also has a performative or secondary sense in which it could be used as a needle. If A foiled the initial needle by taking B's speech as a provocation and replying to it, then B has a further move open, namely, 'I meant it literally'. B's opening remark means *q* literally and *r* performatively. If A takes it performatively, as *r*, and B says 'No, I meant *q*', B opens up an option of condemning A for implying that B is the kind of person to needle A. Such dialogue opens the way for B to trap A into seeming to denigrate the relationship which A and B ought to have. This structure is probably very general.

One must not suppose that *Feindschaft*-sustaining ritualized needlings are disruptive, that is necessarily lead to a break up of relationships. In marriage, where people are forced into intimacy, a complex relationship exists which involves some *Bruderschaft* and some *Feindschaft*. The relative quality of the marriage does not depend on whether *Feindschaft* is totally absent but how it is managed and how sustaining it is.

As Berne (1970) seems to imply, some *Feindschaft* rituals turn out to be highly sustaining to a relationship. He has some convincing examples of action-sequences which, if taken literally, are rather vicious, but since they are played out in a ritual way, simply tend to keep the formal relationship going.

Little is known about contemporary ritual ways of transforming private feelings of enmity into a stable, hostile and publicly realized relationship. Social psychologists have tended to look at attraction and altruism rather than their opposites, and even Goffman has concentrated more on person supportive rituals such as 'face work' than the ritual maintenance of hostility. A great deal remains to be done,

both in the collection of examples and in their analysis and classification and in the investigation of how they work.

In the past there have been much more publicly visible forms of
Feindschaft rituals. I distinguish these into two broad categories. There
are negative rituals where a point of the ritual is a ceremonial and
stylistic display of lack of interaction. The obsolete practice of the
'cut', the stylized refusal to acknowledge or greet someone, was an
example of a negative ritual. Positive rituals, on the other hand,
involve hostile but stylized interaction. The hostile actions are strictly
controlled by rule. A duel does not fit this pattern since it is not a
sustaining of the *Feindschaft* relationship, rather it is a formalized way
of resolving it. Feuds, on the other hand, are sequences of interaction
by which enmity is sustained according to rule. Two avenues of historical research suggest themselves. Feuds seem to have been conducted quite non-violently at times, particularly amongst village
women in rural communities. Anthropologists have studied the violent
or blood feud and there should be little difficulty in abstracting their
material to reveal formal structures useful in the social psychological
study of *Feindschaft*. Finally, a comparative study of violent and non-
violent forms of feuding could usefully be undertaken to try to discern
any formal parallels in the initiation, maintenance and resolution of
the state of enmity.

Monodrama

Throughout this work I have stressed the need to comprehend both
action and talk about action (accounting) in our registration of social
life. The distinction between practical and expressive aspects of social
activity is, I claim, unevenly distributed between action and accounts,
since action has both practical and expressive aspects, while accounting
is primarily, though not exclusively, expressive.

Retrospective resolution of personal/social tension in a dramaturgical mode

In this section I describe a way of resolving a kind of situation where
an actor feels a disparity between how they could be taken to be and
how they want to seem to appear. The solution is to speak in a way
that not only defines the actor's part in the unfolding action of a
drama, but also treats him or her as a cast of characters.

One common device for the drawing of other people into playing
parts is the use of syntactical forms which result in what I shall call,
following Torode, (1977) 'the conjuring up of Voices and Realms'. A
repeated pronoun, for example, is not accepted at its face value as

having identical reference, but scrutinized for its 'voice'. The structure of the discourse is revealed by linking 'voices', not instances of lexically identical pronouns. Thus,

'You never know, do you?'

addressed to another involves two voices – 'You', the voice of abstract humanity (Voice 1), and 'you' (Voice 2), that of the addressee; and via this separation of voices we can understand why the proper response is,

'No, you don't', rather than, 'No, I don't',

since the 'You' who doesn't, is Voice 1. In this way the structure of the stanza comprising the two speeches becomes clear.

Realms are the characteristic territories of Voices and may be more or less well defined in the presentation of monodrama.

The retrospective reconstruction of psychological reality I want to illustrate works by a purely internal constituting of Voices and Realms. As might be expected, monodramatic presentations of social psychological matters involving the self are a prominent feature of accounts. A very common accounting technique involves the separation in speech of 'I' from 'me'. Typically, the account involves a scenario in which the 'I' is represented as losing control of the 'me', who then as an independent being, performs the action for which the account is being prepared. In some scenarios the 'I' is a helpless spectator of the unleashed 'me'; in others the 'I' fails to attend, or loses consciousness, or in some other way is prevented from knowing anything about what the 'me' has been doing. In the former scenario, the 'I' loses control and releases the 'beast within'. In the other, the 'I' in losing consciousness reveals a mere 'automaton within'.

What are the monodramas conjured up in the use of such expressions? Their plots are based upon social vignettes, drawing upon common-sense understandings of commonplace multidrama. By virtue of their origin they have an explanatory function, for example I represent myself as using the same technique of self control as I use to control others when, for example, I say 'I made myself do something which I was reluctant to undertake': or at least, that is how I represent the matter monodramatically.

The self-justifying aspects of the resort to a monodramatic representation of the reasons for setting about reformatory self-work appear clearly when we notice that *my* failings are transformed into personal characteristics of the characters of the monodramatic presentations conjured up in 'I talked myself into it' and so on, thus my reluctance to act or my weakness of character is masked in part by attributing it to a separated and in the plot rather feeble-willed quasi-fellow, the 'me' who can be brought round by the eloquence of 'I'. 'I' as primary self-mover, can hog all the *Herrschaft* ('mastery') available in the little drama.

Thus monodrama is not just presentative of the dynamics of self-management, but is also technique, a way of talking that facilitates self-mastery by separating, as into another person, situation-relative undesirable personal characteristics. Sometimes self-congratulation can also be emphatically expressed by separating off and claiming desirable characteristics for *all* the members of my self-colony of selves as in the little monodrama 'Myself, I did it!'

Projective casting of others into roles adumbrated in the forms of speech

But the same technique can be put to work in trapping others in a self-constituted monodrama. Torode has provided a beautiful example in which a Calvinistic world of exclusion and election is conjured up by a form of speech. I take this example and its general method of analysis from Torode's study of teachers' speech, though the analysis I shall propose is somewhat more elaborate than his.

'We don't have any talking when we do compositions. I hope that is clear.' The first person plural appears here in two voices. The first voice speaks from a transcendent world, the seat of authority and the source of order. The inhabitants of this realm are strict – they 'don't have any talking'. The second occurrence of the first person plural pronoun 'we' denotes a different set of voices, those of the members of the mundane world of the classroom – the subjects, those who 'do'.

Mr Crimond presents himself as a member of both realms – a status to which we shall return – and also as a separated individual able to look at them both from an external standpoint in his character or voice as 'I'. Mr Crimond is the only person in the classroom who is a member of the populations of both realms. He is benevolent towards the citizens of the mundane realm, and he hopes that the message from the transcendent world is clear.

At the same time he is the channel of mediation and interpretation between realms. His hoping is directed to the possibility of his making clear to the members of the mundane realm the authoritarian wishes of the Voices of the transcendent realm. Furthermore, as a member of the transcendent realm, he is elect, while the members of the mundane realm are unable to address the issue of order except through his mediation. However, they are shown the possibility of election. One of them, namely Mr Crimond, is a member of both realms. However, aspiration to membership of the transcendent realm is matched by the possibility of being cast out of 'Heaven' altogether into what Torode calls 'Hell', an act in the monodrama expressed by such phrases as 'you boys . . .' The members of the mundane realm are trapped in Mr Crimond's monodrama. In particular they are unable to address questions concerning the issue of order directly to the source of that order. If they do query these matters, Mr Crimond replies in such phrases as 'We'll have to see', conjuring up an image of lofty deliberation among the immortals and of reserved judgements which may or may not be handed down. It should surprise no one that Mr Crimond maintains a high degree of discipline without recourse to anything other than speech.

Torode also raises the question of different Voices of the 'I', particularly the 'I' of concern (that above which 'hopes') and the 'I' of action and authority, for Mr Crimond occasionally speaks in the person of that Voice, as when he says 'I will not have that sort of thing'.

ACTOR ANALYSIS

In this section I shall be considering a person in action strictly in accordance with the dramaturgical model, that is as analogous to an actor in a staged performance of a traditional scripted play, or an improvised happening. This consideration will throw up some very serious philosophical issues which are treated in detail in the next part of this work, *Personal being*.

Social identity v. personal identity

The most trite yet important distinction to bring to understanding life on the dramaturgical model is that between an actor and his or her parts. As a human being for whom acting is work or even a hobby, the person as actor in the theatre or in a film has an identity distinct from the parts they play. There might be problems for individual actors in keeping the distinction sharp. But clearly, ontologically, stage or film actors are primarily themselves, and stage parts have to be adopted.

When an episode of ordinary life is looked at in accordance with the dramaturgical model, this ontological relation is reversed. Except for machiavellian and socio-pathological individuals, people are primarily the parts they play, and the attitude of detachment that would allow them to see their actions as performances of parts is a frame of mind which has to be consciously adopted and may induce a stultifying self-consciousness inhibiting convincing performance.

The psychological distinction between personal and social identity allows for the detachment of the actor as a person from the part, that is public self-presentations or personas in which one is usually almost wholly immersed. Detachment admits the possibility of control. As one detached from the action one can be an agent. But what can the actor control?

To return to the source-model: on stage an actor must keep fairly close to the script, or in an improvised drama, the scenario, otherwise they will lose the presentation as a part. In very advanced experimental theatre that indeed may be the very effect aimed at. But usually the actor as creating the part is almost without effective agency. Only the ultimate agency remains – to stalk off and abandon the performance altogether. But while playing the part the actor can put a personal stamp on it – make it his Hamlet or her Ophelia. This is done by control of style, of the way the part is performed. As we noticed earlier, this allows an actor considerable expressive power, the power needed to illustrate the sort of person he or she is in the way the actions are performed. Actors allow their personal identities to show through the social identity they are forced to adopt. In this aspect of performance the psychological condition and the ontological category of both stage actor and the performer of daily life are identical. They must both monitor and control the style of the performance without becoming wooden or self-conscious. They must both be agents with respect to these matters, that is fulfilling projects of their own devising, free of promptings and controlling influences from other people and the scenes of the action.

But adopting the stance of an actor and bringing action to explicit consciousness at certain times and moments in one's life can lead to the perception of disparities between presentations, personas, and our conception of character. A particularly prominent example of this phenomenon is the fits of self-consiousness that can overcome an inexperienced or uncertain social actor, so that the reflection of oneself in the eyes of others can become so dazzling as practically to stultify action altogether. I take the form of consciousness which children experience in what we call 'showing off' to be very similar. Struck by the disparity between the presented self and inner being they force embarrassingly over-presented personas on their audience. These are examples of the condition one might describe as 'over-awareness' of the management of one's actions.

In the condition I have just described, the managing self and our conception of how we want to be, and the way we believe we are presenting ourselves, become the focus of explicit attention. But most people act in the social world in an unselfconscious and often unreflective manner, lost in their activities and intent upon their goals. This can lead to an under-awareness of the actor and personal aspects of one's life in the social world. The difficulty of sustaining an adequate conception of the complexity of oneself as a social person has been beautifully described by Doris Lessing: 'This is what it must feel like to be an actor, an actress – how very taxing that must be, a sense of self kept burning behind so many different phantoms.'

To grasp the complexity of the relationship between, and differentiation from an actor and his part, I offer as an example an event which occurred recently in Denmark. A man went into a chocolate shop to buy some confectionary. There was a customer ahead of him – a lady with a little dog. The shop keeper offered the dog a chocolate. The dog refused and left shortly afterwards with its mistress. The man turned to the shop keeper and went, 'Woof, woof!' and was given a piece of chocolate by the proprietor, who remarked, 'You ought to have begged as well'.

The first point to notice is that the legitimacy or propriety of social acts are related to the part in which they are occurring. The man in the social or dramaturgical part of 'Dog' could do things he could not do in one of his other parts, for example university professor. The shop woman was acting with perfect propriety in rebuking the man as 'dog' for leaving out part of the ritual proper to that part; as 'dog' he should have begged as well. But who was she rebuking? It seems to me clear that she was rebuking the individual as managing or controlling self, neither 'dog' nor the 'professor'. It is the managing or controlling self that is the proper object of rebukes of that nature, and, to put the matter more grandly, is the object of moral praise or blame. One might add that the shop keeper had let down the man as managing self rather lightly since as 'dog' he should have wagged his tail after receiving the chocolate. The important point to notice is that social failures occur relative to the parts being undertaken and the personas being presented, and are part of 'drama criticism', but rebukes occur in the moral world and are directed to the man that lies behind the 'dog'.

Techniques for the presentation of social selves

For the most part, the presentations of self as this or that persona proper to a certain kind of social event and amongst people of a particular sort, are achieved not so much in the instrumental activities in bringing off practical tasks such as counting money, driving cars, eating peas, making legal judgements, delivering lectures, screwing nuts on bolts, and so on, but in the style in which those activities are performed. Self-presentation is described in adverbs such as 'reluctantly', 'churlishly', 'gloomily', 'cheerfully', 'carefully', and so on, rather than in verbs of action. Impression-management, as Goffman calls it, consists largely in the control of style. Attributions of character are made to a person by others pretty much on the basis of how they see the style in which he or she performs the actions which are called for on particular occasions. Explicit statements or illustrations of personal qualities are usually unacceptable. They can be criticized as boasting or coming on.

However, the control of style leading to the attribution of character, however effective, takes time, so that to be seen to have authority or strength of character, or to be weak and easily led, excitable or withdrawn, are reputations which may take months or even years to achieve. But the practical purposes of society require certain people to be seen to have personal characteristics such as authority, sympathy, or wisdom directly and immediately. The solution to this practical problem is found in the use of regalia, uniforms, and so on, where the regalia suggest a specific character by framing and determining the persona that can be presented. A glance at the uniforms of the police of various nations is enough to establish the point, but priests and professors, radicals and air line stewardesses are all dependent on the same device. In accordance with the dramaturgical framework I shall call this 'costume'.

The most general form of regalia is clothes, illustrating and commenting upon the body, which they emphasize by concealing. This point has been made most elegantly in the following passage from *The Ogre of Kaltenborg*:

> I observed eagerly how their personalities altered with each [costume]. It is not that they came through the clothes as a voice does through a wall, more or less distinctly, according to the thickness. No – each time a new version of their personality is put forward, altogether new and unexpected, but as complete as the previous one, as complete as nakedness, it is like a poem translated into one language after another which never loses any of its magic but each time puts on new and surprising charms. On the most trivial level, clothes are so many keys to the human body. At that degree of indistinctness key and grid are more or less the same. Clothes are keys because they are *carried* by the body, but they are related to the grid because they cover the body, sometimes entirely like a translation *in extenso* or a long-winded commentary that takes up more room than the text, but they are merely a prosaic gloss, garulous and trivial, without emblematic significance.
>
> More even than a key or a grid, a garment is a *framing*. The face is framed and thus commented on and interpreted by the hat above and the collar below. Arms alter according to whether sleeves are long or short, close-fitting or loose, or whether there aren't any sleeves at all. A short, tight sleeve follows the shape of the arm, brings out the contours of the biceps, the soft swelling of the triceps, the plump roundness of the

shoulder, but without any attempt to please, without any invitation to touch. A loose sleeve hides the roundness of the arm and makes it seem slimmer, but its welcoming ampleness invokes a caress which will take possession of the arm and go right up the shoulder if need be. Shorts and socks frame the knee and interpret it differently according to how low the first come and how high the second.

A socially symbolic object, like any other symbol, is partly defined by syntagmatic relationships with all the possible structures into which it might fit without loss of intelligibility. Sometimes these relationships may be very narrow. For example, roundlensed steel-rimmed spectacles cannot be replaced by any other form of spectacles, say *pince-nez* or horn-rims in a sartorial context defined by Afro-hair, Indian beads and flared jeans, without loss of intelligibility. So the paradigmatic dimension of round-lensed steel-rimmed spectacles is severely restricted. Equally we cannot insert round-lensed steel-rimmed spectacles into the context defined by low-cut shiny black shoes, white shirt, blue tie, grey suit, without loss of intelligibility. 'Just what sort of guy is that?' (Wolfe, 1968) But we can insert either *pince-nez* or horn-rims in the latter context, while horn-rims, though not *pince-nez*, can go into the context, suede desert boots, cavalry twill trousers, viyella shirts and knitted tie, and thick medium-length dark or black hair. Thus syntactically, round-lensed steel-rimmed spectacles are also very circumscribed, which horn-rims have a broader syntagmatic dimension.

Secondly, many symbolic objects do not have a meaning in isolation from their opposites. They mean only as contrasting pairs of symbols. Hair length has once again, in recent times, come into use as a social and political symbol. Historically it has not been the length as such, but the long/short contrast that has had political significance, that is the semantic unit 'long hair' is embedded in the structure 'long/short'. This explains how 'short hair' could be radical in 1640 and 1780, and reactionary in 1965. This example illustrates the way something which may appear at first sight to be a semantic unit in itself is, on more careful analysis, seen to be significant only as a member of a pair. Long hair is currently (or more accurately, was recently) used as part of a heraldic display manifesting a symbol for a radical political orientation. This went with round-lensed, steel-rimmed spectacles, flowing clothes and the like. the semantic unit comprised by the hair length is, for this total object, a diachronic entity '– as opposed to –' which is an opposition over time, that is long hair is worn, not just in opposition to the short hair of the squares, but as opposed in time to short, that is 'long, formerly short'. And of course either length can be a realization of either formula of opposition, the synchronic or the diachronic. The same explanation is available for the apparent contradiction between the role of a brassière as a radical garment in the late nineteenth century and its discarding by certain radical women in the sixties. It was both in synchronic relation to those who continued to wear it, and in diachronic relation to the previous state of the radicals. And in some lexicons it has a meaning in itself, as a way of emphasizing basic femaleness, and of course, in its absence inhibiting physical actions which are deemed proper to the male, such as running or chopping wood.

However, as a general principle the basic form 'x as opposed to y' has no particular temporal order built into it. One could choose an instantiation of the relation now, in anticipation of the appearance of its contrary later. Though peculiarly appropriate to radical heraldry the basic form 'x as opposed to y' has been a very common form for the conveying of social meaning. For example, women have used the up/down contrast in hair style for expressing socio-sexual status, for example to put up the hair showed that childhood had ended and that the woman was marriageable. In a somewhat similar way the contrast clean-shaven/bearded expressed social distinctions amongst the Romans. In early days slaves were clean-shaven and their masters bearded, but in the reign of Hadrian a technological revolution in shaving techniques brought by Sicilian barbers to Rome made shaving much less disagreeable, with the consequence that Hadrian decreed that slaves be bearded, now that their masters were not.

However, as Cooper (1971) has pointed out, both long hair and beards have had a persistent standard meaning despite their frequent appearance as members of contrasting pairs. Long hair has generally been associated with romanticism, femininity and so on, while beards have usually been associated with intellectual and moral status as opposed to political, but *if* political, with conservatism, with the authoritarian father and the like.

The design of people then forms a very striking feature of the person as social actor. It is clear that such heraldic matters as hair-length and type of eye-decoration are parts of a more complex structure, the whole ensemble including clothes and shoes, and ways of walking and holding the arms, and so on. In the American West 'cowboy' is done by some cowhands even in their Sunday suits. It is predominantly marked by a way of walking.

But far the most important structural element in the design of people is clothes. There have been one or two inconclusive studies relating skirt lengths to economic factors, but they have paid little attention to the expressive features even of such correlations, if they could be established. In this chapter I can only draw attention to two features of the clothes in person design, basing my remarks on little more than impressionistic evidence.

The first point to remark about clothes as structured entities concerns their role in socially marking sexual differences, so that one can tell at a glance whether one is going to meet a member of the opposite sex, of the same sex, or a homosexual. Traditionally these have been marked by differential markers in all three possible modes, primary, secondary or tertiary differentia. By primary differentia I mean anatomical differentia based upon genitalia; by secondary I mean anatomical differentia, such as relative hairiness, bone formation, general outline of the limbs, face and so on; and by tertiary differentia I mean markings by different forms of clothes, or by differential regalia, such as different forms of decoration as among the Australian Aboriginals, or by such matters as the length of hair. In societies where 'unisex' fashions in the basic structure of clothing are predominant, such as among Western University students, or in the Muslim world, recourse may have to be made to secondary or primary differentia. Muslim men and women are differentiated by subtle stylistic differences in their *shalwa* and *kemis*, and by the use by women of various forms of face concealment, elaborations on a tertiary theme. Students generally have had recourse to both secondary and primary differentia. When the current fashion was for long hair in both sexes it was accompanied by the growth of beards amongst men, marking them off at a glance. There are, of course, certain surviving subtle modifications of the 'unisex' style so that some tertiary differentia do remain. But in general social marking is by secondary or primary characteristics. The survival of these markers through the transition to different forms of clothing discloses what I should like to identify as a 'social universal' or 'equilibrating principle' that requires that certain differentia be preserved through formal transformations. The way such principles are recognized, learned and promulgated is a much neglected branch of social psychology. Finally one should remark that the contrast heterosexual/homosexual, which *a fortiori* is incapable of being marked by primary or secondary differentia, is usually presented in both sexes by modifications of the basic form of the biologically appropriate clothing and regalia so that they are styled in the predominant stylistic mode of the sex with which the homosexual is identifying. Thus women might continue to wear jacket and skirt, but have them made in mannish materials and styled in a mannish way. The point may be underlined by the choice of accessories from the repertoire of the opposite sex, such as a handbag by a homosexual, and a collar and tie by a lesbian. By these public displays the differentia are the markers of the social dichotomies that go with various socio-sexual categories.

But there are some structural differences in clothing which are manifestly but mysteriously related to the expression of social matters. So far as I can tell, so little is known about these phenomena that I can do little but describe them. Both men's and women's clothing is modified diachronically along a number of dimensions, long/short, loose/tight, what I can only call 'apex up'/'apex down', elaborated/nonelaborated, and there are no doubt others. To illustrate, the 'zoot suit' of the nineteen forties had a very long jacket, while the predominant jacket length in the fifties and early sixties was short. Trousers, which were tight in the Edwardian period, were styled in a loose manner up until the late fifties. In the forties and fifties men's clothes were designed as a triangle with the apex down, wide shoulders and narrow hips, but the introduction of flared jackets and trousers created a silhouette with apex up. And of course elaboration with more buttons, waist coats with lapels, turnups and so on, has come and gone. I would like to put these changes to the social scientist as problematic, through and through, both as to their genesis and their spread through the population of clothes. I believe that in the iconography of clothing there is a ready-made model for all forms of social change, and recommend it for the closest possible study, relatively neglected as it has been hitherto.

KEY CHANGE: ACTORS IN RELATION
TO THE ACTION

Subtle differences in the musical meaning of a melody can be discerned when it is presented in one key rather than another, particularly if the key change is from major to minor. Goffman's (1974) metaphor of the social psychological 'key' draws our attention to the not-so-subtle differences that exist between the way a stage actor is related to his or her portrayal of a simulacrum of some slice of life and the way a person engaged in daily living of the 'same' slice of life is related to their actions. We could express the contrast as that between playing the melody in the 'dramaturgical key' and playing it in the 'reality key'.

What is the difference between play-acting a quarrel and quarrelling? Between play-acting the signing of a contract and really signing one? It cannot be in any of the actions performed. They may be qualitatively identical. The example of the contract gives us a clue. The difference seems to be a matter of commitment. It is not anything in what is done. That is, the difference does not lie in the action. The whole of the difference must reside in the act, since it is by acts that we are committed. The play acting does not create acts. What is done on the stage has no illocutionary force, outside the boundaries of the play itself. The actors know this of course, so therein, I propose, we see the distinction between the seriousness of everyday life and the 'frivolity' of the stage. Those who treat everyday life like a stage play are importing just that feature, namely that their actions have no force as acts, and hence their performance involves no commitments.

Taking an action seriously, in the 'reality key', is to take myself as committed, and this is to take the future of the relationships forged and reforged in the episodes of everyday life, as preempted by the acts jointly performed by the relevant parties to an episode. A making and accepting of a proposal of marriage by the actors on the stage is not expected by either actors or audience to eventuate in a marriage. Why? It can only be because the act-force of the actions is contextually relative. There is a Burkian 'ratio' between scenes and acts.

It follows that the exposition of the rules and conventions of how social life is to be done is not a complete social psychology. It falls short by the crucial issue of commitment. And yet the discovery of the rules and conventions, through which the correctness and propriety of life events is sustained is an essential part of any social psychology.

It remains to remark here that a key change is a change in how things are taken. What does that amount to psychologically? An act of commitment must involve at least the acquisition of some beliefs. Since beliefs are dispositions, acts of commitment involve changes in the dispositions of an actor, as one of the parties to the joint creation of a commitment. The beliefs involved are tied in with and possibly constitutive of attitudes. Again we find ourselves confronting the psychological phenomenon of dispositions. Since attitudes are interactively displayed, and in real cases, drawn from a repertoire of possible attitude displays, acts of commitment must be understood contextually. Much remains to be worked out both conceptually and empirically before an adequate account of the psychology of commitment as a discursive practice is fully understood.

A THIRD MODEL: SOCIAL ACTIVITY AS WORK

A third source-model for the development of analytical and explanatory concepts for act-action episodes is work. I do not propose to deal with this source model in the same detail as the expressive models, since I believe its usefulness to be limited because of the historical rarity of societies in which work, in the sense of the production of the means of life, is the dominant activity. Nevertheless even as a metaphor it throws a useful, oblique light on much that is otherwise obscure.

The abstract form of a 'work' theory

To use a source model to generate concepts, that model must be carefully articulated. The 'work' model seems to me to be naturally separable into two parts, the form of the work-activity and the form of the work-organization.

In general work-activity has to be conceived teleologically in that every form of work has a characteristic product, and the form the work takes is determined by the form of the product and the properties of the medium in which it is realized.

But work is not done with bare hands on a medium found lying about in nature. Both the tools and the work-medium ('raw' material) are already the products of the work of others. Work transforms products by using products to create products. At each stage the producer and the product must be separated for the further transformation and utilization of it by others to proceed. And here is the basic alienation of product from producer, appearing as a necessary consequence of the conditions of work. Bhaskar (1978) has made a useful adaptation of this structure of activities to develop a theory of science as a form of work.

In theory each phase of the process described above could be performed by the same person who could live off the results of exchanging the final product for the final products of others. In practice this form of production is soon superseded by that division of labour which was assumed in defining the simplest form of alienation. Marx, as I understand him, argued that the form of work-organization derived from the form of production – but that seems to be far from universally true. The form of production must be combined with the expressive principles currently available in a society, to define the form of work-organization in detail. For example the sense of dignity and the respect demanded by crafts-workers in many industries forces on the factory a form of work-organization that is far from maximizing the efficiency of the production of the end product. One can understand the way work is organized only by looking at the interactions between the expressive and the practical systems.

Production distinguished by products

The products of social activity are concrete material things on the one hand and reputations, characters, socially and psychologically existing products on the other. We can generalize the production-work theory to include the necessities of the production of reputations and the symbolic devices necessary to represent them. Then this can be formally represented through the use of the idea of symbolic credit. Just as a study of the way work develops requires the concepts of production, the means of production, appropriation of the products of the past, and the alienation of the producer from the product, so an analogous structure could be looked for in the production of expressive products, such as reputations. How do we produce the means for the production of reputations? How do we define the hazards necessary for moral careers? How do we appropriate and change the reputations and reputation creating 'tools' of the past? How far can we tolerate the detachment of our public reputations into an independent expressive order in the control of which we have little influence? The invention of an alternative expressive world by such as football fans or madmen is a possible solution.

The work model is a concrete formulation of the general teleological principle that informs the whole of this study, namely that social behaviour is to be conceived as deliberate action directed towards certain ends. By including social-expressive ends as among the main products of social activity the work model and the general picture of social action converge.

THE REPRESENTATION OF ORDER: ROLES AND RULES

'Rule' as a descriptive and as an explanatory concept

The upshot of the application of the methods of enquiry sketched in Part One and of the use of the models adumbrated in Part Two can be expressed in the form of sets of rules. This is a natural way of writing out a description of the norms that seem to be adhered to by some cultural group, in their daily activities. The task of the social psychologist, as we see it, is the explicit presentation of the tacit knowledge of a group of people. Or to express the point another way, social psychologists look at the world of social interactions in the 'dramaturgical key', while for most of our lives and for most people life is lived with others in the 'reality key'. We find it natural to express what we think we know about the normative conventions of a society as sets of rules. But there are some misunderstandings to which this procedure is particularly liable.

It is tempting to think that if these are the rules, then orderly slices of life are produced by following them. This is the picture that springs to mind when we think of ceremonies and other formal episodes. Indeed, in such cases as the conferment of military honours, the participants may be consciously following explicit rules. But 'conformity to rule' may have a quite different interpretation. We can draw on Wittgenstein's (1953) insights into the matter. He devoted considerable effort to clarifying the role of rules in all sorts of human activities, including calculating. To put the matter bluntly should we take it that rules are the causes, or among the causes, of orderly behaviour? Or should we say that the only active entities in the human world are people, who use rules for a variety of purposes? Wittgenstein argued, through the use of a great many examples, that only the latter view made sense. In outline his argument is very simple. If rules were the causes of behaviour then they would, so to say, fix the future. He imagined a boy being taught to do arithmetic. Adding is a skill, or even a habit. After using the 'add 2' rule to create the set of even numbers as far as 1000, the boy then goes on '1004', '1008' and so on. Of course that is a way of using the 'add 2' rule! But not the way the teacher meant. If the rule were causing the boy's answers then *ceteris paribus* he could not offer those as correct answers. It is not that we are never sure what rule we are using. Rather there is always the question of how we are to apply the rule. Any rule could be applied in countless ways. As Wittgenstein points out there could not be an infinite regress of rules for applying rules for applying rules. We could never act at all if that were so. People use rules, rules do not use people.

The conclusion we must hold on to is that the job of the psychologist is to describe the ways that people do indeed use rules. These range from the use of explicit rules by the actors in formal episodes as templates for action, to the use of a 'rule' metaphor by psychologists to describe the orderly behaviour of pedestrians in the street. Included in this spectrum there is the important case of the use of rules to remind, instruct and admonish people about what they should or could be expected to do. Given this diversity the opportunities for confusion are many.

As a concept for social psychology 'rule' and its natural partner 'role' are terms of art. The 'rules' that social psychologists assemble are of essentially the same status as those that people use to comment on the behaviour of others and to instruct them in proper conduct. We can say that in order to behave consistently with one another people must have tacit knowledge of the rules. But that is not to be taken as an invitation to imagine a hidden information processing mechanism programmed with these rules and causing people to behave in an orderly fashion. Once again one must remind oneself that while the question 'What caused X to exhale violently?' is a proper scientific question, with a proper procedure for finding an answer, the further question 'What caused X to blow his/her whistle?' may have no proper answer. 'Referees should blow their whistles when a player is offside' is not a causal law. Where the citation of rules is germane to understanding what is happening it is best to say that the dichotomy 'caused/not caused' does not apply. If we express these insights in the form of the statement 'rules do not cause behaviour' it sounds as if the statement 'rules do cause behaviour' makes sense and just happens to be false on the whole. The point is rather that these statements do not make sense. They are an illegitimate mix of incompatible concepts.

Recording the rules

Whether we think a rule has application depends very much on the situation we believe to obtain. This is obvious in games. The offside rule of rugby does not have application in American football. Rule citation presupposes situation recognition. From a psychological point of view the latter requires tacit knowledge of a typology or typologies of situations and criteria for applying them. Exactly the same epistemological and methodological considerations apply to situations as apply to rules. Situation recognition is something *people* do, not something that is done for them by a bit of inner machinery. It follows from these considerations that in expressing what a psychologist might discover about the maintenance of social order rule sets must be presented as clustered around situation types. Rules for self-presentation, for the display of the proper persona or personal style, go along with rules for action, and they too are situation specific. In Japanese, persona presentation involves linguistic styles more overtly even than it does in English. Finally research by Hargreaves (1967) and others has shown that propriety of action is tested out by an actor as much by taking notice of the reactions of other people as by reference to explicit rules, whether the actor's own or as cited by a bystander. We might call this 'other', the arbiter.

The structure of tacit knowledge can be presented as follows:

situation 1,	situation 2,	and so on
{rules 1}	{rules 2}	etc.
persona 1	persona 2	etc.
arbiter 1	arbiter 2	etc.

'Role' is as polysemous a concept as 'rule' and as diverse in its application. It does however have a use for us, in that we can compendiously sum up that part of a rule-set and the associated conventions of persona presentation that seems to be an expression of a coherent way of acting adopted by a particular person as a 'role'.

Classifying the rules

There are a number of well-known classificatory schemes for rules that can be used to advantage in this context. There are rules which fix the boundaries of activities, defining them as such. These have usually been called 'constitutive rules'. There are unproblematic examples of such rules used in defining formal episodes, such as the number of players required to field two football teams. Then there are 'regulative rules', those ordinances which are used to regulate the activities in such episodes, such as the 'offside' rule. Then, for agonistic episodes the constitutive and regulative rules for which leave room for more than one outcome, there are tactical and strategic maxims, with which players can regulate their play.

It should be clear by now that the best metaphor for understanding how rules work in social life is that of the instrument or tool. This is a far cry from rule as cause. People use rules in much the same way as they use other devices for ensuring regularities. A straight edge is used by a carpenter to ensure that his saw cut is correct. It is one amongst the tools, which include the saw, the pencil and so on, each having its own proper role in the activity of sawing a plank correctly, that is according to the intent of the carpenter. Only the straight edge is used to ensure a correct line. Rules are among the tools we use for the creation of orderly forms of life.

A rather different way of classifying rules is by reference to their modality. There are rules which are mandatory in requiring that something be done for there to be declared to have been a correct procedure or outcome. There are also mandatory rules which are used to exclude or forbid certain activities. Then there are permissive rules, which neither enjoin nor forbid an activity. Again it is useful to think of these categories as picking out groups of tools used for different purposes. It is also worth remarking that whatever it is that is enjoined, forbidden or permitted by rules must be possible for persons of the kind to whom it is a rule.

There are a number of dimensions along which the impossible – possible polarity might be drawn. Physical possibility is an obvious but rather uninteresting one, except in so far as the way the distinction between the possible and the impossible is drawn among activities depends very much on the state of technology at the time. The interesting cases for social psychologists must be those in which the possibilities are psychological, that is conceptual and cultural. Can people who deploy this set of beliefs, and make use of this range of character types, do this and that kind of thing? This was the question posed by the Frankfurt school with the concept of the 'authoritarian personality' and challenged by Milgram (1974) with the idea of a generic willingness to submit to authority.

PART III

Individual Lives and Social Change

INTRODUCTION: INDIVIDUAL LIVES AND SOCIAL CHANGE

Much of recent social psychology has been focused on small-scale interactions within strictly limited social contexts. These contexts have been limited in cultural variety and in temporal span. If there really were the same abstract general central information processing mechanism (c.p.m.) behind all the teeming variety of overtly distinctive interpersonal modes of interaction the neglect of cultural and historical diversity would make perfect sense. This assumption is nowhere made explicitly but is everywhere evident. Once the assumption of the existence of this alleged ubiquitous mechanism is queried, then even to establish that it does exist, the cultural and historical variety of forms of human interaction will need to be explored. But not by the method long favoured by the majority of cross-cultural psychologists, which is to assume the existence of the c.p.m., and then carry on as before!

I do not believe that abstract information processing mechanisms exist anywhere or have ever existed at any time. There are numberless forms of discursive practice in which human psychology is immanent. In surview they seem to be linked into loose clusters by a network of likenesses and differences. Perhaps Wittgenstein's famous image of an array of family resemblances could be borrowed to try to express the way that the many and diverse discursive practices performed by human beings are related to one another. However I do believe that however various they may be they are employed about a common business. Coordinated action is necessary to the maintenance of life itself. In so far as this is a matter for social psychologists I have called this the 'practical order'. Overlaying it for most of human history and in most human societies of which we have any record, there is another order, the 'expressive order, the creation and maintenance of interpersonal standing as beings of value. A number of recent studies, of which the most famous are Tannen (1991) and Gilligan (1984) have tended to show that just as there were two practical orders in traditional society, one dominated by women and the other by men, so there are two gender-specific expressive orders in contemporary Western society. For men the basic structure appears in hegemonic relations of hierarchies of value. For women the basic structure involves mutual recognition and mutual affirmation of a network of sororal relations. We shall see that they are variously emphasized and differently related in different societies. They can be used to rank social systems in a spectrum depending on the degree to which each pole is dominant in the motivations of the members.

I shall try to show that the long-term patterns of individual human lives are shaped by the interplay between the local forms of practical and expressive orders. In the chapter on individual lives I borrow heavily from the writings of Erving Goffman. Much of life course psychology has been mired in the methodological problems of cohort analysis, and has notably lacked a theoretical framework within which psychological aspects of life structures can be described.

I think it fair to say that no general psychology of social change has been developed so far. This is partly because of the all-pervading influence of the idea that in essence nothing of psychological interest could really change. The topic of social change would be reserved for sociologists and for historians. From the point of view of the psychology of the c.p.m. the same processes must be assumed to underlie social life wherever and whenever it is lived. But if we have abandonded the metaphysics of transcendental information processing, along with other mythical forms of the diaphanous homunculi of the Cartesian tradition, in favour of the idea that there are human agents endeavouring to act in accordance with local systems of rules and norms, and achieving this generic concordance in all sorts of ways, the problem of the explanation of social change becomes acute. Again I shall be drawing on the interplay and tensions between practical and expressive orders to explain how new rule systems come into being, and spread or fail to spread through communities changing them *psychologically* for ever. Arithmetic and democracy are not just devices for calculating the answers to sums and deciding on which candidate shall be chief. They are transformations of the human mind.

Finally one must turn one's attention to the psychology of efforts to manage social change, that is to the psychology of political activity. I am happy to reprint the final chapter virtually as it was first written in 1976, though it did not see print until 1979. The analysis of the social psychology of the politics of the left in terms of the ever-shifting balance between practical and expressive motivations, that I presented there, led to the conclusion that bureaucratic socialism must inevitably decay. The events of the last three years have been a satisfying vindication of the analysis.

7

PRACTICAL AND EXPRESSIVE ORDERS

ANTICIPATORY SUMMARY

The dynamical theory upon which this whole work depends is built around the claim that the social life of every human society displays both practical and expressive aspects, as these have been defined in Chapter 1. The balance between the attention paid to the creation of these 'orders' in the everyday encounters of the folk of particular cultures and epochs will depend on a variety of contingencies, the most important of which are the material conditions of life – just how much effort must be put into the task of maintaining life itself. (Even here there are complications since the value that people give to life itself may depend on the local expressive order.) Should these conditions prove life-threatening and upset an environmental equilibrium already established (such as that which existed in North America prior to the European settlements) practical considerations are likely to come to the fore. In such circumstances the most pressing problems calling for ritualized solutions, such as how the division of labour is to be managed among the folk, are likely to be tied to the practical exigencies of life. In these circumstances the practical order will appear to be the dominant organizing structure in that form of life. But I believe these conditions are rarely encountered by human beings, and rarely maintained for long periods. In most times and places the expressive order is likely to be the dominant aspect of the local form of life. In this chapter I describe a number of examples to illustrate the variety of forms that expressive orders can take and the different degrees to which expressive and practical matters are central at different times and places and under different conditions of life.

LIVES OF HONOUR: CULTURES IN WHICH THE EXPRESSIVE ORDER IS ABSOLUTELY DOMINANT

The Trobriand Islanders

The Trobriand Islanders have passed into anthropological folk lore as the almost mythical locus of the true origins of social anthropology. But besides their mythopoeic standing they live in ways irresistibly exemplary for the theory of society, for they still live a life bounded by and founded upon honour. Their sense of honour is bound up with material things but depends upon a relation to them that is utterly unlike that which appears in the European obsessions with the gathering and the keeping of property. Trobriand honour comes from giving one's 'property' away. In 1922 Malinowski discovered the Kula Ring, an astonishing institution I shall be describing below. But as recently as 1971 Annette Weiner came across a system of exchanges as unconnected with the 'means of life' as the *Kula* and as central to Trobriand lives. While Malinowski's discovery was made among the lives of men, Weiner's was focussed in the life-cycle rituals conducted by women.

To illustrate the separation of work between the practical and expressive orders of Trobriand society consider the cultivation of yams. Relatively small gardens will provide an adequate basic subsistence. But many more yams are grown, and in specially tended gardens. Why? The giving away (not the exchange in our sense) of large numbers of yams is the very stuff of which honour is made. The ability to engage in munificence is publicly illustrated by the size of the yam house built beside one's dwelling. Only rarely are such yams brought down into the practical order as mere food. Their distinctiveness already appears in the way they are produced. Domestic, subsistence gardens are cultivated without the aid of the magic which is reserved for the much larger gardens where prestige yams are grown.

The economy of these people is dominated then by the production of objects for the game of honour. The means of life almost take care of themselves. A very similar phenomenon occurs in Japan in the system of reciprocal gift exchange. In general one does not use the gift one obtains but carefully evaluates its price against an outstanding social obligation and passes it on (Morsbach, 1977).

Trobriand society has evolved two fairly independent systems for the genesis of honour by munificence – the Kula Ring and the *Dala* ceremonials. The former is a system managed by men, the latter by women – though men are also deeply involved.

The *Kula* consists of two cycles of exchange, one in which white shell armbands are the material focus, and the other based upon red shell necklaces. These objects have no exchange value outside the ring of *Kula* objects themselves. Like authorship of a scientific paper their value is transformable only into symbolic credit in the structure of hierarchies of respect and contempt. The cycles move in opposite directions so each member of a Kula partnership exchanges a different category of object with his partner. If my obligation is to give you necklaces yours is to give me armbands. The geographical diameter of the cycles of exchange are immense, involving hundreds of islands and long sea passages.

Possession, though it is a necessary condition for the creation of honour, is not ownership. Every named *Kula* object must eventually be exchanged. Honour accrues from the giving up of possession, of once having had such and such an item. One boasts not so much of what one has now, but of what one has munificently passed along. But that munificence is self-interested. It puts an obligation on the receiver to provide an object of equal reputation. When he receives this the original giver gets yet more symbolic capital since he can now pass that object along in the other direction. His fame and glory increases with each such transaction.

A lesser form of valuable is also exchanged. Minor objects are used to maintain a link when an obligation cannot be fulfilled through the lack of something of adequate reputation to pass along. Such items are constantly being appropriated for personal use, cut up or otherwise disposed of. But that could never be the fate of a genuine Kula object.

The holder of a famous item will gain glory by relinquishing it, but he illustrates the value of the item by the difficulties he raises when asked to give it up. The object itself is supposed to have preferences in these matters. It can be the victim of standard love magic. Weiner quotes a Trobriander as saying, 'Remember, a Kula shell is like a young girl; she looks over every man until she decides which one she likes best. One man is chosen and the others are sent away.'

Malinowski describes the result of a successful *Kula* expedition as follows:

> The temporary ownership [Malinowski's rather misleading expression] allows him to draw a great deal of renown, to exhibit his article, to tell how he obtained it, and to plan to whom he is going to give it. And all this forms one of the favourite subjects of tribal conversation and gossip, in which the feats and the glory in Kula, of chiefs and commoners, are constantly discussed and rediscussed. (Malinowski, 1922:94)

Dala is the substantial basis of cosmic continuity of local geographically based groups. At conception a spirit child derived from an ancestral being (*baloma*) enters the woman's body. The child that is eventually born thus 'has' *dala*, but this *dala* may be cultivated and augmented by certain practices. *Dala* becomes objectified in property, which, though material, is more ephemeral than *dala* spirit. Funeral ceremonies, at the other pole of the life cycle, must be complementarily concerned with the disposal of *dala*. And this is the women's ceremonial preserve.

The mortuary ceremony, in which *dala* is disposed, is like *Kula*, an occasion for acquisition of personal renown by munificent distribution of 'property', valued not for its use, nor for its exchangeability for articles of use, for it has none. It is valued only for the opportunity its temporary holding provides for divesting oneself of it. Women deal in skirts and skirt materials, but so bundled as to have no use value in the making of skirts. These are given away to specific categories of other people in ways parallel to the way men deal in necklaces, armbands and yams.

Trobriand exchange objects, unlike Western money, cannot be detached from the human experience of regeneration and immortality. They are not alienated from the basic concerns of society, and therefore social relations are not merely relations between impersonal things in Marx's terms, but human relations that reify the cyclicity of life, death and rebirth. Thus, Trobriand women and men, exemplified in the objects they exchange, perceive the value of each other through the interface of the value of human beings and the value of regenesis. (Weiner, 1976:218)

Another system of honour: Sudan

Traditionally the Sudanese live according to an expressive order as dominated by honour as that lived by the Trobrianders, but the basis of honour and the means of its preservation are very different. The dynamics of the system can be understood through the explication of four concepts: *ird*, *sharaf*, *karāma*, and *ihttiram*.

According to a detailed account by Nordenstam (1968) the focus of the expressive order is the public character of the women of a family who are expected to be virtuous in all their actions, particularly with respect to sexual matters. Virtuous action leads to the having of the abstract quality of *ird*, or decency. By protecting the quality of the women of the family the male Sudanese protects his honour.

That which a man protects by the moral defence of his family is *sharaf*. It is a quality which everybody except a slave has by nature, though it is a relational attribute, devolving on to a man by virtue of the *ird* of his family. It can be the property of a collective. It does not have to be achieved like our 'character', since everyone is born with it.

Though it cannot be augmented it can be lost, and once lost cannot be re-acquired. Nordenstam suggests that the nearest English equivalent is 'honour'.

But while *sharaf* is the abstract property which one has by virtue of *ird*, it is, as it were, invisible. Its expressive counterpart is *karāma*. Again it is something which is given in full and cannot be augmented. But it can be lost, either directly or by virtue of a decline in the family honour. It is realized as an expressive property both in individual and in collective form. Nordenstam suggests the former should be equated with 'personal dignity'. A family as well as an individual can possess it. The fact that it is an expressive property lays it open to two kinds of derogation. It can be lost by the improper conduct of the one who has *karāma*, or it can be lost by improper treatment meted out to one by others by humiliation or insult.

Interestingly it seems that *karāma* is poised between the expressive aspect of the presentation of selves and the impressions which that presentation makes on others. For instance, the effect on *karāma* of one's own improper actions is always mediated through the attitudes of others to those actions. It has then much in common with what Goffman calls 'character', rather than the ordinary property of dignity.

But for the argumentative purposes of this chapter the most important attribute of *karāma* is its absolute independence from social or economic status. Everyone has *karāma* and has it in full unless by his own folly or by his failure to deal with humiliations heaped upon him by others, he loses it. The acquisition of wealth or property cannot augment one's *karāma*. The only differentiation between men is in the importance attached to the actions by which it might be lost. Thus the pecadilloes of very young men do not count in comparison with the shame a similar action might bring to an older man. There is a sense of 'He should have known better' that qualifies the effect on *karāma* of unbecoming behaviour.

Reciprocal behaviour from others to recognize and thus confirm one's *karāma* is collectively called *ihttiram*, roughly representable as the showing of respect. It appears in a mixture of rituals of deference, actual consideration and good manners. Upon these attributes and upon these alone the Sudanese erect an expressive order, and through them, and exclusively through them, do they value one another.

MIXED CULTURES

The examples so far developed are of societies whose practices are not only dominated by the expressive order and its necessities, but where the economic and practical order are not even represented in the expressive order. That degree of independence is rare. The next range of cases will illustrate progressively more intimate relations between the orders.

Maoris

The practical order serves the needs of the expressive order. Munificence was amongst the virtues most highly prized by the Maoris. It formed part of a complex system of social concepts grounded in a psychological theory of the structure of human beings.

Each person was supposed to be powered by two interacting principles. One, *wairua*, animated the individual and was the efficient cause of their actions. The other, *hau*, controlled moral attitudes and was a kind of repository and a source of virtue. They were each capable of a kind of disembodied but earthly existence. The one might be called the vital force, and the other the soul. Social relations both depended on and engendered accumulations of another principle, *mana*. This principle was not only the source of power in war, or debate, it was also an attribute of the things associated with people who had *mana*. It could be a collective property of families, clans and tribes.

Older commentators, particularly Elsdon Best (1922), have spoken of the Maori social order as if there were no economic differentiation within it at all. Best speaks of the Maoris as having a communistic society, as if all property were held in common. While this seems to have been true of land, it would be better to say that the very idea that the land was 'property' is misleading. It was not so much property held in common as the very being of the tribe, who were deeply associated with it in every way. Other things, such as weapons, clothes and the like were sharply individually differentiated as private property. Cutting through this was the relation of the chief to the food surplus. At first sight it might be thought that since he had disposal of that surplus within the constraints of the democratic debating that accompanied all chiefly decision-making, it ought to have been regarded as his property, at the very most something held in trust for the tribe. But this it seems would be to misrepresent the matter. Munificence enters into our analysis.

To demonstrate munificence, tribes, or sometimes lesser groupings such as the family based clan, the *hapu*, gave extravagant feasts, *hurangi*, involving not only an extraordinary distribution of food at formal dinners, but the construction of enormous wooden pyramidal structures upon which the feasting occurred. Everything was done to amplify the glory of the occasion. But though it was the chief who, as it were, executively set in motion the preparation, and under whose authority the tribal surplus was so expended, it seems that the glory accrued not only to him, but to the *iwi*, the *hapu*, or whatever social unit could readily be identified with the affair.

I remain unclear from the ethnography as to whether the *hurangis* led to increase of *mana*, or whether munificence is an outward expression, an expressive illustration of the *mana* belonging both to the tribe and to the chief. His *mana* in part glorifies the tribe, in part is created by the *mana* of that tribe itself. But much of *mana* does seem to be personal and particular. It is an attribute of places, things and people, but as they are distinct individuals.

Honour in the Pueblo

In small towns in rural Spain a social order with a very high expressive content still flourishes. But unlike the Maori culture of pre-European New Zealand the expressive order and the practical order which is determined by the control of land, water and the resources flowing from them, cross cut one another in the genesis of the forms of daily life.

From the point of view of the expressive order all Spaniards of the same sex are intrinsically as equal as Arabs; but intersecting that principle is a powerful tradition of the privileges of wealth and consequent position (Pitt-Rivers, 1954).

Here we have an expressive order based upon a conceptual relation between personal honour and maleness. All men have this attribute but they may so act as to lose it. Their failure in one way or another to maintain their standing in the table of pride is marked by a savage nicknaming system, through which the community expresses both its collective norms of proper behaviour and its judgements of how well individuals have lived up to them. But so great is the role of pride in the social psychology of rural Spaniards (and women have it too, within their own scheme of virtues) that though one knows one's nickname it is almost never used openly to one's face, since the derogatory judgement it implies would have of necessity to be resented. A detailed account of the nicknaming system can be found in Pitt-Rivers' excellent study.

The idiom of moral discourse with respect to the expressive order is as Pitt-Rivers has it 'frankly physiological'. To have masculinity is to have *'cojones'* (testicles) but to act so as to lower that pride is to be *manso* (castrated). These states are, of course, figurative rather than literal. They embody a rhetoric that reminds one strongly of the chants by which doubts are cast on the masculinity of opposing groups in the aggressive rituals of British football fans. Closely connected to manliness are *amorpropio* and *honor*, which are derivative rather than substantive virtues. The relative weight of pride in the social psychology of traditional and presently rural Spain is illustrated in the predominance it plays in such a study as *The Spaniard and the Seven Deadly Sins* (Diaz-Plaja, 1968). Where pride is linked to epigrams, proverbs, common sayings, and the many exemplary anecdotes that circulate in a society and represent its favoured stereotypes of actions and thought.

The relation of this conception of manliness as the correlative virtue of pride, the defence of that pride be it personal or familial, is obvious in the interpretation of the bull fight and of the standing of the men who take part in it. What, one might wonder, is to be made of the current appearance of a female matador? What virtue does she represent?

But defence of one's own pride is possible only in a society in which one takes care to protect the pride of others. Pitt-Rivers points out how necessary it is for the code of manners to enjoin respect for the pride of others, so public aggressiveness or insult is greatly deprecated. Quarrels do not issue in fights, not even in ritual fights. But just as in the culture of British football fans, the strength of the sanctions against actual bloodletting and the certainty of their realization by the most powerful members of the group ensure that a great deal of bravado can be safely shown. Actual insult or social criticism is practised *sotto voce* or anonymously, and behind someone's back in the invention and use of a derogatory nickname. The institution of the *cencerrada*, the anonymous singing of ribald and personally insulting songs under the cover of darkness, about those who have offended against the moral code of the pueblo, takes the place of the too dangerous play with real public cricitism. In a system based on pride this would have to be recognized and retribution taken or demanded. *Cencerrada* stands in for the duels that can never be fought, not only because one risks killing one's foe, but more importantly because one chances being humiliatingly defeated oneself.

Pitt-Rivers and others have pointed out how the social order based upon the expressive virtue of pride and its defences and support works in with the practical order based upon relative control over the means of production to modify each in essential ways. The possibility of tyranny and exploitation is muted (though hardly eliminated) by the threads of influence that ramify through the society deriving from success or failure in the expressive order. And similarly, as Pitt-Rivers demonstrates in case histories of recent events in the town, the implacable power of institutions based upon public opinion like the *cencerrada* is limited by the power and protection of the rich. Neither order is dominant, and neither determines absolutely the particular social equilibrium between masculinity and femininity that prevails from time to time.

INDETERMINACY OF THE PRACTICAL ORDER

Aztec inversion of status, the cult of the quiet man

Veblen (1899) has accustomed us to the idea that the visible representation of power and position in the economic order is to be represented by conspicuous consumption and flamboyant display. Not all societies have subscribed to this relation between class position and manners. The final step in my demonstration of the independence of the practical and the expressive orders is to show that even where they are clearly related in such a way that the expressive order is structurally determined by the practical order (and its offshoot, an aristocratic lineage based originally on economic power) the determination is not strict. Inversion may occur, for reasons that anthropologists and social psychologists have yet to explore. Soustelle's (1962) splendid ethnography of the classical Aztec civilization includes a detailed account of Aztec manners, a code in which display and overt manifestation of social power and position is inverted into a muted punctiliousness, grounded in a moral theory of service. (Again it is reminiscent of other cultures and other practices, for it has a very similar ring to the traditional code of manners and public morals of the English in the high period of the British Empire.)

The code involved two kinds of conventions: those concerned with the control of the display of feelings, and those to do with the proper humility by which real *hauteur* might best be expressed. Soustelle quotes a Codex to the effect that 'No vainglorious, presumptuous or noisy man has been chosen as a dignitary.'

Soustelle likens the presentational style favoured by the Aztec upper class to the Roman *gravitas*. Again from a Codex we get the advice that a man should present himself as 'humble and not overweening, . . . peaceable and calm.' With this demeanour went a formal code of manners involving a particularly high degree of politeness, both in address and in the practical business of life. Gentlemen were enjoined neither to 'throw themselves upon women like a dog on food', not to 'eat noisily and without care like a glutton'. In short, public presentational style was characterized by the display of the control of the normal appetites. The humility and dignity evinced was itself continuously providing proof of the claim to superiority of those to whom life's accidents had given power and position. Thus Soustelle points out that famous veterans of the wars were permitted great licence in their talk and behaviour, and one might well speculate how far this reflected a consciousness of the fact that their standing had been earned by them alone, in their proper persons so to speak, while others had inherited respect and were called upon to show themselves worthy of it. The dominant language of the Mexican plateau was rich in grammatical elaborations by which the tartness and brusqueness of questions, orders and requests could be dissolved, much as the fast disappearing subjunctive mood used to dissolve the peremptory character of requests in Spanish, or indirect constructions ('I wonder if you'd mind awfully . . .') do in current English.

Along with the code of manners went a strong sense of the obligation of the ruler to those he ruled. Indeed Soustelle is able to show that the anecdotes about a particularly admired ruler have much of the quality of those concerning Haroun al Rashid, that is an almost obsessive care for the well-being (not to say the dignity) of those ruled.

The image of the King or Caliph in disguise in the humble regalia of an ordinary man is a portrayal of the central inversion. To be truly great it is necessary to appear humble. It is another version of the Lion and the Fox of Machiavelli's fable of political power. One can appear to be a Lion only so far as one is known but never seen really to be a Fox.

If we add to this catalogue of cultures nineteenth-century industrial-ized Europe as the socialists saw it, and early twentieth-century United States as Veblen saw it, we will have completed the permutations of the possible relations of the expressive and practical orders. There are instances of societies where the orders seem to have been completely independent of one another. There are societies where, though the systems are independent as orders, nevertheless the total valuation of a person is some product of their valuation in each order. And there are societies where the orders interact with each other so intimately that we can say, without distortion, that the one determines the other. Sometimes the expressive order determines the form that subsistence work shall take. Sometimes the social structure engendered by the productive process influences the whole of the rest of the social relations of a culture. But as we have seen, the Aztecs and the Vanderbilts, archetypes of the cult of display as Veblen saw it, reflected that order in quite opposite ways.

HONOUR AND THE SOCIAL EMOTIONS

Emotional displays are best understood, not as physiological responses to stimuli, but as discursive acts, embodied moral and aesthetic judgements (Harré, 1987). A display of emotion is not only a felt (and sometimes visible) bodily perturbation, but it functions as if it had illocutionary force. An angry person is expressing resentment at someone else's transgression of their proper rights, dignity and so on. The transgression can often be a slighting of one's honour or a slur cast on one's integrity. Just what counts as such a slight or slur and just how upsetting it will be will depend on the local expressive order and one's belief about one's place in it. Sabini and Silver (1981) have shown how the emotion of malign envy arises through and expresses resentment of the conduct or possessions or personal qualities of some other person that seems to belittle or humiliate oneself.

A strong tie between expressive orders and emotions comes through too in Catherine Lutz's (1988) studies of the emotional system of the Ifaluk. In that tight little society enormous importance is given to the ritual recognition of hierarchical relations of social status. Complementary, of course, are the wide variety of ways that these relations can be violated. Displays of the socially central emotions of *metagu* (anxiety, particularly in the presence of social superiors) and *sort* (justified anger at violations of social hierarchy) express complex moral judgements of people's behaviour (one's own included) within the framework of the local expressive order.

The familiar distinction between 'shame cultures' and 'guilt cultures' can be used to identify emotion structures characteristic of expressive and practical orders. The distinctions illustrated in this chapter can be approached from a quite different direction, from a long-standing contrast in the philosophical grounding of theories of morality (Gibbard, 1990).

Two contrasting models of moral judgement can be discerned in the writings respectively of Kant and Hume. The Kantian 'picture' is of a private court of law and a process of deliberation through which a defendant (oneself) is found guilty. The magistrates of the civil courts represent the formalization of the emotion of anger, righteous resentment of transgressions, which are unsafe in the hands of ordinary persons. The Humean 'picture' is of a mocking and contemptuous crowd pouring derision on an offender who is thus publicly shamed. In the Kantian 'picture' the underlying emotional structure is anger/guilt, while for Hume it is derision (contempt)/shame. Hume's analysis of the basis of moral judgement applies perfectly to the social psychology of the expressive order. It is an honour morality. Hume's vocabulary of moral assessment (which I have drawn from Baier, 1992) includes 'honourable and shameful, lovely and odious, noble and despicable'. Contempt for the offender, not anger at the offence is the correlative emotion to a display of vice. An untrustworthy person is 'contemptible, no less than odious'.

I shall be arguing that it is to the expressive order, its honour morality and its 'Humean' cluster of emotions that one must look for an understanding of the temporal dimensions of an adequate social psychology.

Finally this anecdote from Anthony Burgess (1987) illustrates that in the most desperate straits it is the scrap of honour that finally decides the issue. 'There was a man with a cleft palate who had been fitted with an obdurator . . . The patient was to be taught to yawn . . . thus restoring mobility to the soft palate . . . My patient resisted cure . . . Any small distinction, however harmful, is precious to a man. Besides he thought his cleft palate might get him out of the army.'

8

INDIVIDUAL LIVES
AS SOCIAL TRAJECTORIES

ANTICIPATORY SUMMARY

The social psychology of individual lives involves a complementarity between a person's changing and multiple views of their own life course, their autobiographies, and the various and often contradictory views that others hold of them. In the end the life course that matters most to me is my own. My beliefs about what it has been are quite as influential in how it develops as any plans or projects I may have for the future.

An individual life is lived with others in some pattern or array of institutions and material and discursive practices, the societal framework or local 'form of life'. For analytical purposes we can begin with the (disposable) assumption that the framework is relatively stable throughout a life. This assumption is plainly a fiction for the people of recent centuries. I shall use it to set up the idea of a 'moral career'. There are many ways that a life can be viewed, but for the purposes of devising a social psychology of the life course the most fruitful is to see a life in terms of the standing one has in one's own eyes and the eyes of others, with respect to the local criteria of honour, worth and virtue. A life course is not defined just by the events of which it consists, but by the valuations of the person relative to those events. The ways life events are used in the evaluations of persons are embedded in and partly definitive of the institutions that constitute the local form of life.

Two directions of 'fit' can be discerned between lives as moral careers and the institutions that make them possible. In the one institutions are given and the lives tailored to meet their demands. But sometimes institutions are devised just so that certain kinds of lives can be lived.

The 'openings' and 'closings' of lives form complicated patterns as one's biological, psychological and social careers begin and end. The role of ritual is important in these matters, as well as the conventions setting limits to what is taken to be life course of persons. Some of these conventions are discussed in *Physical being* (1991), in relation to issues like abortion and the persistence with technical life support after all signs of psychological life have ended.

From a psychological point of view the beliefs one has about the events of one's life and the value they engender are crucial to the way one plans the future and recollects the past. This fact leads to the need for an idiographic methodology for the systematic study of autobiography, since, at the level at which beliefs about a life are significant for the person who lives it and those with whom it is lived, each life is unique and different from every other. All sorts of philosophical and methodological issues must be dealt with in the development of adequate ways of studying life courses.

LIFE AS MORAL CAREER

Our problem is to devise a conceptual system for analysing and understanding the diachronic structure of a human life as it develops in the eyes of other people and to test it against examples. It will be a system of concepts for analysing the social trajectory of a human life.

The concept of a moral career

Our analysis will be based upon Goffman's idea of a moral career. It is the social history of a person with respect to the attitudes of respect and contempt that others have to them and of their understandings of these attitudes. The attitudes are realized and represented in the institutionalized and ritualized forms in which respect and contempt are tested for and meted out, in particular societies.

A moral career is generated in the first instance by the opinions that other people form of someone from their experience of his or her success and failure in coping with occasions of hazard. An occasion of hazard is a social event in which a person can gain respect by risking contempt. For example, in the moral career that accompanies education an examination is a hazard. It can be treated as a social event, the results of which are publicly promulgated and which a candidate could fail. Respect is gained by passing and contempt is risked in failing.

In this context respect and contempt are not just the private, unexpressed opinions of others about the person, since a moral career is a life trajectory defined in terms of public esteem. The results of hazard will be publicly recognized in social rituals and conventional acts espousing respect or contempt. In reciprocal acknowledgment the moral careerist makes the appropriate response in his or her demeanour to others. By showing condescension, modesty, or whatever may be the appropriate response to the ritual recognition of success, and chagrin, apologetic humility, or whatever is called for in the face of ritualized contempt, a person shows that though they may have failed a particular test they are still a worthy human being. Noble endurance of failure may actually lead to more social credit than arrogant exploitation of success.

However, as I have emphasized in earlier sections, an essential element in the understanding of the social activities of human beings derives from their attributions to each other of permanent moral qualities. I have called this attribution 'character'. It is made up of the attributes that a particular group of people ascribe to an individual according to the impressions they have formed on the basis of that person's expressive activities. These attributes, or rather the beliefs that people have as to these attributes, determine the expectations that a group forms of a person. They are the foundations, as individual beliefs of the willingness of others to defer to, praise, denigrate or simply ignore a person. They are the ultimate basis of that person's moral career. Correlatively, individual social actors form beliefs about themselves concerning their standing in the tables of respect and contempt, that is beliefs about how they are viewed by others. Social psychologists have shown that there is a sustained difference between individuals' opinions about themselves and the views others have of them. In that difference lies part of the dynamics of social life. A moral career, then, is a history of an individual person with respect to the attitudes and beliefs that others have, and the attitudes to and beliefs about oneself that are formed on the basis of one's readings of the attitudes and beliefs of others.

The places of moral careers

Very few people live their moral careers in public space, as it were, gaining and losing character as their reputations wax and wane in the beliefs and expectations of the public at large. Most people live out their moral careers in very limited regions, socially speaking, with respect to a very limited range of other people, and involving a limited number of hazards. In general, then, moral careers are to be understood as relative to institutions, which provide the occasions for hazard. The education system can be looked on as a confederation of institutions in which the sequence of examinations and the public promulgation of their results constitutes a system of hazards sufficient to generate the possibility of moral careers.

Goffman has pointed out the equivocal character of many institutions which at first sight we would describe in an instrumental or practical rhetoric, that is we would describe activities that occur in them as means towards practical ends. For example, a hospital would be unthinkingly described as an institution in which the activities undertaken by the staff and inmates are directed towards the instrumental end of the cure of sickness. But a close examination of such institutions suggests that this rhetoric would be quite insufficient to provide a conceptual system for understanding everything which goes on, particularly those activities which have to do with reputation. In his famous study, *Asylums* (1968) Goffman points out that closed institutions which provide for many moral careers have certain very characteristic common features.

Entry into such an institution is marked by rituals of depersonalization in which in the extreme all traces of the previous moral career of an individual are wiped away. A person may even be given a new name in the course of the incorporation ritual as happens in the entry to monastic orders. A new career with new possibilities for the earning of respect and contempt then begins. In most such entry rituals there is a phase in limbo in which the individual bent on entering is reduced socially to nothing. For example, most armies subject every male recruit to a medical examination in the course of which he is required to appear naked before those who are fully dressed. Looked at sociologically, this nakedness is not just a medical convenience but a stripping off of the conventional marks of prior identity. Similar limbos occur in the examination of potential immigrants to the United States in the Consular Offices of that nation.

In order for there to be the possibility of a moral career within an asylum there must be two complementary arrangements. There must be a system of hazards in the course of which reputation can be gained or lost, and a sequential system of social places in occupying which individuals receive the marks of deference due to them for successful passage through the hazards. Goffman has pointed out that the organization of wards in mental hospitals is best understood by bringing together two conceptions, that of the course of cure and that of the moral career. The passage from one ward to another is read according to the official rhetoric in terms of mental health, but it may be read according to the unofficial rhetoric of perceived moral careers as a rise or fall in prestige, as a matter of punishment or privilege, and so on. Goffman's sociological account has been beautifully amplified in

Kesey's (1976) semi-fictional novel, *One Flew over the Cuckoo's Nest*, the tale of the epic conflict between Nurse and Mac. The story turns on Mac's attempts to gain the moral advantage of Nurse and her ultimately successful efforts to destroy him by causing him to fail at hazard.

The necessity to consider the career of an individual within an institution in accordance with both an instrumental and an expressive or moral rhetoric raises the general question of the degree to which an institution is balanced between those activities. There must be some way of maintaining a sequence of real actions as means to its official ends, against a growing tendency to perform sequences of metonymic actions, only symbolic of real activities. The latter, as we have seen, are functionally related to hazards and their outcomes, and the rituals by which consequential respect and contempt are expressed. For example, an institution may so evolve that none of its activities, even though described in terms of its official rhetoric, are actual performances of what would count as real actions in accordance with that rhetoric. The City companies of London, descendants of the medieval Guilds, call themselves Dyers, Clothworkers, Fishmongers, and so on, but their members have not dyed cloth nor mongered fish in hundreds of years. This example will serve as the occasion for the introduction of a principle which will prove to be of importance in looking at the dynamics of institutions in a later section. All other things being equal, an institution will develop in such a way that its expressive aspect – that is the apparatus for the development of moral careers – will become more and more dominant in the determination of individual action in that institution.

So far we have discussed the concept of moral career in terms of the positive engagement of the social actor in the construction of their career by actively engaging in hazards. By risking failure, he or she is able to enhance reputation. But we owe to Goffman (1968) another important concept, namely the idea of fatefulness and the correlative conception of stigmata.

A fateful action brings about a state of affairs which, if disclosed, would lead to a decline in reputation. It is a threat to moral career. For example, a graduate student who steals a book from Blackwell's Bookshop is undertaking a fateful hazard, for should it become public knowledge their reputation is seriously damaged and their moral career substantially set back.

Stigmata are fateful attributes of individuals, which they can do nothing to remove and which they cannot help but acquire. A graduate student need not steal a book, but someone born into a despised ethnic group cannot by their own actions slough off that ethnicity. Some stigmata, then, have to be managed in the interests of a moral career. The management of stigmata has been admirably described in Goffman's *Stigma* (1968). For the purpose of this work, it is sufficient to draw the reader's attention to the cases described in that book, and the details of self-management there set out.

The problem of similarities in moral careers

An examination of the structure of moral careers suggests that, in many societies, life trajectories considered with respect to the growth and decline of an individual reputation take very similar forms. What sort of explanation can be given for this fact? I shall consider two examples to illustrate two different ways in which life conformities can come to exist. In the first case there is a synchronic structure of institutions and associated hazards which can serve as a template for a diachronic structure of moments of test, in which respect or contempt can be gained. In such a case there is a way of recording the outcome of these moments in public acts and signs. Under these circumstances a moral career takes a standard form. In the other case the members of a society share a theory in accordance with which they each aim at the construction of a life form which exemplifies the most favoured life-trajectory of their society. The question as to why in a particular society there exist shared theories as to the best life trajectory, and why in others life-forms are the products of institutional structures, is susceptible only of a historical explanation.

Case 1. Ordained career

In these cases the *cursus honorum*, the diachronic life-form conceived as a career of respect, derives from a stable and structured social institution. For example, the Ottoman Turkish teaching profession, the *Ulema*, had just such a form (Repp, 1972).

Its basic structure consisted of a graded sequence of *medreses*, universities which were attached to Mosques. In the Turkish Empire the Mosques were sharply differentiated and ordered in relative prestige. This ordering was transferred to the attached *medreses*. The teaching profession was organized around the sequential occupancy of a post in each grade of *medrese* so that an aspirant rose in the learned hierarchy by moving from post to post in successive universities. The criterion for advancement was reputation – that is appointments to higher graded *medreses* were made on the basis of recommendations to the Sultan from members of the learned hierarchy. And here we see the operation of one aspect of the notion of character, as the public reputation that a scholar has with those who are high in the hierarchy of his profession. In order to understand the system, however, it is necessary to notice that it depended upon an expressive and evaluational structure which involved matters other than reputation as a learned man. To each post there was attached a fixed salary. The numerical order of salaries matched the prestige order of the *medreses*. The cash differentials were enormous, of about the order 1:25. Thus, success in passing up the learned hierarchy provided the occasion for the expressive representation of that success according to more general criteria, namely the possibilities for display opened to a person by virtue of his relative wealth.

The system did not, of course, remain entirely unchanged, but it was remarkably stable. It was formalized in the *Kanunname* of Mehmed II about the year 1470.

Our analysis, then, identifies an instrumental hierarchy, depending upon ability in learning and teaching, and an expressive hierarchy of public reputation and social power, depending upon financial reward. In the early days of the *Ulema*, the expressive hierarchy was in one to one correspondence with the instrumental hierarchy. Jobs and salaries matched ability, and ability was reflected in reputation. However, as Repp, the authority on the system points out, the *Ulema* fulfilled the general principle of the evolution of institutions which was proposed earlier in this chapter, namely that in the course of time activities became more expressive and progressively less instrumental. The corruption seems to have been very largely the effect of nepotism. Members high in the learned hierarchy recommended to the Sultan the promotion of relatives independently of their effectiveness as scholars and teachers. The result was a transformation of the *Ulema* from a teaching institution to an expressive institution, in which the salaries were used for the purchase of mere icons for public display. The respect/contempt criteria were transformed. They lost their connection with the official task of the *Ulema* – the activities proper to learned professions – and became associated with public display of outward marks of learning and wisdom, robes of office, portentous speech, and so on.

Case 2. The cult of heroic failure

Similarity of the lives of learned Turks is to be explained by reference to the structure of the institutions in which their careers were made. However, there are other life trajectories which fall into sets of similar form and for which there exists no such institution. The most striking example I know of is the Japanese cult of heroic failure. Each life is constructed by the hero who lives it in a similar fashion to the lives of other heroes, and yet it is a personal creation. I shall be proposing that we understand this in terms of the sharing of a number of inter-connected theories about the ideal life form.

To understand the cult we must compare two main conceptions of the heroic. In the Western conception the heroic life culminates in success. The correlative emotions are pride and contentment, or satisfaction. The Japanese conception of the heroic life culminates in failure after a high peak of initial success, and the correlative emotions are sadness and regret.

Of course, each culture contains in minor form the heroic life form of the other. In Western literature the tragic hero bears some similarity to the most popular form of Japanese heroic life, while the Japanese themselves recognize, though do not greatly admire, the heroic life in the Western mould. According to Ivan Morris (1975) whose study *The Nobility of Failure*, examines the Japanese conception of the heroic in detail, the admiration which the Japanese give to the life of heroic failure is to be explained by the imposition of characteristic aesthetic categories on the life trajectory. According to Morris, a central aesthetic principle realized in Japanese art forms is that beauty is to be seen in decay, in the falling of the cherry blossom, in autumn, and so on. 'Yet in the very impermanence and poignancy of the human condition, the Japanese have discovered a positive quality, their recognition of a special beauty inherent in evanescence, worldly misfortune and "the pathos of things".' A tragic life form, the moral career of the failed hero, could be seen as yet another symbol realizing this conception. As Morris puts it, 'his [the hero's] fall represents in human form the quintessential Japanese image, the scattering of the fragile cherry blossoms'. Morris produces a great deal of evidence for the claim that for millenia the Japanese have chosen to admire and sometimes to construct lives which fulfil this aesthetic design. He claims, for example, that the phenomenon of the Kamikaze pilots is to be understood in terms of this aesthetic principle. The kamikaze phenomenon, so he argues, depended heavily on the perception that Japan had already lost all hope of winning the war. The young men who piloted the suicide planes were not seeking immortality like heroes in the Valhalla tradition, but rather in making a useless sacrifice on the declining stage of the war they were fulfilling their traditional conception of the heroic life form.

The explanation, then, for the similarity of many Japanese moral careers, including the recent suicide of Mishima, the Nobel prize-winning novelist, is to be sought in aesthetic theory and a shared conception of the heroic. There are no Japanese institutions which impose this form upon life. Indeed, rather the contrary. One can compare the careers of the brothers Yoretomo and Yoshitsune. The former was the founder of the traditional Japanese state. His influence persisted for six or seven hundred years and, in consequence, he holds a place of muted respect in the Japanese hierarchy of great men. But as a hero he is overshadowed by Yoshitsune, his younger brother, who, after a spectacular beginning as a revolutionary leader, failed completely in his campaign. He eventually committed suicide in the traditional Japanese fashion, almost alone, under a pine tree beside a lake.

This example draws our attention to a further and very striking feature of this cult, namely the role of time in the consciousness of the individual who is constructing his own life form. It is very different from the role it plays in the heroic life of Western tradition. For the Japanese adventurer, intent upon the heroic, the culmination of his moral career and the reputation he acquires in the eyes of others may be postponed until long after his death. He is seeking respect from succeeding generations, and he buys this at the cost of being seen as a failure by his contemporaries. Such a conception requires a further shared idea, namely a belief in the persistence of the essential forms of Japanese culture. Amongst a people who have no sense of the longevity of their national culture, the Japanese cult of the heroic would make no sense.

In Morris's classical study of this cult there is a notable weakness, a weakness which I am in no position to resolve. He has no well-worked-out theory to account for the preservation and continuous sharing of a conception of the heroic over so long a period. Morris offers two rather lame explanations. He suggests without much conviction that the persistence of Mahayana Buddhism may have been a contributory factor to the stability of the aesthetic conceptions upon which the Japanese heroic life form is based. But one might equally argue that it was the persistence of the aesthetic ideals that sustained the Mahayana form of Buddhism. The geographical features of the Archipelago, for example its earthquakes, he proposed, might have led to the ideas of evanescence, of impermanence, becoming implanted as permanent features of Japanese conceptions of the beautiful and the good. But the Greeks and the Icelanders are equally plagued by earth tremors and consequent disasters, and have developed no such aesthetico-social theory. Indeed, the Icelanders, I suppose above all, have been proponents of the Western cult of heroic success.

The free construction of institutions for unofficial moral careers
The cases I have just been considering are embedded in coherent and well-formed societies where institutions and shared theories are strong. The construction of moral careers in more open societies, and particu-

larly societies where the conceptions of a well-ordered life are very diverse, is a much more difficult and uncertain matter. Indeed, for many people moral careers are lived wholly within institutions. However, it has been pointed out by Goffman and others, that in industrialized society many people undertake a secondary career in the pursuit of respect which lies outside the main institutional structures of the society and is catered for by special arrangements in special places.

Simmel (1971) proposed the term 'adventure' for the social activities which take place in time-off, so to speak, and which can be seen as engagements in a series of hazards. Only a limited reputation can be gained in these activities since they must either be secret or occur in places far from the location of the normal occupations of the individuals involved. Goffman has drawn attention to the possibility of treating gambling as a form of 'adventure'. In Nevada the adventure has degenerated into a form in which the display of the expressive attributes of character occurs merely in the sight of machines.

The kind of activities that Goffman and Simmel have in mind are generally developed by someone other than the adventurer they are provided for. I want to consider briefly an example of the construction of alternative moral careers where the institution is created and sustained even against the hostility of the surrounding societies by the adventurers themselves. A recent phenomenon in British society has been the elaboration of formalized rituals by football fans. Marsh's studies have shown that the lads taking part in these events are generally devalued in the official careers that the society at large provides for them. They are those whose life in school has been a progression of humiliations and ritual affirmations of their valuelessness to society. It becomes apparent to them that in the official world there is no possibility whatever of their obtaining respect. But on the terraces of football grounds on Saturday afternoons they bring into existence a highly structured and hierarchical society in which a moral career, the growth of a public reputation through a series of hazards successfully overcome, can be attempted. In brief, a lad may begin such a career sitting on the concrete wall separating the spectators from the field of play watching and learning from the actions of the competent members of the group arrayed before him on the terraces. Slowly he acquires the 'gear', the regalia symbolic of his position in the hierarchy. Eventually, after a year or two's apprenticeship, he takes his place on the highest tier of seats. As the years go by and he comports himself successfully in the 'fights' in which his fellow-fans engage, he moves down, each descent marking social advancement. At first he acquires the uniform in all its splendour and then, as his reputation becomes established, sheds it bit by bit. Enough successful actions and his reputation as a 'hard' man is established. Finally he reaches the full glory of 'town-boy' whose personal fame is sufficient to allow him to dispense with any symbols of glory such as scarves, rosettes and so on.

The occasions of hazard are represented by the fans as 'fights'. Close empirical study of these encounters has shown that they are to be treated as events of much the same kind as aggressive threats and ritualized territorial defences seen amongst many animals. They are more matters of the display of the signs, marks and instruments of aggression than they are of actual bodily encounters. In fact, bodily encounters are very rare. The result of a successful 'fight' is the retreat of the enemy and the enhancement of the reputation of the protagonist of the side who has forced the other to back down. The well-ordered hierarchical micro-society provides a clear *cursus honorum*. It is an institution, stable over time but created by the very people who use it to develop their moral careers. It has the form of a Turkish *Ulema* but it is a creation independent of the over-arching society. Nor is there any constitutional device such as the edicts of the Turkish Sultan which publicly represent and hence serve to determine the form of the hierarchy. It is an institution constituted by custom and preserved by tradition.

THE BEGINNINGS AND ENDS
OF SOCIAL CAREERS

I turn now to consider the ways in which we can see a social actor coming into existence and ceasing to exist. We must sharply distinguish social careers from biological careers since it is by no means clear that the beginning and end of a social career is identical with the birth and death of an organism.

The birth of an actor

It has sometimes been assumed that an infant is born into the world as an empty vessel or *tabula rasa* and becomes a social actor by a process of learning, of socialization. This has sometimes been called 'internalizing the norms'. An infant is supposed to acquire, bit by bit, skill by skill, and even, according to Piaget, in a necessary sequential order that reproduces the phylogeny of civilization, the knowledge and abilities which eventually emerge in adulthood as the competence of a social actor. Recently both these ideas, the *tabula rasa* and progressive staging, have been challenged (Bryant, 1974).

Richards (1974) and others have criticized the traditional view of the infant as an empty vessel into whom first his mother and then the other adults and children who form his social milieu pour an increasing amount of social competence. They have proposed that a child should be imagined as a component of a synthetic but complete social individual – the mother-child dyad. The mother, as an independent social being, interacts with this dyad, as if it were another social entity. Careful studies of the way mothers speak to infants, suggest that much of the mother's speech serves to complete the infant by attributing intentions, wants and plans to it. She does for her child what that child cannot presently do for itself, so that it is always part of a fully competent, social individual. For example, she systematically and routinely attributes cognitive states and operations to the infant on the basis of faint, and sometimes false, cues in its movements and expressions.

The birth of an actor could be said then to occur at the moment at which the mother-child dyad is formed – that is when she takes on the completion of a social individual of which the infant is, for the first part of its life, merely a component. This picture of social maturation is of the transfer of responsibility for certain functions from one component of a complete being to another. There never is a *tabula rasa* out in the social world. As Trevarthen (1974) has demonstrated the mother, as herself, interacts with the mother-child as a pseudo-self, in many conversations and games.

There are good empirical reasons for seeing this symbiosis continuing until a child is about four years of age, at which point most of the transference from the mother component to the infant part of the dyadic but socially unitary being has been achieved. In the next phase of life, adult skills and methods of social action are rapidly developed in social activities fairly well isolated from adult influence. Social apprenticeship begins in the underlife of school, in the playground, and the unattended parts of home. Here, the children create an autonomous precursor world. They engage in symbolic activity such as the exchange of tokens as a binding of friendship; they arrange the creation and maintenance of aspects of social order, such as turn-taking, by the use of rituals. They control their interactions by means of systems of rules; and they defend their persons by a whole series of equilibrating procedures ranging from protests against failures of distributive justice to insulting rhymes by means of which a person can restore the dignity he or she has lost when brought low by the actions of adults. Detailed studies of both the infant period and the autonomous precursor world present a very different picture of development from that of the sequentialists, Piaget and Kohlberg (Kitwood,

1977). Studies of the lives of children when they are not in interaction with adults suggest a very high level of social competence, but exercised upon a material and social content which is quite alien to the adult world. For example, there is a strong verbal contractual basis to orderly and rule-governed activity in the playing of marbles. Furthermore, Kitwood's extremely detailed studies have shown that the idea of stages in the moral competence of a child can not be sustained empirically. It seems that most children are in command of most moral theories most of the time, but apply them in a highly situation-specific manner, so that they are sometimes intuitionists, sometimes utilitarians, and sometimes even depend upon the categorical imperative.

Once socio-psychological symbiosis has been dissolved and the child separates from the mother as a competent individual, he or she is in possession of most of the skills that will be needed to manage an adult life. A child's problem is to bring these skills together in situations where one or more seem to be called for at the same time. Piaget's settings for his investigation have characteristically led to an uncertainty as to which of a pair of principles a child should use in solving a problem. The confusion is resolved as one principle comes to mask others which might be applicable in these situations. Later, the principles separate. The unmasking of an old skill has been taken by Piaget to be the staged, sequential appearance of a new skill. The Piagetian and Kohlberg picture of stages seems to be quite unsustainable empirically with respect to social activity. A seven-year-old co-operatively creating and sustaining a complex social world in the playground of a school is already operating with a very full bouquet of the skills required of an adult. The situations in which he or she uses them, however, are neatly separated, so that conflicts that acquire multiple operations are very rarely encountered.

The death of an actor

An actor, as conceived in this study, is a social being, though necessarily embodied. The ending of a life trajectory involves a complex interaction of processes closing off different aspects of a career. In particular, a person's life must be rounded off as an agent, as a bearer of character, and as an embodied being. Death may not be simultaneous in each mode and indeed, there seems to be very good reason for thinking that it is not.

In general in contemporary thinking, the dissolution of embodiment is treated as a progressive phase-by-phase process. There are serious philosophico-legal problems about the precise point in this process at which a human life should be thought to be terminated. These concern, it seems, the physical signs of person-termination, and of course depend upon specific embodiment theses as well as particular philosophical doctrines as to the nature of persons. There is a complex interaction between the concept of agency, consciousness and physical death, which it is not part of my purpose here to analyse. All that we need to notice is that with respect to the biological progress, an arbitrary point of closure is defined which is closely related to legal and other considerations. However, for ceremonial purposes a simulacrum of embodiment may be produced. For example, the body of a person may be embalmed and so decorated as to seem to be alive, that is to seem to be still a member of a social world. Leave-takings may occur in which one of the participants is a corpse.

The argument developed in *Personal being*, concerning the nature of the self as agent, suggests that our conceptual apparatus calls for persons to be attributed an abstract, contentless agency capable of being exercised on any concrete matter whatever. It is logically possible for agency in this sense to survive the abstraction of any particular content entailed by the organic death of a person. If the agency is pure, it could be transferable in principle to any content whatever. However, in a further stage of the argument, when we analysed the conditions for the existence of selves, human persons, abstract agency turned out to be a metaphysical representation of a process feature of the physiological system, which forms the material basis of human individuals. It represents the indefinitely multipliable possibility of one part of the system being able to represent and control another part. This abstract agentive capacity is materially grounded. So the logical possibility of the survival of agency beyond organic death will never actually be empirically realized. But this is a contingency, and whether we hold it true or false is very closely related to the kind of embodiment mode which we take to be associated with human agency. For example, if it were possible to sustain the Cartesian mode as an empirically possible form of embodiment, then the history of the self with respect to the history of its physical bearer, its point of application under the Cartesian mode, would be quite different.

From the actor's point of view, the concept of the self as agent that is relevant to the closures of death is the capacity of the self to reflect upon its own contents. The capacity of the self to act in the world is a relevant property only as far as determination of agency as a social or public matter is concerned. We have already seen the close connection between criteria for deciding the point of physical death and the ending of action in the world as it is experienced by other people. But, as far as the actor is concerned, it is rather the possibility of reflection upon any of his or her own mental contents than the possibility of action that is the crucial issue. Action in the world and reflection can be radically distinguished. They are aspects of the distinction between and joint necessity of both autonomy and reflexivity, the distinction we found to be central to the concept of a person-in-society. From this point of view, the actor's appropriate stance in the face of organic death is a form of Pascal's wager: If the self as reflexive agent survives the end of the physical career it will have some content to reflect upon. But if the self in this sense does not survive, then there is no standpoint from which its failure to survive might be regretted.

From the actor's point of view, death is a presentational moment which can be managed in the interests of completing a moral career, that is, it is a very important testing point for persona management and the completion of character. The contemporary custom of removing the moment of death from a public or social milieu is, from the actor's point of view, disastrous, in that he or she has no chance of completing that character, or even revising it, by making a good death. 'Nothing in his life so became him as his leaving of it.' According to the theory advocated in this work, the management of death in other epochs was socially very much more satisfactory. Opportunities were provided for deathbed repentance, for speeches at the foot of the scaffold, and so on. The management of death as a presentational moment was placed firmly in the hands of the actor, and he or she was surrounded by a supporting cast who enabled the performance of the last dramaturgical activity in the best interests of the character an individual would leave behind (McManners, 1975).

Organic death, however, even on the scaffold, is not the end of moral career, for that is completed by the funeral. This is the occasion for a rite of passage involving the ritual disposal of the persona, and the generation of a 'document' to represent the character, the public repute, of the individual whose moral career is being closed. This takes the form of funeral oration, or an obituary, in which an attempt is made to sum up the reputation of the individual actor. It rounds off the moral career. This is in sharp contrast to the moral careers of Japanese heroes, as I described them in a previous section, in that they look to a reputation which has to be achieved in the eyes of others long after the moment at which, in Western societies, an obituary would have been published and a funeral oration would have been given. There are, of course, in the Western world, such activities as the reconsideration of the reputation of an important person, the waxing and waning of public esteem for musicians, artists, novelists and the like. So, character, even in the Western world, is for certain people at least, a long-term property. However, I take these to be exceptional. For most people moral career ends in a funeral oration.

A METHODOLOGY FOR THE STUDY
OF LIVES

The problem of developing a conceptual system and an associated methodology for the study of the psychological aspects of a human life course centres on the perennial problem of empirical psychology, namely whether an extensive method aimed at investigating the common properties of a large class of individuals is to be preferred to an intensive method in which individuals are examined, one by one, with no prior assumptions about the similarities or differences that may emerge among them. Traditional life-course psychology has been based on the extensive method. Large numbers of individuals at different ages have been investigated and the common properties of each age-set determined. The results have been as disappointing in fact as they might have been expected to be in theory. Almost all that has emerged from this kind of analysis is a re-affirmation of the known biological differences between one age cohort and another. The arguments in the critical chapters of this book concerning the traditional methods of psychology have pointed to the necessity to employ an idiographic method as part of an intensive design, that is to study individuals one by one, without any prior assumptions as to the generality of the psychological processes revealed. The point can be put quite sharply in terms of the concept of ergodicity. It cannot be assumed that if we study life forms by looking at different individuals, one for each time-slice, we will find a profile of change that is identical to, or sufficiently similar to, the profile of change that we would find by allowing one individual to evolve his own life form over time. In short, life-course properties are very unlikely to be ergodic.

Du Mas proposed three empirical domains: D1: The distribution of properties over individuals at a time; D2: The distribution of individuals with respect to a given property at different times; D3: The idiographic domain, the distribution of properties of a given individual over times. Since the domains are orthogonal, it is obvious that the structure of the idiographic domain cannot be deduced from knowledge of the structures of D1 and D2 unless the study has already incorporated D3 by exhausting D1 and D2. It follows from this that there is at least the possibility that the psychological histories of each individual may turn out to be unique. The principles of sequence and order in each member of the idiographic domain may turn out to be unlike the principles of sequence and order of any other members of that domain. The way one individual's life evolves may show certain longitudinal, structural properties, to be called themes, which may, in principle, be different from those of any other individual.

Methods for the study of the psychology of individual lives must then be developed in Du Mas' idiographic domain. The De Waele method, the only systematic idiographic life-course psychology so far developed, consists in the construction of documents which represent an agreed account of the distribution of an individual's psychological attributes at different times, including such matters as emotions, beliefs, accepted rules, experiences of the self and others, and so on (De Waele & Harré, 1977).

Broadly speaking, there are two kinds of life-course documents, the biography and the diary. These documents are generated after the events they describe, but they are written on the basis of those events. The diary is a contemporaneous record of the psychological life-course, whereas the biography must be constructed from a past which must be revived before it can be described. In consequence biography and autobiography are epistemologically distinct from diary.

An autobiography is characterized by the relative conceptual sophistication of the analysis and interpretation which it contains. It involves events from the past as they are interpreted in the light of the knowledge and experience which a person has at the time the biography is constructed, which may be much later than the events described. Of course, correspondingly, an autobiography is historically problematic. The method of autobiographical construction that I shall describe has been developed for the study of the lives of murderers but it can be generalized to any human life. The construction of an autobiography can be conceived as a process by which very large-scale accounts are successively negotiated with an individual encouraged to show his or her actions to have been reasonable at the time of their performance.

De Waele uses two main methods for the construction of an autobiography, methods which interact with one another.

The participant prepares an autobiography which is partitioned into time slices, each representing a distinct phase in life. The phases are identified from the autobiography. They are not defined with respect to any *a priori* scheme for the analysis of lives. The team of investigators – let us suppose that there are six – is each offered a slice and has the task of reconstructing the rest of the biography, using common-sense social and psychological knowledge. The reconstructions are then negotiated with other members of the team and then with the participant. In the final phase, the products of these negotiations are brought together into an agreed version.

The second stage of the investigation involves a different set of investigators and a different partition of the autobiography, this time into theme slices, such as work, education, relations with the opposite sex, and so on. A similar process of reconstruction and negotiation is undertaken, the final stage of which is the construction of another agreed autobiography.

In the last phase of this part of the investigation, the time reconstruction and the theme reconstruction are finally brought together.

And there are, of course, difficulties with the very idea of 'the way things were then'. There is no solution to the ultimate problem of historical accuracy. In the De Waele method historicity is abandoned as a criterion in favour of authenticity; that is, do the recollected features of the events of the life course form a coherent thematic order? This is not to be confused with a criterion of consistency, since it is not suggested that the various themes of an individual's life should be expected to fit together into a consistent whole.

A life may show a number of themes both in its public actions and private interpretations. A theme can be thought of as a distinctive style of action. For instance, in one of the Brussels biographies, the dominating theme of the life of one individual was 'simplification'. Any form of complexity, moral, physical, practical or theoretical, is routinely denied or avoided. The approach of that individual to the successive problems posed to him by life has always been 'Simplify'.

What of the status of the knowledge that has been generated in the person under study as his or her autobiography has been developed? And how do the changes in the participant during the autobiographical reconstruction relate to the historicity or authenticity of the final document? It follows from the above considerations, that it is impossible to say whether we have discovered the truth about an individual life course, or whether we have created in a participant a current conception of their life relative to the point of view that has now been reached. Psychologically, the effect of a Brussels investigation on a participant is to enlarge their knowledge of their own lifeform. This knowledge now becomes part of that person's resources for generating action and action-plans. In rare cases it can be reduced to 'That's the sort of person I am', in which the whole life-form is condensed into a pre-given instance of a typology. But in most cases such a condensation is impossible, and indeed the participant is very unlikely to undertake it. The status of a biography, then, is not that of a simple historical document.

However, this is insufficient to complete the study and a further set of investigations are now undertaken. The final agreed biography can be seen to contain a whole range of situations which are felt by the participant to be problematic or to have involved some sort of conflict. Once these situations are identified their formal structure can be discovered, for example, did the problem emerge from a sequence of similar, but solvable situations, and so on. In the next stage of the investigation the participant is expected to relive episodes which are formally isomorphic with those which he represented in his agreed biography as problematic and agonistic. The participant is not told which of the events in his past the artificial problem and conflict situations are supposed to replicate. Indeed, in an ideal application of the method he is brought to experience a wide range of possible forms of such situations. In the course of this experience of artificially constructed problems and conflicts, he is asked to remember those situations in his past life of which he is reminded as he experiences the emotions, the frustrations, the methods, by means of which he deals with those which he is presently undergoing. The structure of the situations of the past can be inferred from the predetermined structure of the situations which he is currently experiencing. Predetermination affords some leverage against the besetting epistemological problem of all life-course studies, namely how far do recollections of the past accurately represent the events as they occurred. The results of this phase of the investigation are then combined with the agreed biography to produce the final document which is now organized for themes – that is for longitudinal lines of similar occurrences according to criteria provided by the participant himself.

The De Waele method, which I have outlined above, is an exceedingly powerful empirical method, generating a well-ordered and very rich psychological biography of an individual. However, there are philosophical problems of an epistemological character at which I have already hinted.

The idiographic method reveals in a very detailed way, the self-conception that an individual has developed in the course of life, and which has been amplified and modified in untestable ways in the course of the experience of constructing the biography. The biography, then, is partly a representation of the individual's current psychological structure.

The first level of philosophical inquiry relative to the implications of the method can be reached by assuming what will later be questioned, namely the continuous identity of the individual participant, P, whose autobiography we are assisting, together with the idea of there being some sequence of events el, . . . en, which we take to be P's life course, as it happened. Against this background the first problem emerges.

Since there seem to be no sharp criteria for deciding determinatively whether the (auto)biography considered as a collection of hypotheses about the life course events el . . . en are true, what is the status of the autobiography under these conditions?

This question is readily answered if we distinguish the cognitive state of P, the participant at the time of the beginning of the De Waele experience, a young man who has committed a murder, from his condition at the end. As an active participant in every phase of the autobiographical construction P has become knowledgeablè about his past life to the extent that the content of the autobiography at the end of the experience is almost identical with his conception of his life course as he now believes it to have been. As explicit knowledge it is available to him as part of his resources for action at times running even some distance into the future. But if a man's cognitive resources are the bases of his action-planning and so on, then our knowledge of them enables us to predict his acts and actions in parallel to the way they enable him to form intentions to perform acts and actions.

This accounts for the success of De Waele and his team in predicting the future life course of a prisoner in their parole reports. It is not as if they had succeeded in showing the prisoner to be an instantiation of some ideal type, nor his actions to be predictable from a covering law, unless it is the banality that people often do what they intend.

But the assumptions upon which this discussion was based are themselves questionable. Whose autobiography have we constructed? The question arises in this dramatic form against the background thought that the state of the participant after a year's investigations may be so different from his state at the beginning of the De Waele experience that we need to register an ontological change. He is no longer, we may feel inclined to say, the *same person* as he was.

We might, in certain cases where there has been profound change in knowledge, attitude and so on, be ready to say that though it was P1, who entered the experience at the beginning, and who lived the history el . . . en, it is P2 who has come into being in the course of constructing the autobiography. Only P knows that he lived it. The paradoxical status of the 'he' in the last sentence cannot be wholly resolved since at least P2 must be able to remember that 'he' was once P1. But there can be no philosophical solution, since in these cases P2 has access to some of the features of P1 that figure in judgements of personal identity.

But this question and its philosophically indeterminate answer is itself embedded in a nest of further assumptions concerning the description of a life course. It is assumed that the episodes we have crudely represented by el . . . en are able to be given a univocal description, as if finally there was only one perspective on a life course. And behind that lies the assumption that there is indeed a singular sequence, *the* life course, as one and only one thing. This assumption has been called in question by Schutz (1972). As a person shifts from one 'perspective' to another in the interpretation of their life, they transform the events under each interpretation. Though these events may have spatio-temporal identity, they are not socially singular. The life course must be treated as indefinitely multiple while no criterion for limiting perspectives is to hand.

The shift of significance of 'an' event with shift in perspective has been nicely illustrated by Helling (1977) in the case of the life story of a man working as a carpenter. An incident in which he was asked to do some work in the boss's house is referred to twice in a fragment of autobiography. In one instance it is embedded within a perspective which is used to illustrate the man's position in society as a fall from previous heights. He is now the sort of man who can be ordered around by the boss. In the other perspective he is to be seen as rising to a position of trust, the kind of man who can be relied upon to do a good job even when not under supervision. Was *the* incident an occasion for feelings of pride or of humiliation? The question can now be seen to be ill posed. Spatio-temporal identity does not entail social uniqueness. One event occurred, but contemporaneous with it were two 'incidents'. They were both real in their effects upon the sense of personal worth experienced by the carpenter and illustrated in the perspectival duality of his account.

9

A SOCIAL PSYCHOLOGY OF SOCIAL CHANGE

ANTICIPATORY SUMMARY

The phenomena of interest to social psychologists can all be shown to be attributes of the discursive matrices of social interactions, which develop within locally valid normative frameworks. It is our tacit knowledge of these frameworks that fits us to be members of a community. The task of the social psychologist is to make this tacit knowledge explicit, and to search amongst the local systems for anything which, at some well defined level of abstraction, might be a universal feature of interpersonal discourse.

In Chapter 7 I illustrated the wide diversity of ways that the balance is drawn between the practical and the expressive orders of different societies, and how diverse are the forms that these take. In this chapter I address the problem of diversity in the temporal dimension. The first step will be to provide a general criterion for identifying changes against the background of the invariants that survive transformations in both practical and expressive orders.

Taking the psychological foundations of social activity to be expressible in terms of the metaphor of 'rule-following' the psychological problems raised by the fact of social change can easily be identified. They are all aspects of the problem of explaining how changes in 'rule-systems' occur. I shall be trying to develop a theory which avoids any assumptions of the positive causation of new social forms. The general framework of this theory will draw on an explicit analogy with the latest theory of biological change. However this analogy leaves the question of the origin of mutant social and material practices, the analogue of the mutation in the biological theory, untouched. By developing and refining the idea of a dialectic resolution of tensions between opposing systems of motivations, I shall be able to use the idea of tensions originating in mismatches between people's locations in their local practical and expressive orders to invoke a 'dialectic of honour'. In that dialectic I shall show how the origins of mutant social practices can be discerned.

Finally I shall apply the whole scheme, involving both dialectic and selectionist formats, to some examples, particularly the contemporary women's movement. I should emphasize here, to avoid the kind of misattributions to which anyone dealing with the psychology of sensitive subjects is liable, that offering an explanation of the rise of the women's movement is not a covert way of devaluing the aspirations of those active in it. This ought not to need to be said but unfortunately it seems always to need reiteration.

SOCIAL CHANGE

The problems of social change cannot be identified without some careful prior distinction drawing. We must distinguish first of all between the changes that might take place in institutions and societies considered as people-structures, for instance redistribution of respect-relations in contrast to changes that come about in social practices, for example the revision of ritual forms in act/action structures. In both cases there are complexities. People-structures may change in such a way that the 'essential' nature of the people remains the same and only external relations among them undergo a differentiation over time. However, since most social relations are internally related to the natures of the members, institutional and societal changes will usually involve changes in the people as well as in relational structures. There are several ways that social practices can change. While the acts to be performed remain the same, they may come to be realized in different action-structures. But it may be that through a series of imperceptible changes different acts come to be performed by means of given action-structures. For example, a ceremony which was once taken to be the performance of one act may become emptied of that content, and though retaining its action-structure, become the performance of some other act. I shall be concerned to develop concepts for formulating theories of change of social practices and for devising theories of the change of institutions and societies, so that the social psychological processes involved can be clearly identified.

However, change of practices and of institutions are not independent of one another. Social practices in institutions or societies are linked in an essential way. People-structures are realized in day-to-day living in act/action structures. For example, a hierarchical people-structure is realized in everyday practice in the act/action represented. In many cases the relation between change in social practices and change in institutions and other people-structures is so close that the distinction is analytic rather than material, that is one sort of change should not be seen as the cause of the other. Nevertheless, change in act/action structures must be considered independently of change in people-structures, even though they are intimately linked.

To understand change both the sources of stability and the sources of modification must be identified. Change can be discerned only against a background of stability. So it is necessary to identify some invariant properties in the institution or practice we are investigating. The first task will be to examine various possibilities for the location of universals or invariants in social life, in people-structures and in act/action structures. Having adequately identified what it is that is changing against what it is that is stable, a social analyst is in a position to begin to look for the sources of influence that bring about the changes have been identified.

THE SEARCH FOR INVARIANTS

In the course of the early chapters of this study detailed analysis of various reductive theories of social life were undertaken and their limitations exposed. However, they must be considered again in that such theories do offer some hints of possible invariants. I propose to recapitulate briefly the arguments against reductive theories but with the emphasis on possible sources of hypotheses as to social invariants.

Biologically-based invariants

The biological basis of life has, as we noticed in earlier chapters, been taken by some theorists as the source of a universal theory of social activity, and consequently of social invariants and change.

The simplest such theory holds that there are, built in as it were to human beings, a set of fixed drives, the realization of which is triggered by contact with environmental stimuli. On this view the existence of drives is all that is required to explain the fundamental activities of social life. If there are such drives, they would be invariants. And if they were conserved through all changes one would expect to find them in every society. Differences in institutions and practices could arise only in the means by which the goals set by drives were realized. But this theory is either trivial or tautological. It is indisputable that every human being from time to time feels thirsty. But the drive to satisfy that bodily need, when it appears as a felt want, comes under the control of a meaning system and thus enters social life only through the meaning it has for members of a particular social group. For example, according to those who adopt a form of social life in which mortification of the flesh is a dominant social good, thirst will be only barely satisfied and on special occasions not satisfied at all. The same is true to an even greater extent of other postulated drives, such as that for dominance, for mating and the like. The drive theory, with respect to the problem of social invariants, is trivial. Alternatively, if every kind of differentiated behaviour is taken as the ground for the postulation of a drive, the drive theory is tautological in the absence of any independent evidence for the existence of such drives. The theory need not detain us.

Much more important in contemporary social theory is the ethological analogy. It has been argued by many biologists, and even some social theorists, that there are invariant routines in human life in just the way that there are invariant routines in animal life. Human social practices have a biological utility, it is argued, sufficient to justify the claim that the source of these routines is genetically determined. If so they will be invariant through all changes and universal in the species. I shall concern myself now only with the logic of the analogical reasoning which identifies certain forms of human action with the routines of animal life. Cultural elaboration suggests that the likenesses and differences between act/action sequences and animal routines are not alone sufficient to ground an ethological theory. To test the idea the negative and neutral aspects of the analogy must be explored by an independent examination of the human case. It is not a sufficient ground for the claim that, say, the human propensity to defend territory is genetically grounded, that we can demonstrate an analogous pattern of social activity in the life of the robin. It would have to be established that the ordinary processes of social learning of a culturally devised solution to the problem of space-aportionment and the like were not operating in the human case, before the ubiquity of the practice of defending the home ground could be arguably grounded in genetics. Secondly, even if it were possible to establish that there were genetic sources for certain human social routines, for example male and female reproductive strategies, the differences in their meaning in different societies raises the problem of the origin of culturally specific social meaning attached to these strategies. Clearly these are unlikely to be explicable in ethological, that is genetic, terms.

But a more fatal objection can be raised to the whole ethological analogy programme. Writers on this topic such as Ardrey (1968) have taken for granted that the appropriate analogies are to be sought in the activities of wild animals. Territoriality, ritualization, displacement, aggression and so on, have been studied in feral conditions and treated as analogous to human institutions like war, property, defence, urban living and so on. But of course, human beings are not wild animals. They are domesticated by the work of mothers, psychiatrists, priests, policemen, teachers and so on. The appropriate analogies, to my knowledge, have never been explored. No one has asked how closely are those human life practices similar to the life forms of pussy cats, pet dogs, pigs, cows, horses, gerbils, budgerigars and the like. It is to the social psychology of farm animals and pets that we should be looking for useful analogies to sources of the patterns of lives of human kind. And by parity of reasoning these considerations suggest that the forms of life of domesticated animals are much more dependent on those of their human owners than they are on genetic endowment.

The alleged biologically grounded universals I have just considered are all supposedly to be found in social action of various kinds, in the defence of territories, in attacks on other animals and so on. There is another category of genetically determined features of the social life of animals which might more plausibly be ascribed to the activities of humans. These are the structural invariants ethologists call 'bonds'. As Tiger and Fox have argued (1971) there could be genetic programming for various kinds of bonding. There could be a tendency to form male-male bonds, realized for instance in football fan groups. Nor does it seem implausible to assume that the male-female relations of mating and the adult–infant relations of child rearing are genetically grounded. However the evidence for such a claim is at best indirect. Discounting the enormous cultural differentiation and local elaboration of these relations in actual institutions, it could be argued that the ubiquity of the relational structure so revealed is explicable only through the hypothesis of a common genetic endowment. Tiger and Fox use the slow rate of genetic bio-evolution to argue that modern humans have the genetic endowment of their hunter-gatherer ancestors (if indeed such there were). If we suppose that that form of social organization was the last pre-civilized 'natural' life form, and that the bonding relations claimed to be discernible in the social lives of all modern human beings were adaptive in a biological sense in the hunter-gatherer conditions, there is at least the sketch of an argument.

But however plausible such an argument might be it is not conclusive. Similar patterns and similar relations and structures may be homologous, that is identical both in function and origin. But they may be no more than analogous, similar solutions to similar problems but arrived at and maintained by some quite different mechanism. It is a clever move to promote institutions that affirm the solidarity of any kind of social formation that strengthens the reproductive success of the members of a culture. And male bonding might well be adaptive for hunter-gathers. Though people may appear to be both clever and social, it may be that, by nature, they are just clever. They could have invented sociality as the best solution to the problems of living, and as part of sociality the institutions that illustrate and reinforce (in a non-behavioural sense) useful bonds.

In general, then, human biology enters social reality only as it is embedded in a culture. On this view biological phenomena are given specific meanings by members. Perhaps the clearest example of the dominance of culture over biology is the varying interpretations of sickness. Illness is explained on the one hand as a result of an organic defect or infestation and on the other as punishment meted out for some sin.

Cognitive preformation theory

It seems that the idea of taking the biological basis of life as the source of universal and invariant properties of human social routines and social structures cannot be plausibly sustained. However, recently two theories have been proposed which skirt the issue of biological origins, while at the same time making strong claims for the existence of universal and invariant properties of social forms and social practices. In these theories it is claimed that analyses of certain human activities reveal universal structures which can be explained only by the hypothesis that they reflect fundamental features of the human mind. There are, it is supposed, cognitive preformations which have been realized in the activities identified as structurally alike by the theorists.

Levi-Straus's (1968) theory of the structural basis of human society in a system of binary oppositions in the thinking of all people is a theory of this sort. He argued that certain invariant properties of social practices and the mythological stories associated with them are the surface features which reflect deep binary oppositions in the way the human mind operates. Cultural and tribal differences are to be explained by the idea of cultural *bricolage*. The way a society represents to itself the underlying structure of the human mind which determines its forms, is differentiated by what it has available through historical accident as the material in which to realize these forms. Totemism, for example, is the realization of the logical properties of sets with respect to social groupings in a rhetoric which is derived from the taxonomies of animals, plants and minerals which such societies find essential to their survival. These taxonomies are what a tribe has to hand; they are their bricolage. Though it seems to me that such a theory is philosophically impeccable, I understand that its empirical grounding is now regarded as weak. I shall assume that it would not generally be regarded as an adequate theory of social universals.

Linguistic studies have recently been the focus of a theory of deep structure which proposes universal and invariant forms underlying the grammar of all human languages (Leiber, 1975). The Chomskian theory of deep structure is not, of course, a theory of the social practice of speaking, but rather of certain invariants which are supposed to be present in the forms that knowledge of language take in every human being. According to the Chomskian theory, each human being is born with a physiologically grounded apparatus which enables them to selectively receive and learn certain, and only certain, properties of the sound sequences uttered by others. Thus, generation by generation the learning of language appears to repeat certain fundamental forms. The assessment of this theory is really extremely difficult, since it is protected from empirical investigation by a number of subsidiary hypotheses and more particularly by the distinction which locates these universals in knowledge of language rather than in linguistic practice. However, I take it that the theory is not now widely accepted, either by linguists or by developmental psychologists and we can safely shelve it along with the invariants of Levi-Straussian structural anthropology in the category of 'not proven'.

Universal social conventions

Three different rule systems and interpretative procedures seem to be at work in generating the forms of social life; etiquettes, game-ritual principles or rules, and dramaturgical maxims. No claim is made for the universality of etiquettes since there is every reason for believing that the action sequences which realize social acts in different societies are very different from one another. However, it remains a possibility that there is a range of social acts required to maintain *any* mode of social life as, for example, the acts of binding and loosing people to various kinds of social commitment, the ritual disposal of the dead, the incorporation of strangers and so on. It may be that these acts and others like them are universals. However, such a theory is empirical and it would need to be shown that every society depended for its creation and maintenance upon just such social acts. It is by no means certain that that has been established. At best, it remains a possibility.

The third kind of regularity, the dramaturgical, the compendium of social roles or ways of presenting oneself as a certain social persona, seems rather unlikely to be universal. Some widespread categorial differentiations have been identified by Argyle and Little (1972) in their study of the personas displayed by middle-class people in different situations. There seem to be corresponding differentiations recognized among the Japanese. There seem to be four or five well-differentiated and socially distinct modes of presentation of a person, depending upon whether a person is acting among close family or distant family, strangers or intimates, officials or friends. Again, though these are possible universals, it is by no means clear that a sufficient empirical grounding has been provided for them.

The upshot, then, is a cautious rejection of all the *a priori* theories of invariants that have so far been proposed, since they are either manifestly defective, for logical and conceptual reasons, as we have seen with the drives theory, or they lack empirical support, as seems to be the case with cognitive preformation theories. Or the empirical support available is suggestive, but by no means conclusive, as in role–rule theories. We must turn now to a more promising line of investigation, namely the attempt to show what sort of conditions would lead to the postulation of some form of social universal.

Compensating changes as signs of an invariant

Instead of arguing *a priori* for certain kinds of social universals or invariants, and then examining social institutions and practices to try to find them, an alternative strategy is to look at changing practices and changing institutions to see if in the transformations that actually occur, social universals can be discerned. If one kind of change is generally associated with another kind of change and the former can be seen to be compensated for by the latter, then it may be plausible to propose as an invariant the relation and practice or attitude or whatever which has been preserved by means of the compensating changes.

The main example I shall consider in this chapter is the contemporary women's movement. I understand this as a parallel and linked series of changes in social practices and social theories which has been marked by a sharp alteration in the way in which certain spokeswomen have accounted for the form of social practices and social institutions involving women. This can be seen particularly in the transformation of female accounting by the introduction of a political rhetoric. Women have come to speak of their sex as a social class, and of their relationship to men as class-exploitation. This change in accounting techniques and resources has been paralleled by a rapid change in fashion, that is in the clothes, hairstyles and other accoutrements by which men and women are symbolically differentiated as male and female. As I shall argue we are dealing here with two distinct but related processes. The change in fashion has, at first sight, a paradoxical air, in that while there has been a shift to 'unisex' clothing in which men and women dress in very similar garments, there have been other changes which amplify sexual differences.

These changes can be understood as compensatory movements around a social invariant, the man/woman difference. Before the current fashion changes began the differences between men and women were visibly marked by differences in tertiary properties, such as distinctive clothing, and distinctive ways of dressing the hair. The association of particular tertiary properties with this or that sex is clearly arbitrary. But since these associations are matters of historical origin it perhaps would be misleading to speak of them as conventions.

The obliteration of tertiary distinctions in the fashions of the 1970s came about through the adoption of men's clothing by women and women's hair styles by men. The traditional sign system for marking the sexes as distinct had become much diminished. If the male/female distinction was functioning as a social invariant we would expect compensating changes to occur in other presentational possibilities to restore the representation of the difference. This is indeed just what we find. As hair styles became more and more similar so beards and moustaches become more and more prominent. Secondary differentia take over the role of social markers from tertiary. Unisex clothing becomes tighter to allow basic anatomical differences to show through. In these latter ways primary differentia were emphasized as markers. The net effect of the changes has been to preserve the capability for immediate recognition of the sex of most other human beings. The presentational ambiguities of tertiary marking, exploited by transvestites and homosexuals, have been reconstituted in secondary and even in pseudo-primary differentia.

At the same time there was a revival of traditional women's clothing, particularly long skirts and Victorian styles, which served to re-emphasize the traditional female role and to illustrate as sharply as possible the social differentiation of men from women. The value of the traditional role is illustrated, for those who hold to it, by an exaggeration of traditional tertiary markers.

How is this to be understood? We are concerned in this example with two universals: the universal differential male/female which is a purely biological invariant and the social invariant, namely the differentiation man/woman as social identities. The shift in rhetoric which tends to blunt the distinctions between men and women is compensated by a change in fashion which, by emphasizing the male/ female difference restores the man/woman universal.

It is possible to state a general principle which lies behind the analysis I have just proposed. Compensating changes will occur on two planes, that is a change in accounting resources and modes will be compensated for by a change in expressive modes so as to preserve a social universal.

The most important man/woman institution is that of marriage or some informal equivalent, having similar stability. It is possible to trace distinct differences in the theory of marriage simply by examining the image of marriage in popular songs. In the 1940s, in what one might call the Sinatra era, marriage is represented in popular music as a trap set by women for men, so that they will be supported in idleness by men's work. In contemporary accounting, popular music hardly mentions marriage at all and the relationships between men and women are differently identified. But the women's liberation rhetoric treats marriage in our era as a trap set for women by men so that they will get sexual mates, domestic help and so on at the cheapest possible rates.

It is also important to notice that in some cases the compensating changes occur in different institutions. The institution that seems to have brought about the change in rhetoric and accounting modes is what one might call the intellectual-journalistic establishment, since those changes occurred by means of the publication of books, the writing of articles and so on. The compensating change in fashion, which preserves the man/woman universal as an invariant, is brought about by the inventions and reactions to demand of the artistic-fashion establishment. Though distinct, these institutions are linked, particularly through journalism. One could identify here an interesting sociological problem, which it might not be too difficult to solve, namely how are these compensating changes brought about? How does the link operate?

THE LOCATION OF SOCIAL CHANGE

Practices

Theoretically there is a limited range of categories of possible social change. Broadly speaking social interactions can be divided into the instrumental, co-ordinated activities bringing social and material products into existence; and the self-presentational where the outcome is a step up or down in public reputation and moral career. Leaving aside material production and concentrating only on social activities which have social ends, the core of social episodes can be found in sequences of public actions in the course of which social acts are performed. By 'acts' I mean events which have distinctive social meanings, such as insults, marriages, convictions, cementations of friendships and so on, and by 'actions' the locally accepted conventionally associated ways by which acts such as the above are performed. We can now lay out the range of changes that could occur in small-scale social interactions.

1   A new convention might appear associating a different action with the same act: for instance, there has been a systematic change in the titles of respect used to perform acts of social deference; while arguably the acts have remained stable.

2   Sometimes the same action is performed as heretofore, but it is now understood as the performance of a rather different act. For instance a modern industrial strike can no longer be regarded as a simple protest against economic exploitation, but seems to be the performance of a self-presentational drama publicly emphasizing workers' power and dignity.

3   A more complex kind of change can occur when a novel act/ action structure appears but the social microstructure that it generates seems to be much the same as that generated by the old act/action sequence which has been superseded. A contemporary example seems to be the spread of common law marriage, where the institution that is created is much like the old, but the ritual steps leading to its establishment are different.

Similar kinds of change can occur in presentational activities. Changes occur in the acceptable range of personas and characters admitted as legitimate and proper presentations in a society. These are often accompanied by changes in the stylistic and symbolic devices by which they are publicly displayed. So we find the same persona/ character presented in different ways at different times. Sometimes different personas are presented with what seem to be traditional devices, while there may be changes in both.

And of course, along with these go changes in the accounting resources and the conventions that govern the selection of material that can be brought forward for use on accounting occasions. A splendid example of this kind of change is the growth of the use of Freudian and pseudo-Freudian concepts in accounting, the spread of which has been studied by Moscovici (1961).

We must take account too of changes in the practical order. These could be called changes in techniques.

Institutions, considered as complexes of people-structures and admissible social practices, characteristically exhibit two life forms. There is an overlife, the realization in those structures and practices of the official theory of the institution. That theory appears in a rhetoric for speaking of the activities of the overlife. But the human demands of the expressive order, originally nicely linked to the practical order as set forth in the official rhetoric, soon lead to the appearance of an underlife. Within this alternative social order there are moral careers for those for whom the overlife provides little opportunity for advancement. I take this duality to be the normal condition of institutions.

We can look for change in two dimensions. There may be changes in the practical order as improvements (or indeed mere changes) are made in the techniques by which the tasks of the practical order are accomplished. These may infect the expressive order by bringing about changes in the official moral career structure, by leading to the introduction of new role positions and so on. This kind of thing can be sensed in the turmoil produced by the mere proposal to appoint worker-directors to the boards of management of companies. But more inexorable by far are the changes that occur as the demands of the expressive orders of both overlife and underlife come to be felt more and more strongly. Soon they begin to dominate the motivations of members of the institution. This too will, in its turn, be reflected in the practical order, leading to routinization and formalization of the tasks which it demands. And sometimes the point may be reached when there is no more than an empty simulacrum of a real task performance.

Law-making as registration and record

If there were formal devices by which the managers of society could decide upon and promulgate explicit rules of action to which some coercive agency ensured the folk conformed, the problem of social stability and change would be solved. One could simply identify and describe the institutions and practices by which this was effected. One might be tempted to turn to the study of the law and its informal sibling, custom, as just such an institution. Could it be that the law is the source of order and stability in society and the nexus for social change? It might be argued that the political process is no more than the process of inventing new laws and devising changes in old laws in order to bring about changes in society in conformity with them. I take this view to be naive, since notoriously laws are enforceable only if they are, in a sense, already adopted. I shall not argue this point here since I am not concerned with the history or sociology of law. I shall assume that as far as the social psychological mode of enquiry is concerned laws and customs are secondary phenomena. They are rhetorical representations of the perception of tendencies to social stability and change rather than any part of their causes.

From the social psychological the point of view, the central matter of law is the institutions in which it is socially realized. The courts, the prisons, interview rooms, police stations and the forces that inhabit them, are matters to be investigated. The official rhetoric concerning the law should be brought in question, since we ought not to be too ready to accept it as providing an unproblematic theory of those institutions. One might be tempted to say that Parliament and other law-giving corporations are places where performative utterances are exchanged to contrive public/collective commitments to courses of action and so to determine the future. I suggest this naive theory deserves just as much scrutiny as the theory that hospitals are for curing people. Law and the rhetoric that supports it becomes something to be explained. The legal institutions do not figure among the explainers of social stability and change. On this view, law is a historically generated adjunct, a way for remembering past decisions, for recording the outcomes of meetings, discussions and debates. To think of the law as an instrument of stability and change is a misunderstanding of its place in the regulation of social life. With respect to the activities of people in society, it is a memorial device, a series of reminders, and a resource for a rhetoric of blame and praise. It is not, in this view, part of the causal apparatus involved in continuous creation of the social world.

THE SELECTIONIST ASPECTS OF A THEORY OF SOCIAL CHANGE

Social life, I have argued, is produced by competent actors shaping their actions in accordance with local systems of rules and conventions. The explanation for changes in social practices and processes, immanent in which are the phenomena of interest to social psychologists, must be sought in changes in local rules and conventions. How does one set of rules and conventions become partially or wholly displaced by another? The theory of the social psychology of social change, to be expounded in what follows, is directed to answering this question.

Mutation-selection formats

Some novel practices spread, that is are copied by lots of people and are adopted as one of their habits or customs or institutions; some do not. This is the general framework of the populational account of social change. At least two matters of philosophical interest are implicit in this simple formulation.

By what criteria do we identify and individuate practices and consequentially of what is the 'population' formed?

The fact of differential spread calls for explanation. The concept that suggests itself is the relative adaptiveness of practices to the social conditions in which they appear. What might be meant by 'social adaptiveness'? By what range of criteria would a judgement of more or less adaptiveness be made? The possibilities are broad, and we must consider social, psychological and biological aspects of the matter. I shall return to a detailed discussion of these issues below.

Before considering the details of the bio-evolution/socio-evolution parallel, relative to the borrowing of the more detailed conceptual apparatus, there are some differences to be remarked upon at the most general level of the transfer of the bare mutation/selection (M/S) scheme; particularly that the scheme has univocal application to the understanding of bio-evolution, but admits of several variants in application to socio-evolution. Three important cases of this form of difference need to be remarked before we turn to examine detailed parallels.

For the most part bio-evolution maps change and stability onto the individual/environment distinction. In consequence mutation conditions have their point of effectiveness at individuals (though individuals at which level of analysis is a point of dispute to which we shall be obliged to return). In general selection-conditions are identified with a relatively stable environment. Biologists do, however, recognize cases where more or less the same mutant appears many times, while its spread waits upon a change of environment. This is to reverse the mapping of the change/non-change distinction, *at a higher level*, since each repetition of the 'same' mutation is a departure from the form of its immediate predecessor in the lineage.

But in socio-evolution the mapping of change/stability onto the M/S conditions is as likely to require repetition of the same mutation awaiting suitable conditions to appear as to work at the lowest level of mutant individual practices in stable social (economic, geographical etc.) environments.

A distinction easily confused with the one just elaborated is that between evolutionary explanations in which the mutant is individual and the selection conditions collective, and those in which the selection conditions are individual and the mutant collective. This is quite simply inadmissible in biology. But it could be held that it is a possible reading of certain social phenomena. Fashion often follows the Darwinian model, an innovation appearing in whatever is individual, for example Mary Quant's miniskirt, the first Punk band and so on, and the environment within which such an innovation must spread is formed from the expressive and practical order of some contemporary collective.

But consider attempts by African governments to introduce new economic structures requiring novel practices from farmers. The failure of these collectively promulgated innovations to spread could be put down to the individual intransigence of each farmer. With respect to a personal property like 'intransigence' or 'conservatism' farmers are a mere aggregate of individuals.

Objections to treating these cases as distinct might be raised on two points. It is not clear that the innovatory reform programme is 'onto-logically' a collective property, if the conservatism of the farmers is not. At least as it comes to affect a nation's farmers it has to be promulgated in the form of lessons from individual agronomic experts, particularized notices and regulations, and personal readings and consultations. Nor is it clear that the social kind, 'farmer', could be instantiated in individuals defined wholly in terms of external relations, that is as a mere aggregate of individuals. Lukes has argued fairly convincingly that there are no categories of persons whose members could be individuals of that sort.

It might be that cases of this kind are more aptly treated as Durkheimian conjunctions of social facts than inverted Darwinian selective elimination of variants. So treated they could be subjected to analysis into a structural network of individual interactions in the manner proposed by Bhaskar.

Neither case so far cited serves to make an uncontroversial and absolute distinction between bio- and socio-evolution.

In advocating an M/S type of conceptual system for formulating explanations of social change we are not confined to a purely Darwinian form of explanation. Provided mutation conditions and selection conditions are both analytically and existentially distinct a continuum of M/S explanation schemata can be defined with respect to the degree of causal coupling between the two kinds of conditions. In a Darwinian schema-type M-conditions and S-conditions are absolutely causally independent. In the present state of biology I take it all explanations of organic change are strictly Darwinian. In other fields Popper has required an exclusive use of Darwinian schemata. But in a Lamarckian schema-type M-conditions and S-conditions interact causally in such a way that they are mutually dependent. Lamarckian schemata are still populational schemata, though the mutual causal influence between M-conditions and S-conditions ensures that indeed the mutant forms will soon necessarily dominate the population provided the environment remains more or less stable.

But between the pure forms of these explanation-types there are indefinitely many M/S schemata differing in the degree of coupling between mutation and selection conditions. In application to the explanation of social change we must admit the possibility of some degree of coupling between M and S conditions (Toulmin, 1972).

This means that we should expect people to conceive innovations, not merely by random reshuffling of their knowledge, beliefs, rules of conduct, habits, social practices and customs, but by deliberate design in the light of the conditions that the creative and rebellious amongst the people anticipate will occur. Further, in a record-keeping society experience of the fate of previous attempts at innovation can be retained and fed into the later processes by which M-conditions and S-conditions interact. In short, change in societies with collective memories will tend to become actually more and more Lamarckian, though we have no reason to suppose that knowledge will ever accumulate to the extent that the process will become Lamarckian in fully coupled form.

In differentially drawing on different M/S schemata socio-evolution is in a quite different case from populational theory in the biological context. Here we seem to have a distinction of profound consequence between the M/S conceptual scheme as applied in different fields.

Table 2

Type of Theory	*Summary* Relation of Conditions
Darwinian	M independent of S
Early human social conditions *************************	M weakly coupled to S *******************
Later human social conditions	M strongly coupled to S
Lamarckian	(i) M coupled to S (ii) S coupled to M

When M is coupled to S in a commercial enterprise we have the phenomenon of market research, in which the design of a product is determined by beliefs about the state of the market. But when S is coupled to M we have advertising in which the selection conditions or market is manipulated to favour the spread of a predetermined M.

Any relatively Darwinian view is required to deal with an apparent paradox. Evolutionary theories are offered as explanations of the changes in collectives, as rivals to the Durkheimian type of theory, which supposes that a social fact can be changed by altering another social fact. *A fortiori* the organic model, as a strictly Darwinian theory, offers no account whatever of the way in which selection conditions can change mutation conditions and be changed by them. So, if a weak Darwinian theory is offered anywhere on the spectrum between the Darwinian and Lamarckian extremes, it must, it seems, have a non-Darwinian theory of how interaction between conditions might be brought about. In practice this gap reduces to the need for a theory of how large-scale phenomena are represented to individual consciousness and for a theory to understand how a myriad of interpersonal interactions form collectives. We shall return to sketch solutions to both these needs.

An important consequence of the perception that an evolutionary theory need not be strictly Darwinian, is what one might call the politicizing of anthropology and history.

The descriptive ethnographies of *anthropology* could be treated as accounts of alternative forms of human association. By becoming known they enter into the process by which mutant social practices and social formations are created in a contemporary society, let us say, Western Europe. To learn from an anthropologist that a certain way of organizing social life exists elsewhere, with novel ways of performing the rituals by which social life is forwarded, and that people lead apparently satisfactory lives in accordance with it, opens up for us the possibility of other ways of life for us. It is not trivial either to remark that science fiction may have the same effect, in that conceptions of new forms of society – in this case imaginatively created – if popular and widely promulgated, can become effective agents in the social process. They can serve as models for the conceiving of possible social forms contemporary people might try to realize.

Selection conditions, on the other hand, can obviously become better understood by the study of *history*. The effect of knowledge of history on the cognitive and imaginative resources of human beings is not only to alter the possible forms of mutation by allowing people to make use of knowledge of how mutants have been selected by specific selection conditions in the past, but by bringing about an increasing degree of interaction between mutation and selection conditions social change becomes more Lamarckian. Under these conditions any adequate theory of social change and consequential form of political action also becomes more Lamarckian. Success in the utilization of specific theories will reflect back still further upon the spectrum of possible ways of social change, continuously making successive theories more and more Lamarckian. It becomes apparent, then, that the incorporation of anthropological and historical knowledge in public shared conceptions of what is possible and what was actual, alters not only the process but demands a progressively different social theory to understand it.

The general idea of a populational or M/S theory of historical change encompasses a great variety of specific forms. Since they are of rather different structure it will be necessary to be fairly precise about which form of populational theory is serving as the source-model for the construction of a theory of social change. I shall try to develop and to delimit the analogy between bio-evolution and socio-evolution through the best version, so far as I can ascertain, of the gene (-complex) selection theory, popularly expounded by Dawkins (1976) and extended and modified by Hull (1978).

All populational theories conceive of change as defined in terms of the replacement of a population of one type by a collection of individuals of another; under the condition that there exists a real relation between the members of the successive populations. All organic evolutionary theories of the M/S form meet these conditions whether they are Darwinian or Lamarckian.

To identify evolutionary theories in more detail Hull has developed a set of concepts out of Dawkin's original concept of replicator.

The first central concept in any populational theory is that of 'lineage', a sequence of individuals in a real relation that leads from one population to another. In the biological case the individuals are not organisms, but genes. For example an ancestral descent tree from a common family ancestor is a lineage. So is a sequence of better and better pumps, if each design arose by making improvements on the preceding one.

A lineage can be formally defined on a set of sets and a relation, that is as a sequence of populations together with a reproductive relation between members, say some form of copying.

The second central concept is that of replicator, the kind of entity through which identity and difference is actually transmitted at the reproductive stage. In general lineages are populations of replicators.

To define a mutation-selection or M/S theory a further concept-pair is required, interactor and environment, since it is in the real relation between interactors and environments that the differential effect on replicators occurs.

Dawkin's main contribution to the clarification of the logical structure of evolutionary theories is the clear statement of the principle that replicators and interactors may be distinct existents, requiring a consideration of what real relation may obtain between them. In general interactors are generated by replicators, but their existence is a necessary condition for replicators to form a lineage. In the organic application of the theory replicators are genes or gene-complexes, and interactors are organisms. The evolving population is then a collective of gene (-complexes).

To form a lineage, a sequence of replicators must satisfy two conditions: there must be real causal relations between one member and the next; there must be sufficient structural similarity between successive members. For these conditions to be known to be satisfied there must be criteria by which the identity and individuation of replicators could be determined. According to Hull lineages are the proper subjects of the verb 'to evolve'. A lineage will be said to have evolved when, with respect to the relevant properties, replicators late in the succession are different from those earlier in the chain.

At least in the biological applications of this explanation-format the criteria of similarity and difference between successive replicators depend on structural isomorphisms between them. If to be a gene is for an assemblage of molecules to have a particular structure then a metaphysical problem looms. What ontological commitments does the theory have? Are the genes the structures or the particular molecular realizations of the structures? Much of the language of biology suggests the former, for example 'gene-pool', 'the same gene appearing in different generations' and so on.

We seem to be presented with alternative pictures.

1 Replicators (genes) are assemblages of particular molecules, and are differentiated by structural properties. Evolution, as defined above with respect to lineages, is the replacement of old replicators by new, which are, in varying degrees, structurally similar to and structurally different from the old. No basis of continuity is required to sustain the lineage.

2 Replicators are the material realizations of a structure. It is the structure that is the gene. Evolution is the change of the structure through time and successive realizations. The picture requires some basis for the continuity of the structure, since for us to say the structure has changed, something must be preserved unchanged as the time-

independent referent. But there is no material basis for the continuity since successive replications are realizations in new molecules. We are required, it seems, to postulate some abstract entity as the bearer of continuity.

It seems that the facts, so to speak, and the explanatory format, admit of either alternative. We are then free to choose whichever accords best with our metaphysical principles. In the light of a general materialism and under the discipline of Ockham's razor, I choose to treat replicator identity and lineage change in accordance with the first picture. An immediate effect of this choice is to dissolve the rather ill-focussed notion of *a* gene into two components, particular molecular assemblages on the one hand, and the structural properties of those assemblages on the other. If genes and gene-complexes are to be identified with the structural properties of assemblages and two distinct molecular assemblages can have the same structure, two distinct molecular assemblages can be the bearers of the same gene (-complex). It follows that the replicators cannot be genes or gene-complexes. They must be the material bearers of genes.

Transfer of concepts: socio-evolution as parallel to gene selection

The general distinction between dialectical and evolutionary theories allows for a rather weakly framed socio-evolutionary explanatory format. At that level of generality one borrows the mutation/selection distinction, and one can speak vaguely of mutant practices, socio-economic selection environments and so on. The sharpened account of the fine structure of modern bio-evolutionary theory that I have just set out allows for a second stage of borrowing. Can we use the gene-theory as a source of concepts for developing ideas about possible generative mechanisms of social continuity and change? We could avoid a general commitment to teleology while explaining naturalistically the appearance of some measure of adaptiveness between social practices and social economic and ecological conditions.

The replicators are cognitively rather than molecularly realized as 'memes' (Dawkins, 1976). Replicators can be fixed as the sources of the structure of interactors. Let us take the interactors to be social practices, then the replicators should be the sources of social practices. We may, for want of a better term, call them 'rules'. We now have the following structure:

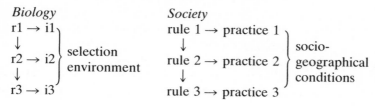

Mutation is defined on the rule-sequence as a lineage, and selection on the adaptiveness of practices to the environment, relative to which practices spread or do not spread; are kept or dropped by a community. For simplicity of exposition I shall be maintaining the fiction that each practice has its distinct rule. I shall drop that fiction later, since there are some negative aspects of the transfer that require us to consider whole rule-systems.

Though the transfer schema above is more refined than the Popper-Toulmin borrowing of the M/S framework, it is still vague. Before we can examine the analogy between bio- and socio-evolution carefully two further steps are required.

An essential feature of the replicator/interactor theory is the principle that only replicators replicate. There is no direct real causal relation between successive interactors. To reach the next interactor the system must pass through a replicator node, where a new replicator is generated which in its turn controls the generation of the next interactor.

Under the transfer mapping proposed above the social practices of one generation are conceived not to generate the social practices of the next directly. There must be a replicator node. In socio-evolution this would be the replication of the rules held to by one generation or by the same generation at different times. New practices would be produced by the following of a new rule. In effect this condition on socio-evolution is equivalent to the condition that social change must involve a social psychological theory, involving the changing competences of the individual members of the collective. This consequence is very welcome.

Lineages of rules offer the same metaphysical alternatives as did lineages of genes. Should we speak of a sequence of individual, structurally similar rules, or of the changing structure of a temporally enduring rule? In short where are we to locate a rule ontologically? Again I propose to adopt the least exciting picture. Rules are to be individuated as the cognitive resources of individual people over reasonable time-spans, so that if you and I are said to be 'following the same rule' that will be treated as a way of saying that the rule I am following is structurally isomorphic, or in some other appropriate way similar, to the rule you are following.

Social practices are equally metaphysically uncertain. To formulate clear ideas about the way socio-economic and geographical environments could actually affect the way people behave I propose to treat practices in the same way as I have treated rules. Each occasion on which an act/action sequence is produced will count as a distinct instance of a practice. The expression 'the same social (or other) practice' as in 'the farmers of today are using the same practices as their forefathers' will be taken to mean that several successive concrete act/action sequences are structurally or in some other way similar. And to say that *a* practice has spread throughout the community will be taken to mean that the concrete act/action sequences produced by people on particular occasions are similar in suitable respects to some other concrete, prior and particular act/action sequences, and differ from others.

In drawing the positive analogy I have assumed that the rule concept is an analogue to the gene concept as replicator, and is, like a gene, individually and internally realized in an organism. But rules can also be social and public. And temporal sequences of social, publicly promulgated rules could be imagined. There have been successive forms of the Highway Code and the Marriage Service. Such sequences would meet the requirements for constituting a lineage, and they would produce sequences of differing sets of like social practices.

But this dissimilarity seems to me to lie within the range of possible replicator-interactor theories. The general form of the theory and its major categories and relations are preserved. This feature of the mechanisms of socio-evolution does however open the possibilities of other kinds of mutation process than the merely personal fluctuations and innovations suggested by the strict analogy with biological applications of the replicator-interactor format. There may be such mutations as errors in the transcription of the documents in which rules are written down, or other forms of misrepresentation. The merging of cultures with explicit publicly represented rule-systems, such as codes of laws, could lead to a mixing of the systems of laws, parallel to the genetic mixing of sexual reproduction. One might find an instance of this in the imposition of an alien framework of law on tribal custom in a colonial regime.

In record-keeping societies the lineage of replicators is likely to be linked in more complex ways than in simpler cultures. In the biological version of the theory the n+1th replicator is produced from the nth replicator, and the influence of all those before the nth can be exerted only through whatever of their features are represented in the nth. But in rule-replication in record-keeping societies there is knowledge of many past rule-systems available to influence the way the n+1th rule in a lineage of rules is formed. The records allow past features long since eliminated from the lineage to be reintroduced. Lineages of rules under such a condition are not just simply ordered structures like this

$$r1 \rightarrow r2 \rightarrow r3 \rightarrow \ldots\ldots rn \rightarrow rn+1 \rightarrow \ldots\ldots$$

but more complex lattices like this

$$r1 \rightarrow r2 \rightarrow r3 \rightarrow r4 \ldots\ldots$$

In organic evolution, selection pressure acts directly on interactors (organisms) and only indirectly on replicators (genes). But in socio-evolution social approval and disapproval could act on either rules or practices. Indeed a proposed new rule could be eliminated from a culture before it had ever had a chance to be tested through realization in a social practice. Some legislative debates could be regarded as pre-selection processes in which proposed rules are tested by imagining their realization and its consequences, selection pressure acting directly on the replicators.

In bio-evolution mutations occur through imperfect copying of the structure of the nth replicator in the formation of the n+1th. One might look upon mutation as a defect in or prevention of the normal replication process. Learning the rules from one's family, one's teacher or one's peers could be thought of as the corresponding natural process in socio-evolution. a social mutation would be an inaccurate or imperfect learning of the rules. But in human affairs it may also be possible to encourage the replication of new rules as replicators which would not 'naturally' be copied. One might think of a school as an institutional realization of such a process. Stability is deliberately ensured and mutations prevented by testing the learning to make sure that each generation has indeed accurately replicated the knowledge and principles of action of the past.

The bio-evolutionary application of the replicator-interactor theoretical structure requires that the successive interactors, each produced by a replicator, are not causally linked. However the possibility of direct, mimetic reproduction of practices, customs, style and so on, could occur without the intermediate fixing of the practice in individually represented rules. For instance a Maori *tohunga* might know how to perform some practical task, and be followed by an assistant who has merely copied his every move, without the assistant acquiring an individual, explicit representation of the practice. Transmission in socio-evolution could be by interactor-interactor replication without passing through the stage of replicator.

Finally one should notice the possibility of interaction among the rules. In the social application the replicators may interact with each other to produce compensatory changes maintaining a stable form for an interaction. Many rules, like many genes, are required to produce a practice. We have already noticed the equilibrations that occur around important social presentational distinctions such as male/female. This could be expressed in terms of the replicator-interactor theory as reactions of one part of a rule system to changes in another so as to yield the same social phenomenon. Some interaction between genes is now considered likely in bio-evolution.

In summary it seems that theories of biological evolution have something to offer social psychologists looking for concepts in which to formulate theories of particular social changes. Again, the underlying motivation that brings bio- and socio-evolution together is the wish to explain adaptation without recourse to any stronger teleology than the nature of the beings involved (people) can sustain.

The limits of change in the mechanisms of social change

Could the processes of social change and the theories required to understand them become wholly Lamarckian? The answer, I think, must be an unqualified 'No'.

Some of the selection conditions to which interactors and replicators are subject, though they can become known by historical study, could not be changed to favour a particular mutant. Nor are these conditions the product of the spread of social practices which are the surviving mutants of past generations. I have in mind such non-social features of the environment as the weather, natural resources and so on. However, not every non-social element is stable. The growth of scientific knowledge and technical capacity may lead to some apparently non-social elements, such as the weather, succumbing to socially motivated technical intervention. It is a commonplace of economic theory that the extent of finite resources available to a society is not fixed by absolute physical quantities but by such matters as social desirability of extraction processes, capital investment and so on. It is not even clear that the laws of nature are immune from some sort of change under social influence. What we take them to be is, as we now realize, a compromise between changing forms of thought and the intransigent behaviour of the universe.

I have been assuming, though with reservations, that the selection conditions for mutant practices are, in general, to be found amongst the properties of the groups that human beings form in their various modes of association. For the interaction between mutation and selection conditions to form a closed circuit, it must be possible for these collective properties to be altered by human action. It is by no means clear to me that we have good reason for thinking this to be possible. I have reservations – one metaphysical and one epistemic. The metaphysical reservation has to do with the nature of collective properties. It may be because of the inevitability of at least some unintended consequences of human action that some main features of society will always be beyond the reach of intentional action. Every intentional action to alter something, which we have come to understand, will have, at least in principle, its own flux of unintended consequences. At least as far as human attempts to alter the collective properties of society by intended action are known, we have a record ranging from the merely dismal to the utterly disastrous. The epistemic reason is more conditional, in that in order to know what it would be rational to do, we must have some conception of the collective property which is serving as a selection condition and it is by no means clear that a methodology which reliably produced knowledge of collective properties could be worked out. It does not seem to me, however, that it is beyond human ingenuity to create such a device, but there seems to be no hint of how it might be done. Despite this pessimism, there seems to be no difficulty in principle in supposing that human collectives have distinctive properties, but it is not my purpose in this work to investigate the tension between epistemic pessimism and the metaphysical optimism that I feel on this matter.

I have already suggested that the application of an evolutionary schema must be qualified not only by limiting the degree of absolute Darwinism according to which it is constructed, but by borrowing from the organic sciences the idea that the selection environment might be subject to change. If the processes of social change are seen to be at their most effective in daily life in the selection of mutant practices by a social environment, and that environment itself is changing, a fully adequate theory of social change would have to include a way of explaining change of environment.

Could the Darwinian-Lamarckian spectrum, so plausible as a format for accounting for microsocial practices that maintain the social order of daily life, be generalized to provide an evolutionary account of the change in environment by the simple device of ordering environments in such a way that each environment could be thought of as under selection pressure from a wider environment, and so subject to change? An encouraging presupposition for this approach is to be found in Marx's important observation that human collectives can be defined by the fact that they reproduce their methods of sustaining life, albeit, I would wish to add, imperfectly. This suggests there might be some level of analysis at which collectives are themselves treatable as individuals undergoing mutation. If that is the case, then it seems reasonable to look for an environment of either greater scope or of higher order which can contain the selection conditions for collectives whose properties are now the mutant element in the system. The geographical conditions of the earth might constitute such an environment. But more interestingly, there are selection conditions internal to collectives, in which the collective constitutes its own selection condition. What I have in mind here is the generalization of the biological concept of lethal mutation in that a lethal mutation eliminates an individual because it leads to the formation of organs which do not form a viable system with the other inherited organ structures of an organism of that type. Novel social practices that are suicidal in existing socio-economic conditions would be an example. Finally, and still as an effect internal to the collective, are the appearance of non-standard human beings, or non-standard practices which can serve to drastically alter the conditions under which a mutant practice can survive.

Reflection upon these points leads us to a co-ordinated pair of solutions to the problem of the mechanism of change raised by the generalization of the evolutionary theory as an explanation of change in environments. The problem turns out to be soluble along two dimensions. In the one, the physical geographical conditions of the earth constitute an environment for all social environments, relatively stable with respect to social change, though not wholly immune from interaction with it. On the other hand, the properties of a collective, coupled with certain individual mutations, can serve as a selection condition for that very collective. This is possible only because the selection conditions and the collective and its properties do not exactly coincide, nor do collectives exactly reproduce themselves in the practices of successive generations.

The argument so far depends upon a number of assumptions about the way in which collectives are constituted out of and yet independent of their individual members' assumptions which have neither been defined nor defended. The next step is to show how in a relatively straightforward and simple way, the individual/collective relationship can be schematized for the purposes of understanding how an evolutionary theory of a quasi Lamarckian form can be effective.

Social adaptiveness

The concept of adaptiveness is correlative to that of function. A general criterion of adaptiveness is easily defined. A practice, institutional structure, mode of self-presentation and so on, is well adapted if it subserves the social function and personal projects of that practice and so on. But to say this is merely to display the conceptual connection between function and adaptation. Both concepts are based upon a root-idea of 'means-ends'.

Nevertheless, the display of this conceptual connection is not wholly useless. It provides a schema for formulating concrete, empirical questions about the spread or the failure to spread of innovations. The phases of an investigation might run as follows:

1 In what means-ends relations can we say a certain practice stands? Hypotheses about the functions of practices must not be just collective-sociological (the sin of functionalism) nor just individual-psychological (the sin of individualism) but reached by a negotiation between commentators on and members of a society.

The formulation of means-ends hypotheses is made more complicated still by the necessity to separate, at least analytically, the expressive and practical orders. The 'same' practice may have to be located in two or more networks of means-ends relations. For example, a strike may be able to be seen to be functionally adaptive to the expressive end of demonstrating dignity, but functionally maladaptive to the practical end of improving standard of living.

2 With some means-ends hypotheses to hand, the next phase would involve the theoretical contemplation of alternative means to the given ends. But these means must be contemplated against a background of what is known about the historical conditions, and particularly the current psychology of the folk. Survival of a novel practice is, I argue, determined by an interplay between individual-psychological possibility and collective-social necessity.

In short, I presume there are no universal criteria of social adaptiveness that are specific enough to explain particular cases of the spread of a practice. But particular questions of why some innovations spread and others do not ought to be looked at in a means-end framework, with both orders in mind.

AN EXAMPLE OF THE SOCIO-DIALECTIC
EXPLANATORY FORMAT

In analyzing any social change we are in effect analyzing a social movement. The women's movement is a very complex phenomenon, involving numerous strands and often conflicting points of view. However it is possible, I believe, to discern an overall pattern to the movement, in which the origins of the social changes that it represents can be understood through the application of the theory outlined in the previous sections. The first step will be to try to identify the dialectic of tensions between the way women experience their locations in the current practical and expressive orders. Were the latter to express status in the former no dialectic of tensions would exist and no mutant social practices would occur. Was there a common disparity between the positions of some articulate women in the practical and in the expressive orders? One must add the observation that during most of postwar era the expressive order has been realized in customs and practices that represented a practical order in which the social world was fairly neatly divided into two spheres, in one of which women were socially dominant and in the other, men. Each had its own practical order.

In this analysis I shall follow commentators such as Shirley Ardener (1975) in distinguishing between the movement for women's rights, which is concerned with access to locations in the practical order ('practical feminism') and the less tangible but even more important movement for a change in the way the value of women as persons is recognized and ritually confirmed ('symbolic feminism'). In what follows I shall be assuming that the movement I have called 'practical feminism' has enjoyed a large measure of success, changing the location of women in the practical order. It seems to me that explanations for this success must also be sought in a selectionist theory, in which the two world wars and the transformation of the techniques of manufacturing and of marketing must play a large part as an environment favouring mutant practices in the way women are located in the world of work. A 'mutant practice' is simply a new way of organizing the social structure of production. Pursuing that issue further is a matter for sociology. Symbolic feminism has arisen, I shall argue, through the rhetorical redescription of perceived incongruities between the location of women in the current expressive order and their locations in the world of work. (In our time there has come to be more and more of social life lived in just one practical order, as the importance of the domestic scene has declined.)

Of course, one should notice that the practical and expressive orders, which I am treating as analytically distinct, intersect and interact. For instance some of the pressure from women to enter certain professions, such as stockbroking, could be explicable in part in terms of the expressive advantage of being seen to be in that kind of job, rather than through any consuming interest in the tasks to be performed. There is no reason to suppose that in such matters women's motivations are so very different from those of men.

Let us list some of the expressive acts that have been perceived by women to be incongruous with their position in the contemporary practical order: the custom that the man should pay for meals taken in restaurants, the custom that cars should be driven by men, who race around to open the door for the women passengers, even when those women are world champion athletes, the custom of holding doors open for women to pass through, and so on. The 'old fashioned courtesies' by which women were honoured as wives and mothers, in the old expressive order, become the vehicles of acts of condescension and patronization in the new. The actions persist, but the acts they are taken to perform change.

There is a more subtle aspect of symbolic feminism which is worth remarking. In the old divided or dual practical orders, the family purse strings were more often than not held by the women. Domestic and economic power, in the sense of whose views ultimately prevailed in matters in dispute, more often than not, belonged to women. As the boundaries between the two practical orders became more and more permeable the equality of regard that was growing in the expressive order tied to the world of work, subtly contradicted the asymmetry of men's and women's locations in the old domestic order. Many women, happily located in the old practical and expressive orders, felt themselves devalued by the *expressive* representation of the new locations in the new practical order, which symbolic feminism was intent on creating. It seems to me that in the nineteen nineties symbolic feminism is in process of transition to yet another form.

But felt tensions and contradictions do not provide occasions for the invention of new social practices unless there is some rhetoric available in which they can find expression in a set of interpretations drawn from familiar insitutions. Late Medieval symbolic feminism, the beguine movement, drew on the rhetoric of religion to interpret local social practices as expressively demeaning. The necessity to call in a male priest to intercede between religious women and God was so interpreted. In our times a political rhetoric has been employed in giving a concrete form to expressive dissatisfactions (Greer, 1984). In the light of the religious rhetoric new religious practices were invented in the later Middle Ages, while in our time a range of mutant expressive practices have been invented in the light of the political rhetoric. A very simple but nice case of this kind of expressive invention is the new range of personal titles to which we have become more or less accustomed, so that 'Miss' has gone from the repertoire.

Secord and Guttentag (1988) suggest a common demographic factor in both the genesis of the original tension and as the selection environment. They demonstrate that in conditions where the number of females actually available as partners for suitable males is large relative to the number of such males, changes in attitudes to marriage and sexual relations in both male and female valuations of the female are to be found. In these conditions 'women's movements' appear. Secord and Guttentag use demographic data. They base their conclusions upon correlations of the demographic conditions and the public visibility and institutional representation of women's expressive demands. The historical ubiquity of the phenomenon suggests the search for a causal mechanism. We might find it by imposing a primarily evolutionary explanatory format in two complementary phases. At the level of individual behaviour the format would produce a theory like this: men, always liable to be promiscuous, find that when there is a superabundance of females they can get away with changing partners more often than they could before. Many women experience these individual abandonments and betrayals as in conflict with the dominant expressive order, which emphasizes a protective and supportive attitude as proper for men to show to women. And so the dialectic begins to develop as a psychological phenomenon. And once set going the separation of a successful 'practical feminism' becomes the source of a secondary dialectic tension with the revision of the old expressive order demanded by 'symbolic feminism' (Ardener, 1975).

Within this combination of populational (evolutionary) and dialectic formats there is no difficulty in understanding how a demographic condition could have power to generate individual choices of behaviour and attitude, since the changing demographic condition merely favours an existing male behavioural tendency, experienceable by women.

But the evolutionary format can be reapplied at a collective level of analysis. Secord and Guttentag point out that the spread of an innovatory rhetoric to become a movement can be explained by seeing the history of these matters as the intersection of two cycles somewhat out of synchronization. There is always somewhere or other an incipient women's movement, and it rises and declines in intensity according to causal processes which are presently unknown. But it will only become a movement and lead to changes in the social world generally if it is on the rise, so to speak, at a time when the demographic cycle of changing proportions of men to women has reached a point where there are more women than men at the appropriate age. The demographic cycle serves as a changing selection environment for repeated mutations in the perception by women of their role in the social world.

The social psychological problems in this theory can be defined in terms of the three-fold questions: perception? motivation? action? Secord and Guttentag propose a theory of social perception – namely that individual women perceive the demographic conditions in the behaviour of men – men, fulfilling the reproductive strategy typical of males, as demeaning. Motivational resources and action templates derive from the contemporary rhetorics. People draw on what there is currently available to theorize about their situations – as they perceive them.

An advantage of the use of the two formats, the dialectic and the mutation-selection, is that one can conduct detailed social psychological research into the one, while leaving the operative element in the other inexactly specified. All that is needed for the application of the methodology of negative causation is the assumption of some selection environment, which will permit the spread of certain mutant practices and not others. It is not necessary even for the selection environment to favour one practice rather than another, merely not to impede their differential diffusion.

10

THE SOCIAL PSYCHOLOGY OF POLITICAL ACTIVITY

ANTICIPATORY SUMMARY

A political philosophy is a moral position. The development of a theory of the psychology of political change inevitably requires a consideration of the basic moral commitments one would wish to make to the most general specification of what would be socially desirable. I propose three: to a degree of personal autonomy; to a measure of social order; and to the right to speak and to be heard. The last is the most fundamental, according to the theory sketched in this book, since both personal autonomy and social order are discursively constituted. Following André I argue for a three-dimensional classification of political philosophies. There is the dimension of rhetoric, running from reason to unreason. There is the dimension of expressive hierarchy, running from mutual respect to ritualized contempt. Thirdly there is the dimension of degree of autonomy. Acceptance of the moral commitments sketched above would lead to the favouring of a political system based on the joint maximization of reason, respect and autonomy, in so far as that was socially psychologically possible.

How might such an ideal come to be realized? Proposals for political programmes are proposals for social change, so must rest in social psychology. Their overall viability will depend directly upon their conformity to the most general features of human social psychology, and their local feasibility will depend on the local practical and expressive orders. The considerations advanced in this book tend to show that both *laissez faire* and socialist political systems are paradoxically unstable and inevitably evolve away from the morally desirable ideal identified above.

There are two ways by which one might try to change a society. One can directly confront an existing social order and attempt its overthrow. Or one can begin to live an alternative life form within the existing society which one hopes will be taken up by more and more people. The former is doomed to fail for social psychological reasons. The latter is conformable to the social psychology of social change, as I have outlined it in chapter 9. However there is no way that a deliberately designed mutant social formation, can be insulated from selection pressures of the larger social, geographical and economic environment. It must take its chance, along with whatever spontaneous microsocieties spring up in the resolution of tensions between the current practical and expressive orders.

Finally one must distinguish transformations of the practical order of a society, leaving its expressive order more or less intact, and transformations of its expressive order, through which and only through which can the moral quality of human associations change. I argue that it is changes in the expressive orders of societies that are the most fundamental. Yet those expressive orders are the most resistant to revision.

A MORAL STANDPOINT

Any general psychological theory must make use of a certain conception of human kind. But a social psychology, as I have tried to argue, depends on assumptions about the possible forms of social life as well. While a psychology owes its readers an explicit statement of the moral position which underlies it, a social psychology is doubly bound. One owes one's readers an explicit statement of the political consequences of one's view of people in association, and the political possibilities which the adoption of that view would open up. In what follows I attempt a sketch, and it is no more than a sketch, of the political consequences of the position advocated in this book.

To develop a sketch of a political philosophy on the basis of our psycho-sociological conclusions a moral standpoint must be imposed upon the material. As almost all moral philosophers have argued it is impossible to derive moral principles from social or other facts without introducing an ultimately factually arbitrary assignment of moral worth to some human attribute, social practice and so on.

Two basic principles emerge naturally from the earlier analysis of the necessary attributes of socially competent persons. I showed that we needed to attribute both autonomy and reflexivity to human beings to ground their main psychosociological capabilities. Autonomy was the capacity to act independently of any given influence, whether external or internal, and reflexivity was the capacity to bring lower order motivations and even causes of action under motivations and principles of higher order, in an indefinite hierarchy.

These capacities or powers vary considerably from person to person, and in any given person from time to time. They can be augmented by education, and reduced by training. Two divergent moral systems can be constructed by taking the issue of the augmentation or the dimunition of personal powers as the locus of the arbitrary choice of moral principle. I shall say, following Shotter (1975), Kant (1965) and many others, that the augmentation of personal powers is an ultimate good. Diverging from this locus are the moral theories of Skinner (1972) and many others, who hold that the dimunition of personal powers is an ultimate moral good.

Closely connected with the principle of the augmentation of autonomy and reflexivity as personal powers, is a principle which leads to the limitation of the exercise of these powers in a social context. Again I try to identify a locus of the ultimate assignment of moral worth. The analysis of the social interactions of human beings led from many different directions to the idea that the search for order is pervasive in human life. It is achieved in the structuring of actions, in the formation of hierarchies of respect and contempt, in the relative status that people assign to themselves. Contrary to some strands of social thought I shall be arguing for a radical theory from the very principle that social order (though it will be a social order fragmented into indefinitely many forms of association) is an ultimate moral good.

It should be evident that the elevation of the facts of personal autonomy and reflexivity and of the universal appearance of social order to moral principles leads to a system with a strong internal tension. I hope to show that each cluster of moral assignments provides the limiting conditions necessary for fruitful development in actual institutions, of the other. The need for order limits the exercise of personal autonomy by the necessity to co-operate with others in the creation and maintenance of order by dramaturgical means, and the power of autonomy and reflexivity limits the rigidity of socially maintained structure in actions, institutions and so on.

In the next stage of the argument I try to relate personal or psychological attributes to traditional political philosophies. In this way my choice of moral principles as ultimate attributions of moral worth to certain personal and psychological properties of human beings can be related to a choice of a broad political position, as deriving its worth from the basic moral principles.

The argument however proceeds with yet another assumption of a relation between value and fact. At the heart of the analyses of social activity in Part II of this study lay speech. Speech appeared contingently as part of the action, but necessarily as the prime means of accounting, the theorizing about and criticizing of action so characteristic of human life. Theorizing opens up the possibility of the contemplation of alternatives, and as Secord and I argued in our critical study of social psychological method, accounting ultimately depends on the existence of reflexive consciousness. This line of argument would locate speaking as a necessary condition for the possibility of political activity, since it is closely related to the possibility of the private-personal conceiving and the public-social promulgating of ideas of alternative social orders to those currently being maintained by personal public activity within existing social collectives. But I want to take a further step. I want to attach worth to speaking as accounting in its own right. From this I immediately derive the principle that since, as a person, everyone has as a matter of fact the power to give an account, they must also have the right. The moral 'must' comes from the relation of that right to the conditions for being a person at all. This seems to me an independent moral principle, and I set it forth as a third locus of the association of value with fact.

PSYCHOLOGICAL DIMENSIONS OF POLITICAL THEORIES

The lethal mutation as psychological impossibility

The rapid disintegration of most attempts at new forms of human association is not wholly to be explained by reference to the hostility or indifference of the host society within which they come into being. A survey of a wide range of such novelties, including modern communes, suggests that some forms of association for the people of a certain historical time and cultural origin are psychologically impossible. Even the most successful new societies, such as the Oneida Community, founded in the midnineteenth century in Upper New York State, depended for the longevity of its social forms on the personal power of one man. The survival of the community after his death was possible only because profound changes were made in its organization. The community quickly became indistinguishable from others around it. It retained its identity largely through the silver plate manufacturing for which as an industrial corporation it is still famous. It seems that a lethal mutation was incorporated within the original Oneida Community. It is easily identified. Access to the sexual favours of the women at Oneida was distributed by rank within a male hierarchy, appointment to which was in the personal gift of the founder. This proved a psychologically untenable basis for a social organization as the younger men acquired their psychological predispositions and moral opinions from the circumambient communities with which they worked.

The psychological conditions under which a particular social arrangement has to be lived act therefore as internal limiting conditions on the viability of those arrangements. Sometimes they make demands which the members can fulfil only under the control of a powerful leader. The limiting conditions lurk as latencies in the members of the society, ready to destroy it when the leader departs or is overthrown. Novel social arrangements which demand unrealizable psychological conditions are rather like lethal mutations in the biological sphere. Once special life-support systems are removed such an individual quickly perishes. These considerations raise the general question of the psychological conditions of reform and the psychological dimension of political thought.

Varieties of psychologies in theories of political association

The argument in this section is based upon some distinctions made by J. André in a series of unpublished papers. He distinguishes political theories and their associated programmes by reference to the underlying socio-psychological assumptions upon which they are based. Essentially these assumptions amount to theories of motivation. Motivation, like intention and want, is a curiously and importantly dual concept. It has a place in the public world of planning and the attachment of a person to their project. André's classification, I believe, tacitly depends upon this important duality, but he does not explicitly identify it.

André distinguishes three different forms of psychological foundation for social life in accordance with an identifiable political theory. He differentiates them according to what he calls 'dimensions'.

A linear political theory proposes that the basis of political and social action is a single, fundamental, socio-psychological aspect of human beings in association. For example, the thesis that seeking and exercising power is the source of all forms of political association would be a linear theory.

A two-dimensional theory proposes that the form of a political association and its practices derives from the intersection of two axes of motivation. Political forms are differentiated as people are more or less committed to and interested in these motives and call upon them in the rhetoric of their accounts. André is able to show that analyses such as Hyeck's two-dimensional representation of political

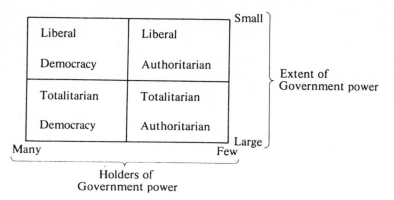

Figure 6

philosophies (Fig. 6): and Rockeach's two-valued theory of political ideology defined in terms of a Cartesian product of degree of freedom and degree of equality are reflections of a general two-dimensional theory of political motivation. He argues that on one dimension lies the attitude of individuals to the exercise of personal power and on the other their willingness to form associations. For example, if they have no interest in the personal exercise of power and no wish to form highly ordered institutions, society comparable to that envisaged in the final form of Communism would arise, if those were the only motivations of the people.

André holds that two-dimensional motivation theories are inadequate to the variety of known forms of political association. He proposes a third dimension. In my terms it represents the degree to which reference to reason figures *in the rhetoric* associated with the making of day-to-day decisions in the political arena. By adding the third dimension André is able to propose a much richer classification represented in a psychopolitical cube (See Fig. 7).

To take account of the central psychological importance of moral career I collapse the 'power' + 'association' dimensions into a single axis representing degree of autonomy, and add an axis representing the socio-psychological representations of worth, respect/contempt hierarchies.

Equality of worth cannot be achieved when there is one and only one system of criteria for evaluating people and their actions. If the giving of respect and showing of contempt for people is as fundamental as I am supposing then respect-hierarchies will never disappear from human life. Equality of worth could be approached only by the

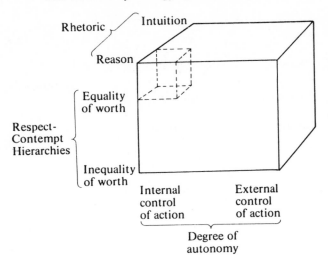

Figure 7

growth or provision of multiple respect hierarchies, with widely different criteria.

The distinction between internal control and external control is partly a psychological issue, partly determined by whether controlling bodies are participatory or representative. There will be external control whatever the claim to be the representative, be it majority vote (Parliament), historical necessity (Communist Party) or divine right (Medieval Kings), when decisions are made for people by others. The cell which we will inhabit is theoretically identified according to the argument of this work as that located at that vertex of a psycho-political cube where equality of worth (for me the giving of multiple possibilities of achieving respect) freedom (for me the right to give an account and have one's account attended to), and reason (for me the utilization of a rhetoric of rationality for accounting for actions and decisions) are realized.

It seems, then, that in terms of different theoretical orientations and different modes of attachment to the necessities of political association, it is possible to provide a taxonomy of political theories on the basis of a socio-psychology of motives, projects and intentions provided they are interpreted in terms of the public/private duality. In the course of the remaining sections of the study I intend to argue for the inevitability of the discovery that one, and only one, cell of the psycho-political cube contains a mode of political association which is wholly appropriate to human life as I have analysed it. However, it is no part of my theory that the inevitability of the discovery of the theoretical uniqueness of that cell is a good reason for believing that it will inevitably come to be, for reasons which I shall consider in detail.

PROBLEMS IN THE DEDUCTION OF A POLITICAL PROGRAMME

The general political paradox

A society consists of a network of relations among individuals. It is quite likely that the network has properties that are different from a mere aggregate of individual actions. It is theoretically possible that the steps which have to be taken to realize changes in the interpersonal networks that make up a society, will lead to changes in the situation of an individual that that person thinks are undesirable. This, of course, is the classical political paradox. How is it possible to reconcile the interests of individuals and society? And it is a paradox since the society consists of those individuals, one of whose interests ought to be the best interests of all. Philosophers have offered a variety of solutions, none of which, in my view, is without serious difficulty. I do not propose to rehearse the arguments of classical political philosophy in this work. General solutions to the basic political paradox fall into two main groups.

There are those which emphasize collective properties of society and see individual life fulfillments in terms of them, and those which concentrate on features of individual lives in the hope that some summation of these will constitute a social advantage. Neither seems to me to locate a possible social psychological base for a theory of political association. Whatever theory is advanced must take account of the possibility that the properties of collectives are distinct from the properties of their individual members, and yet must restrict intentional concepts to individual members and their projects. I hope it will be seen that the approach in this study preserves just such a structure.

Pragmatic paradoxes of specific political programmes

The deduction of a political programme from any socio-psychological theory of human action is faced not just with the general political paradox but with specific difficulties which infect large classes of practical activities. There are two such paradoxes which are of central importance in the deduction I am about to undertake, the paradox of *laissez faire* and the paradox of socialism.

How is it possible for freedom in the moral sphere – that is freedom to construct one's life-form and to build one's personality and character for oneself – to be achieved without leaving open freedom in the economic sphere – that is the freedom to exploit others and the environment in one's own personal interests? The paradox arises from the opportunity which the giving of absolute freedom to all opens to some, the strong and the greedy, to limit or eliminate the freedom of many. How is it possible to partition the fields of activity of human agents in a principled way? This has been the difficulty which has beset anarchistic programmes of political reform in the past. I do not propose to treat this as an issue of principle but rather as a socio-psychological problem. I shall propose a solution by paying attention to what we know and might come to know about the springs of human action.

The perception of the paradox of *laissez faire* was, of course, one of the sources of the socialist proposal that a form of state should be devised in which the activities of all the citizens should be managed in the interests of the most exploitable group in that society. This has, of course, led to its own destructive pragmatic paradox. A necessary condition for the management of the activities of the citizens is the setting up of institutions of managers who, in principle, will act in the interests of all. But the managers form an institution, and institutions evolve in such a way that expressive activities and motivations come to dominate the instrumental ends for which the institution was founded. The managers are in danger of becoming a new exploiting class. The paradox, in short, follows from the impossibility of preventing the rise of new exploiting classes without setting up a class yet more powerful. Again, I do not propose to treat the paradox of socialism by philosophical argument. I shall examine the paradox and the possibility of its solution with respect to socio-psychological considerations having to do with the nature of human beings and their forms of association.

I take both the paradox of *laissez faire* and the paradox of socialism to be consequences of reflection on the actual nature of people and their modes of association. They are reflections of features of human life on which no programme of education, or moral exhortations, and no newly invented institutions, will have the slightest effect. Any attempt to alter these basic features of human life can only slow down the inevitable socio-psychological processes by which the paradoxes manifest themselves in actual public activities.

I have expressed these paradoxes in traditional political terms but in contexts which are essentially contemporary, that is in terms of political movements that have characterized the last 150 years, but of course, both paradoxes are reflections of the age-old paradox of liberty and equality. Both liberty and equality are desiderata of the moral state but the consequences of allowing ourselves liberty clash with the conditions of our equality and, on the other hand, the conditions of human equality clash with the necessary conditions for human liberty.

Before I proceed to the development of an argument for a political programme based on the socio-psychology of this work, it is worth pausing to examine a well-argued and seemingly attractive solution proposed by Steven Lukes (1973b) in his book *Individualism*. Lukes' solution is based upon a concept which is also central to the argument of this work, namely the idea of respect for persons. In Lukes' argument this allows for a theoretical resolution of the specific pragmatic paradoxes, and the classical paradox of liberty and equality.

The paradox of *laissez faire* would disappear if economic exploitation could be made to seem a kind of contempt, and the paradox of socialism would disappear if the transformation of the managerial *cadres* into an exploiting class in the course of a shift from instrumental to expressive motivation was seen to involve contempt for their clientèle. These suggestions are highly theoretical and contain no hint of how such reforms of fundamental human attitudes and activities are likely to be undertaken. Lukes offers a practical solution. He supposes that the realization of respect for persons is a technical matter. It can be brought about, he thinks, by some form of state management which is so organized as to see to distribution of both wealth and power. Lukes takes these to be the practical forms in which respect for persons is realized.

However, Lukes's theory falls straight back into the old difficulties. It is not clear that the realization of respect in wealth and power is a sufficiently universal feature of human societies to form the basis of an *a priori* formulation of a political programme, since both are highly problematic as goods. Traditional wisdom has it that wealth and power seem attractive only to those who have not attained them. When they are attained they are realized to be burdens. Paradoxically, the revelations of those who have attained wealth and power are never believed by those who follow after. Traditional wisdom has it that wealth and power once attained become the source of a new range of motives, which would lead one to abandon them. Only perhaps a neurotic compulsion for security compels one to hold on to them. Of course, in a social organization which provided forms of security and modes of respect other than those associated with wealth and power, the tales brought back from the summits might have some likelihood of being believed and in being believed the search for wealth and power would itself be sabotaged. The idea that power is an unqualified good whose redistribution by means of some state apparatus would resolve the pragmatic paradoxes, is again equivocal in that traditional wisdom holds that power over others entails, for most of those who attain it, the burden of responsibility; and that the burden of responsibility comes to outweigh the satisfactions of the exercise of power. Whatever may be the psychological law involved at this point, it is clear that wealth and power are not unequivocal as ultimate goods.

Even if Lukes were right in identifying the key socio-psychological goods associated with respect for persons he falls into the pragmatic paradox I have associated with classical socialism, in that he supposes that the state, or what of course amounts to the same thing in practice, a bureaucracy, can achieve the practical marks of respect for everyone in the redistribution of wealth and power without creating a new exploiting class, that is a new class which uses its instrumental activities for the purposes of expressive presentations of self. I believe this belief to be unfounded for the reasons I have argued in detail, and so I believe the political society Lukes envisages to be impossible of actual realization.

Whatever way we take which avoids the central problem, that is avoids confronting the relationship between the inevitable development of the closed societies of bureaucrats and the nature of human association, will fail. It is an irremedial feature of human association that bureaucracies will always develop towards total institutions and shift from the instrumental to the expressive mode. Human association must have a symbolic base, the symbols become detached from the instrumentality of the institution and become the sole content of action.

These features of the social psychology of bureaucrats are well known and have been the subject of much critical thinking amongst anarchist social philosophers. For example, Bakunin took it as a fundamental principle that a socialist bureaucracy was bound to generate a new ruling class, irrespective of the origins of those who came to compose it, whether they were drawn from the working class or were renegade intellectuals. Machevski even went so far as to argue that Marxist Socialism was an ideological device by which the intelligensia proposed to seize power and become a new ruling class. Sorel pointed out that revolutionary leaders could succeed only on condition that they adopted despotic practices. Any party of revolution will, of necessity, lead to a new oppressive society with the party as the new ruling class. These criticisms point to the surface phenomenon of the transformation of closed institutions without delving deeply into the socio-psychological conditions of human association from which they inevitably follow. The argument of this work has been in part designed to lay bare the empirical and theoretical foundation for these intuitive perceptions and to found anarchist criticism of socialism on a sound footing.

It is not difficult, it seems, to locate the weak point in Lukes's programme which occurs despite the depth and power of his analysis of the moral properties that any individual in a society must preserve for that society to be counted as morally approvable. The paradox arises because his sketch of a practical programme for the realization of those moral properties involves conditions incompatible with them, given the social psychological principles of the development of human institutions. If, as I have argued throughout this work, those social psychological principles are deeply rooted, indeed are the fundamental nature of people and integral to the most deep principles of human association, no programme like Lukes's could ever succeed. It follows that the occasion for the transformation of a society from a form in which every human being has a sufficient measure of respect and the means to achieve it, to one in which a new oppressive class appears, is mediated by one and only one feature, namely the coming into being of a class or institution of social managers. Our problem, then, is to consider the design of a society in which the paradoxes of *laissez faire* and of socialism can both be avoided, that is a society which contains the machinery for the elimination of exploitation without realizing that machinery in a bureaucracy.

Lastly in this romp through centuries of political theory, I want to turn briefly to Marx's solution, namely to give the management of society to the most exploitable class, the proletariat. Of course, this is an attractive solution in principle, but difficulties abound, not least the practical one of setting up an institution by means of which that management could be undertaken. And any institution which is set up must, of course, develop according to the trajectory of all managerial institutions. The necessity for some form of representative institution which manages in the interests of the most exploitable class, follows from the practical impossibility of that class exercising management for itself. The moment such an institution of management is set up the iron laws of the social psychological development of societies come into effect. Bureaucracies, I must emphasize, are total institutions in Goffman's sense, that is, they will transform themselves so that the moral careers of the functionaries become dominant over the official work of the institution unless there are other institutions which can conduct a continuous assessment of that total institution and occasionally bring it to heel. But if the institution of which we are speaking is the state apparatus itself, the central bureaucracy, there is no other institution to bring it to heel. We should expect to find formalization of the official rhetoric which describes the apparent instrumental activities of the bureaucracy. Our efforts to understand what we see to be happening in that institution demand the explicatory power of drama-turgical model and the analytical concepts associated with the idea of moral career.

THE DEDUCTION OF A POLITICAL PSYCHOLOGY OF SOCIAL ACTION

The stage is now set for the deduction of a theory of political change and social action consequent upon the various theories and insights which I have proposed in earlier parts of this study. The first step in our argument will be to identify the necessary conditions for political activity to be possible. These can be set out as follows:

Psycho-social conditions
It should be possible for the members of a social collective to envisage a form of life different from that which they currently live, and they must be able to conceive of a programme by which what they take to be the most desirable form could be brought into being.

Moral conditions
They should have criteria by means of which judgements of relative desirability can be made between the forms of life which they can conceive to be possible. They must be able to compare those forms of life with the conditions under which they believe themselves to exist.

The possibility of a programme based upon a judgement as to the best form of life does not entail that it can be realized by political action. I shall be arguing that this requires that the theory that members of the collective hold as to how a desirable form of life can be brought into being is based upon an adequate conception of the nature of social change.

If we assume that the political spectrum with which political theory confronts us, namely that between those who wish to preserve (or conserve) social formations that already exist, and those who wish to change them, is naive, we must look more deeply into the forms of possible political action. I am interested only in forms of radical politics in terms of which people might set about changing society. The basic distinction is between a political radicalism which I shall call 'the confrontation mode', and a political radicalism of the alternation mode.

In a confrontation mode, the members who are intent upon a revision of society identify what they take to be the major structural properties of the existing collective and set about attempting to change them. This is a process of confrontation, of direct attack in one form or another upon the existing structure of the collective and the social practices which reproduce it.

It is not difficult to see that this is a paradoxical form of political activity. There are good historical grounds to sustain this objection. In many cases the social formation which the radicals are intent upon changing is neither well-articulated nor particularly well-defined. The effect of challenging it is to force its supporters to formulate their view of society more fully, thus making it more real. In short, the effect of confrontation radicalism is sometimes to stabilize and to make more fully realized the very social formation against which the radical programme is directed. The existing society becomes conscious of itself and thus comes to wish to defend what it now takes to be its social order in the course of such a confrontation.

At the same time as this is happening to the structure which is the subject of the programme of change, a corresponding alteration is occurring in the organization of those who are confronting it. As the existing structure becomes better and better defined, so the organization of the radical party must match it more and more closely to have a chance of successfully overthrowing it. Whatever organs come into existence on the conservative side must be matched by the radicals. This, I think, is the simple explanation of the often-remarked historical fact that in the course of a revolution the revolutionary party comes to be a mirror image of the party which is defending the status quo.

In short, we can say that with respect to the original task of altering the old social order and replacing it with something new, the confrontation programme is almost irremediably paradoxical. The conditions under which it can exist are precisely those under which it cannot succeed.

This suggests that we should look for a different form of political activity in the hope of avoiding the paradox. The programme of alternation politics offers just such a possibility, but as we shall see, though it avoids the difficulties and pitfalls of confrontation politics it has difficulties and pitfalls of its own.

It is clear that any programme which is likely to succeed must base itself on the processes of social change which we already know to occur. If the arguments of this work are correct, then some mixture of dialectical tension resolution and evolutionary selection of mutants is responsible for social change. A political programme should therefore be based upon a combination of these processes. In general, then, we should be trying to formulate a political programme which utilizes the mutation/selection conception of the way social trends fall and introduces new rhetorics to amplify tensions between the practical and expressive orders. An alternation politics will set about defining and bringing into existence mutant forms of social practice and association and novel rhetorics within the existing society. That society, its rhetorics, practices and even its ecology constitutes the selection conditions for mutants. If these spread then in the course of the social change thus deliberately brought about, the collective as selection condition will itself change, favouring some mutants rather than others. This process need not be the helpless social tinkering of the Popperian social theory, since, as I have argued earlier, the introduction of anthropological, historical and social scientific knowledge into the system ensures that the processes of social change are not pure Darwinian but go some way towards being Lamarckian in form.

Given this general picture, how might it be possible to formulate a prescription for an alternative social formation?

THE BASES OF THE ALTERNATION POLITICAL PROGRAMME

I have argued in earlier chapters that the moral basis of society is to be found in the criteria by which human beings are accorded respect and contempt as persons. This idea derives from the micro-sociological studies of Erving Goffman which have revealed the extent to which the ritual expression of respect and contempt are the cement of day-to-day relations. The first steps in an alternation programme must be to envisage a society in which the criteria for the attribution of respect and contempt for people are radically different. The first step in freeing these criteria for imaginative reformulation is to detach them from their contemporary connection with the economic system, so that the criteria for and marks of respect or contempt for a person are separated from the accumulation of wealth or goods. But such a separation is only a necessary, but not a sufficient, condition for the setting up of a quasi-Darwinian social order, since if the detached respect and contempt criteria still form a single system, the possibility of mutant forms of these criteria is still precluded. The next step, then, must be to multiply respect hierarchies indefinitely, either by looking for and amplifying existing small-scale and local respect hierarchies, or by inventing more as a deliberate act of policy. If the moral basis of a society lies in its respect and contempt criteria, then the multiplication of respect and contempt criterial hierarchies will lead automatically to multiplication of alternative micro-societies and consequently to an increase in the possibility of political change.

But the moral basis of this political psychology so far has provided only a more elaborated necessary condition for the bringing about of a new social order. The multiple alternative societies as I have so far described them exist only in the imagination of political authors and science fiction writers. There must necessarily be some revolutionary phase. As I have already argued, a confrontation revolution is certain to fail. Because of its paradoxical relation to the old structure it must lead, after a series of confrontations which could be violent and destructive, to a society which is in all respects except nomenclature and personnel, identical with the one it replaces.

In order to understand the nature of an 'alternation' revolution it is necessary to notice that the respect-contempt hierarchies have to do rather with the expressive devices which society can call upon than anything simply practical. Respect and contempt must be marked by conventional signs and these markers are part of the expressive order of the society. They might be clothes, manner of speech, deferential forms for address, certain kinds of possessions, or the ability to display a necklace which one has been able to persuade someone to lend one, as in the Kula ring, and so on. If all other properties of the society have changed, except the expressive devices, the continuity of the respect/contempt practices of the old society is ensured. The reproduction of the expressive hierarchies will lead to the reconstruction of a new base structure which is formally isomorphic with the old. At the heart of the imaginative anticipation of new social formations must be the conventions of an alternative expressive order by which social relations are to be actually constituted on a day-to-day basis. These, of course, will be the expressive devices by means of which persons present themselves as worthy, and the rituals by which respect and contempt are marked.

I propose to call the efforts of a group of social reformers to change the major structural properties of a society, such as the means by which the legislative activities are regulated, or the relative wealth of the inhabitants is arranged, a primary revolution. The deeper changes in the moral basis of society which would be brought about by a change in the criteria for expressions of respect and contempt I will call the secondary revolution.

The distinction between a radical revision of the practical order and the attempt to create a new expressive order was foreshadowed in the French Revolution. Forms of address were altered, weights and measures were changed, and even the old names of months replaced by new. From our point of view one of the more interesting expressive innovations was the insistence on driving and riding on the right. Traditionally the gentry had ridden on the left, to bring their sword arms into convenient relation. The peasantry walked on the right, to face the oncoming traffic so to speak. Riding on the left was aristocratic, walking on the right, proletarian. The expressive effect of keeping to the right must have been considerable. Chairman Mao's 'cultural revolution' seems to have been directed at the expressive practices through which the day-to-day order of old China was still being reproduced long after the primary revolution. But by choosing a confrontation mode he doomed the secondary revolution of failure.

It seems clear to me that primary revolutions can occur with little effect on the expressive order of society. Is the reverse true? Could there be a secondary revolution, a drastic change in the personas people project, in the moral careers open to categories of persons and so on, which had no real effect on the practical order? I think not. If, for instance, skin colour ceased to be a criterion in the respect/contempt hierarchies of certain societies would not the position of black people in the practical (more specifically in the economic) order change? I believe it would.

These theses are empirical. The arguments I have so far brought forward hinge on the central perception of this chapter that a political philosophy which lacks an adequate social psychology will be impotent to alter the moral basis of society, though it might well be highly effective in altering its gross structural properties.

If this argument is correct, then it follows that the mutants or alternative societies which I have been arguing are a necessary condition for a quasi-Darwinian, quasi-Lamarckian change in the moral quality of a social collective, must be brought into being through small-scale local, secondary revolutions. They would involve the setting up of institutions and social practices in which new criteria for the giving of respect and contempt in new expressive systems come into daily operation.

And with new expressive practices go new rhetorics, in which and through which the folk are able to theorize about themselves and their social conditions, and in so doing create their own social identities.

DIFFICULTIES WITH ALTERNATION PROGRAMMES

This sounds an attractive theory at first sight, since it seems to have a satisfactory moral basis and to be related to a plausible theory of social change. However, like the confrontation programme, it has problems. These problems, though, I believe are not of the fatal paradoxical kind, which infect the confrontation theory.

There is no doubt that there is plenty of historical evidence that the attempt to set up mutant microsocieties within a circumambient society frequently leads to a violent attack upon that mutant. The circumambient society as a collective, acting as a selection environment, is generally hostile. If there is to be alternation politics, directed to secondary revolutions, there must be some way of protecting mutants from this hostility until they are viable and capable of being copied, that is of reproducing. It has been argued that in most societies there is a kind of sub-world composed of a variety of different kinds of individuals which is in general immune from the effects of the surrounding society and within which mutants can begin to exist. For example there is a close relation between those who pursue artistic vocations and the various strata of society that are on the borders of crime. Certain conditions would have to be fulfilled before any pocket of the under-life could serve as the nursery for nascent novel practices and the trial ground for new personas. Much that passes for an underlife is tightly bound, at least emotionally, to the over-life, the official orders of society. For instance an adventurer who feels anxious or guilty relative to the prospect of official discovery is leading an underlife whose motivational structure is but a mirror image of the over-life. For a new expressive social formation to be possible the alternative life (perhaps lived only part-time by a Simmelian adventurer) must be quite detached from the over-life. Its rules of action, its conventions as to the emotions it is proper to experience, its admissible styles of self-presentation and so on must be independent creations, and not just contrary reflections of the expressive order of the over-life. Perhaps we should speak of the 'under-under-life' to distinguish the practice of a genuinely alternative expressive order. But the mere existence of this sub-world is not sufficient to provide the basis for an optimistic prognosis for the existence of most mutants. Of course, I would be consistent in arguing that a society which protects its own mutants either by apathy or by deliberate policy is a morally superior society to that which destroys them, but such a pious observation is not a sufficient ground for a social-psychology of political action based upon the possibility of alternative micro-societies.

It might be objected that the general outline of the theory which I have been proposing has already been the basis of a *laissez faire* political system, the result of which is far from desirable, namely nineteenth-century social Darwinism. For my version of alternation politics to take on the moral tone I have been trying to sustain, a collapse into social Darwinism must be avoided at all costs. In terms of this discussion, social Darwinism could be defined as that form of selection which favours the most ruthless and self-regarding actors. On this view existing collectives should be transformed so that they have attributes which are lethal for all radically alternative practices, whatever they might be, that represent parity of regard between persons. So that far from being a possible basis for a radical political programme, the evolutionary conception, if taken as a guide to political action, can lead only to the worst alternative.

The reply to this objection can be found in the first section of this chapter, the acts by which the attachment of value to represent one's fundamental tenets as to the Nature of Man are accomplished. I have argued that within the constraints imposed by the historically conditioned social psychologies we already exemplify, and the intensely conservative effects of the social apprenticeship served by our children in their autonomous microsocieties, the knowledge acquired through the use of the new approach in social psychology puts us, the folk, in a position to design new forms of association. Historical and anthropological studies can show us the possibilities human beings have already explored. The task of the reconstruction of society can be begun by anyone at any time in any face to face encounter.

REFERENCES

Allport, G.W. 1954: *The nature of prejudice* Cambridge, Mass.: Addison-Wesley.

Ardener, S. 1975: *Perceiving women* London: Dent.

Ardrey, R. 1968: *The territorial imperative* New York: Dell.

Argyle, M. and Cook, M. 1976: *Gaze and mutual gaze* Cambridge: Cambridge University Press.

Argyle, M. and Little, B. 1972: 'Do personality traits apply to social behaviour?' *Journal for the theory of social behaviour* **2**, 1–35.

Atkinson, J.M. 1979: *Order in court* London: Macmillan.

Austin, J.L. 1961: 'A plea for excuses' in G.J. Warnock and J. Urmson (eds) *Philosophical papers* Oxford: Clarendon Press Ch. 6.

Backman, C. 1977: 'Explorations in psycho-ethics: the warranting of judgements' in R. Harré (ed) *Life sentences* Chichester: Wylie pp. 98–108.

Baier, A. 1992: 'Moralities and cruelty: reflections on Hume and Kant' (Paper presented at Georgetown University).

Berkowitz, L. 1962: *Aggression* New York: McGraw-Hill.

Berne, E. 1970: *Games people play* Harmondsworth: Penguin.

Best, E. 1922: *Spiritual and mental concepts of the Maori* Wellington, N.Z.: Dominion Museum Monograph.

Bhaskar, R. 1978: *A realist theory of science* Brighton: Harvester.

Billig, M. 1987: *Arguing and thinking* Oxford: Blackwell.

Blurton-Jones, N.G. 1972: 'Non-verbal communication in children' in R. Hinde (ed) *Non-verbal communication* Cambridge: Cambridge University Press.

Bourdieu, P. 1973: 'The Berber house' in M. Douglas (ed) *Rules and meanings* Harmondsworth: Penguin Ch. 18.

Brenner, M. 1978: 'Interviewing: the social phenomenology of a research instrument' in M. Brenner, P. Marsh and M. Brenner (eds) *The social context of method* London: Croom Helm pp. 122–139.

Brillat-Savarin 1970 (1826): *La physiologie de la gout* trans A. Drayton as *The philosopher in the kitchen* Harmondsworth: Penguin.

Brissett, D. and Edgley, C. 1974 (eds): *Life as theatre: a dramaturgical source book* Chicago: Aldine.

Brown, P. 1973: *The Chimbu* London: Routledge and Kegan Paul Ch. 9.

Bruner, J.S. 1990: *Acts of meaning* Cambridge, Mass.: Harvard University Press.

Bryant, P.E. 1974: *Perception and understanding in young children* London: Methuen.

Bullock, A. 1962: *Hitler: a study in tyranny* New York: Harper and Row.

Bullock, A. 1992: *Hitler and Stalin: parallel lives* New York: Knopf.

Burgess, A. 1987: *Little Wilson and big God* London: Heinemann.

Burke, K. 1945: *A grammar of motives* Englewood Cliffs, N.J.: Prentice Hall.

Chance, M.R.A. 1988: *Social fabrics of the mind* Hove and London: Erlbaum pp. 3–9.

Clarke, D.D. 1983: *Language and action* Oxford: Pergamon.

Chomsky, N. 1965: *Aspects of the theory of syntax* Cambridge, Mass.: M.I.T. Press.

Cooper, W. 1971: *Hair, sex, society, symbolism* London: Alden.

Coulter, J. 1992: 'Bilmes on internal states: a critical commentary' *Journal for the theory of social behaviour* **22**, forthcoming.

Danziger, K. 1990: *Constructing the subject: historical origins of psychological research* Cambridge: Cambridge University Press.

Dawkins, R. 1976: *The selfish gene* Oxford: Clarendon Press.

De Waele, J.-P. and Harré, R. 1976: 'The personality of individuals' in R. Harré (ed) *Personality* Oxford: Blackwell.

Diaz-Plaja, F. 1968: *The Spaniard and the seven deadly sins* trans J.I. Palmer London: Gollancz.

Douglas, M. 1966: *Purity and danger* London: Routledge and Kegan Paul.

Douglas, M. 1972: 'Deciphering a meal' *Daedalus* (Winter).

Durkheim, E. 1915: *Elementary forms of the religious life* London: Allen and Unwin.

Duval, S. and Wicklund, R.A. 1972: *A theory of objective self awareness* New York: Academic Press.

Etchemendy, J. 1988: 'Models, semantics and logical truth' *Linguistics and philosophy* **11**, 91–106.

Fransella, F. and Bannister, D. 1977: *A manual of repertory grid technique* London: Academic Press.

Garfinkel, H. 1967: *Studies in ethnomethodology* Englewood Cliffs: Prentice Hall.

Gergen, K.J. 1973: 'Social psychology as history' *Journal of personality social psychology* **26**, 309–320.

Gibbard, A. 1990: *Wise choices: apt feelings: A theory of normative judgements* Cambridge, Mass. Harvard University Press.

Gilligan, C. 1982: *In a different voice* Cambridge, Mass.: Harvard University Press.

Goffman, E. 1968: *Asylums* Harmondsworth: Penguin.

Goffman, E. 1968: *Stigma* Harmondsworth: Penguin.

Goffman, E. 1969: *The presentation of self in everyday life* London: Allen Lane, Penguin.

Goffman, E. 1972: 'Facework' in *Interaction ritual* London: Allen Lane, Penguin.

Goffman, E. 1972: *Relations in public* Harmondsworth: Penguin.

Goffman, E. 1974: *Frame analysis* Cambridge, Mass.: Harvard University Press.

Greenwood, J. 1991: *Relations and representations* London: Routledge Ch. 5.

Greer, G. 1984: *Sex and destiny* New York: Harper and Row.

Grice, P. 1989: *Studies in the way of words* Cambridge, Mass.: Harvard University Press.

Hamilton, D.L. 1991: 'Interpersonal perception: on charting the terrain' *Psychological inquiry* 2, 383–397.

Hargreaves, D. 1967: *Social relations in secondary schools* London: Routledge and Kegan Paul.

Harré, R. (ed.) 1987: *The social construction of emotion* Oxford: Blackwell.

Harré, R. 1983: *Personal being* Oxford: Blackwell; Cambridge, Mass.: Harvard University Press.

Harré, R. 1991: *Physical being* Oxford: Blackwell.

Helling, I. 1977: 'The carpenters of Konstanz' in R. Harré (ed) *Life sentences* Chichester: Wylie.

Holiday, A. 1987: *Moral powers* Brighton: Harvester.

Hollway, W. 1984: 'Gender difference and the production of subjectivity' in J. Henriques et al. (eds) *Changing the subject* London: Methuen pp. 227–263.

Hume, D. 177 (1975): *An enquiry concerning the principles of morals* Oxford: Clarendon Press.

Joiner, D. 1971: 'Social ritual and architectural space' *Architectural research and teaching* 1, 48ff.

Jones, E.E. and Nisbett R.E. 1971: *The actor and the observer: divergent perceptions of the causes of behavior* New York: General Learning Press.

Kant, I. 1785 (1961): *Groundwork of the metaphysics of morals* trans H.J. Paton as *The moral law* London: Hutchison pp. 108–113.

Kelly, G. 1955: *The psychology of personal constructs* New York: Norton.

Kesey, K. 1974: *One flew over the cuckoo's nest* New York: Viking Compass.

Kitwood, T. 1979: *Conversations with a stranger* London: Routledge and Kegan Paul.

Labov, W. and Fanshel, D. 1977: *Therapeutic discourse* New York: Academic Press.

Laing, R.D. 1969: *The divided self* New York: Pantheon.

Le Bon, G. 1979: in A. Widener (ed) *Gustave Le Bon* Indianapolis: Liberty Press.

Leiber, J. 1975: *Noam Chomsky: a philosophical overview* New York: St Martin's Press.

Levi-Strauss, C. 1968: *Structural anthropology* London: Penguin.

Lewin, K. 1935: *Principles of topological psychology* New York McGraw-Hill.

Lodge, D. 1992: *New York review of books* **XXXIX: 7**, p. 56.

Lukes, S. 1973a: *Emile Durkheim: his life and work* London: Allen Lane.

Lukes, S. 1973b: *Individualism* Oxford: Clarendon Press.

Lutz, C.A. 1988: *Unnatural emotions* Chicago and London: Chicago University Press.

McManners, J. 1975: *Reflections on the deathbed of Voltaire: the art of dying in 18th century France* Oxford: Clarendon Press.

Malinowski, B. 1922: *Argonauts of the Western Pacific* London: Routledge.

Marks, I.M. and Gelder, M.G. 1967: 'Transvestism and fetishism' *British Journal of Psychiatry* 113, 711–729.

Marsh, P., Rosser, E. and Harré R. 1977: *The rules of disorder* London: Routledge and Kegan Paul.

Middleton, D. and Edwards, D. 1990: *Collective remembering* London: Sage.

Milgram, S. 1974: *Obedience to authority* London: Tavistock.

Miller, G., Galanter, E. and Pribram, K. 1960: *Plans and the structure of behavior* New York: Henry Holt Ch. 2.

Mills, C. Wright 1974: 'Situated actions and vocabularies of motive' in Brisset and Edgley *op. cit.* pp. 162–170.

Mischel, T. 1964: 'Personal constructs, rules and the logic of clinical activity' *Psychological review* 71, 180–192.

Mixon, D. 1971: 'Behavior analysis treating subjects as actors rather than organisms' *Journal for the theory of social behaviour* 1, 19–31.

Moghaddam, A. and Harré, R. 1992: 'Rethinking the laboratory experiment' *American behavioral scientist.*

Morris, I. 1975: *The nobility of failure* London: Secker and Warburg.

Morsbach, H. 1977: 'The psychological importance of the ritualized gift exchange in modern Japan' *Annals of the New York Academy of Sciences* 293, 98–113.

Moscovici, S. 1961: *La psychoanalyse: son image et son publique* Paris: Presses Universitaires de France.

Moscovici, S. 1985: *The age of the crowd: a historical treatise on mass psychology* Cambridge: Cambridge University Press.

Nisbett, R.E. and Wilson, T.D. 1977: 'Telling more than we can know' *Psychological review* 84, 231–259.

Nordenstam, T. 1968: *Sudanese ethics* Uppsala: Scandinavian Institute of African Studies.

Overington, M.A. 1977: 'Kenneth Burke and the method of dramatism' *Theory and society* 4, 131–156.

Park, R.E. 1972: *The crowd and the public* H. Elser (ed) Chicago and London: Chicago University Press.

Parker, I. 1987: *The crisis in social psychology and how to solve it* London.

Parrott, J. and Harré, R. 1992: 'Smedslundian suburbs in Wittgenstein's city' *Psychological Inquiry* 2, 358–361.

Pitt-Rivers, J.A. 1954: *The people of the Sierra* London: Weidenfeld and Nicholson.

Plutchik, R. 1980: *Emotion: a psychoevolutionary synthesis* New York: Harper and Row.

Polanyi, M. 1962: *Personal knowledge* London: Routledge and Kegan Paul.

Potter, J. and Wetherell M. 1987: *Discourse and social psychology* London: Sage.

Repp, R.C. 1972 in N.R. Keddie (ed): *Scholars, saints and sufis* Berkeley: California University Press, pp. 17–32.

Richards, M.P.M. 1974: *The integration of a child into a social world*

Cambridge: Cambridge University Press.

Robinson, D. 1992: 'Psychology as its history' *Annals of theoretical psychology* **9**, p. 4.

Rosaldo, M.Z. 1980: *Knowledge and passion: Ilongot notions of self and social life* Cambridge: Cambridge University Press.

Rosser, E. and Harré R. 1976: 'The meaning of "trouble"' in M. Hammersley and P. Woods (eds) *The process of schooling* London: Routledge and Kegan Paul.

Ryan, A. 1970: *The philosophy of the social sciences* London: Macmillan.

Sabini, J. and Silver, M. 1981: *Moralities of everyday life* New York: Oxford University Press.

Sahlins, M. 1974: *Stone age economics* London: Tavistock.

Saussure, F. de 1974: *A course of general linguistics* trans W. Baskin London: Fontana-Collins.

Schank, R.C. and Abelson, R.P. 1977: *Scripts, plans, goals and understanding* Hillsdale, N.J.: Erlbaum.

Schama, S. 1989: *Citizens* New York: Knopf p. 525.

Schegloff, M. and Sacks, H. 1974: 'Opening up closings' in R. Turner (ed) *Ethnomethodology* London: Penguin.

Schutz, A. 1972: *The phenomenology of the social world* London: Heinemann.

Secord, P.F. and Guttentag, M. 1988: *Too many women: the sex ratio question* Beverly Hills: Sage.

Shotter, J. 1975: *Images of man in psychological research* London: Methuen.

Shweder, R.A. 1991: *Thinking through cultures* Cambridge, Mass.: Harvard Univesity Press.

Signale, S. 1891: *La folla deliquenta.*

Simmel, G. 1971: *On individuality and social forms* Chicago: Chicago University Press.

Skinner, B.F. 1972: *Beyond freedom and dignity* London: Cape.

Smedslund, J. 1988: *Psychologic* Berlin and New York: Springer-Verlag.

Soustelle, J. 1962: *The daily life of the Aztecs* trans P.O'Brien New York: Macmillan.

Stearns, C.Z. and Stearns, P.N. 1987: *Emotions and social change* New York: Holmes and Meier.

Tajfel, H. 1972: 'Experiments in a vacuum' in J. Israel and H. Tajfel (eds) *The context of social psychology* London: Academic Press pp. 69–119.

Tannen, D. 1986: *Conversational style* Norwood, N.J.: Ablex.

Tannen, D. 1991: *You just don't understand* New York: William Morrow.

Theroux, P. 1988: *Riding the iron rooster* London: Hamish Hamilton.

Tiger, L. and Fox, R. 1971: *The imperial animal* London: Secker and Warburg.

Torode, B. 1977: 'The revelation of a theory of the social world as grammar' in R. Harre (ed) *Life sentences* Chichester: Wylie pp. 87–97.

Trevarthen, C. 1979: 'Communication and cooperation in early infancy' in M. Bulowa (ed): *Before speech: the beginnings of human cooperation* Cambridge: Cambridge University Press.

Toulmin, S.E. 1972: *Human understanding* Princeton: Princeton University Press.

Triandis, H.C. 1991: 'Cross-cultural differences in assertiveness/competition v.

loyalty/cooperation' in R.A. Hinde and J. Groebel (eds) *Cooperation and prosocial behaviour* Cambridge: Cambridge University Press pp. 78–88.

Veblen, T. 1899: *A theory of the leisure class* New York: Macmillan.

von Cranach, M. 1981: 'The psychological study of goal-directed action: basic issues' in M. von Cranach and R. Harré (eds) *The analysis of action* Cambridge: Cambridge University Press, Ch. 2.

Weber, M. 1957: *The theory of social and economic organization* trans. A.M. Henderson and T. Parsons, Glencoe: The Free Press.

Weiner, A.B. 1976: *Women of virtue, men of renown* Austin and London: University of Texas Press.

Weinstein, E.A. and Deutschberger, P. 1964: 'Tasks, bargains and identities in social interactions' *Social forces* **42**, 451–456.

Weightman, J. 1990: in *The European* 3–5 August 1990, p. 5.

Williams, M. 1976: 'Presenting oneself in talk: the disclosure of occupation' in R. Harré (ed) *Life sentences* Chichester Wylie, Ch. 5.

Wittgenstein, L. 1953: *Philosophical investigations* trans G.E.M. Anscombe Oxford: Blackwell.

Wittgenstein, L. 1969: *On certainty* G.E.M. Anscombe and G. von Wright (eds) Oxford: Blackwell.

Wolfe, T. 1968: The great electric kool-aid acid test London: Black Swan.

Wrightsman, L.S. and Deaux, K. 1981: *Social psychology in the 80s* Monterey: Brooks/Cole.

Yates, F. 1966: *The art of memory* London: Routledge and Kegan Paul.

Zajonc, R.B. 1968: 'Attitudinal effects of mere exposure' *Journal of personality and social psychology* (Monograph supplement) **9**, 2–27.

Zajonc, R.B. 1980: 'Feeling and thinking: preferences need no inferences' *American psychologist* **35**, 151–175.

Index of Names

Index of Subjects